IMAGES
of America

GRAHAM

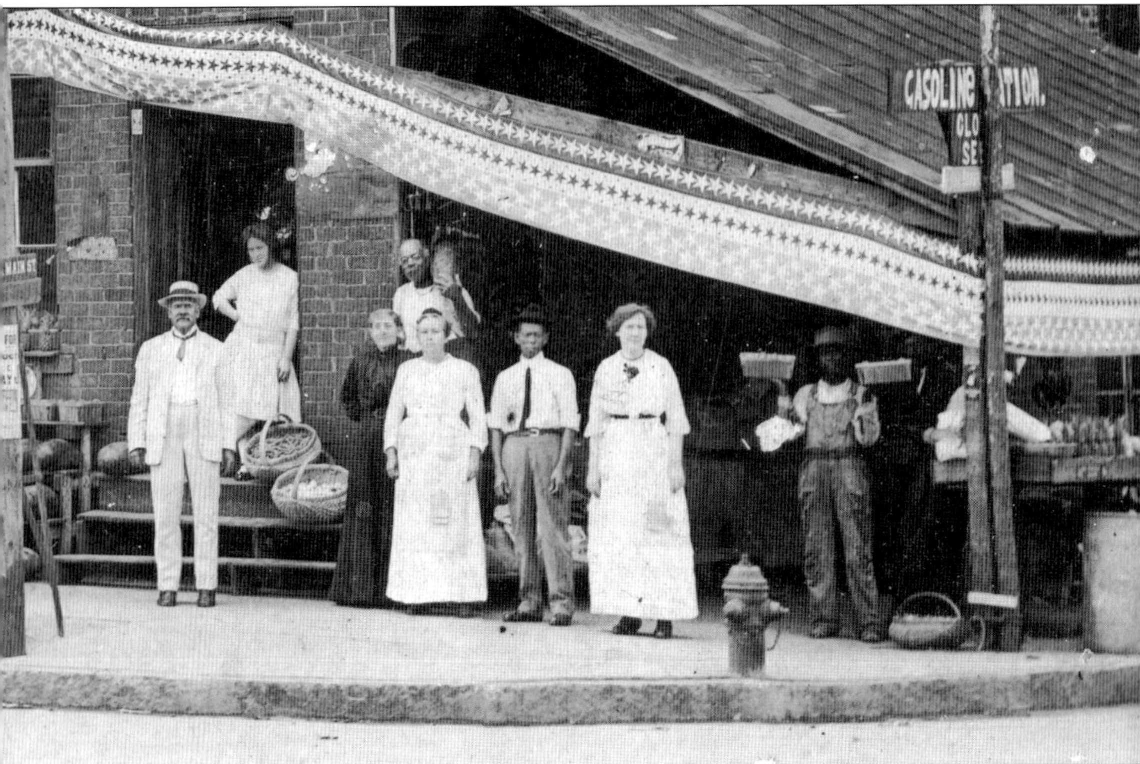

In this closer view of the photograph on the front cover, preparations for the Independence Day celebration are underway. Standing in front of W.J. Nicks General Merchandise, from left to right, are (first row) W.J. Nicks, Betty Nicks Thompson (Nicks's sister, wearing black), Minnie Fowler Nicks (Nicks's wife, wearing white), Sing Lee, who operated the laundry to the right of the store, and two unidentified persons; (second row) Nicks's daughter Enita Nicks (standing behind Nicks in the doorway) and unidentified. (Courtesy of Graham Historical Museum.)

On the Cover: W.J. Nicks General Merchandise was owned and operated by the Nicks family for more than 70 years. W.J. Nicks, who lived on the second floor of his business, bought and sold goods for cash or trade. Items bartered included furs, grain, beeswax, plants, ice, and coffins. The store was among the first to sell ice and gasoline in Graham. Gasoline was kept in five-gallon cans that were emptied into a car's tank. This photograph was taken on Saturday, July 3, 1915. Since the Fourth of July fell on Sunday, the celebration took place a day early. (Courtesy of Graham Historical Museum.)

IMAGES
of America

GRAHAM

Amy Edwards Barr and Jerry Peterman

ARCADIA
PUBLISHING

ISBN 978-0-7385-9813-0

Published by Arcadia Publishing
Charleston, South Carolina

Printed in the United States of America

Library of Congress Control Number: 2012945077

For all general information, please contact Arcadia Publishing:
Telephone 843-853-2070
Fax 843-853-0044
E-mail sales@arcadiapublishing.com
For customer service and orders:
Toll-Free 1-888-313-2665

Visit us on the Internet at www.arcadiapublishing.com

To David Barr and Jan Peterman, for their support and understanding during the writing of this book, and to the citizens of Graham, who are the reason we love to call Graham home

Contents

ACKNOWLEDGMENTS

We are grateful to the many people who so generously provided the photographs for this book. Without the help of so many of Graham's residents, the book would not have been possible. People opened their homes to us and enthusiastically shared special images and memories of the town. M.J. Wilkerson, director of Alamance County Public Libraries, provided the vision and support to begin this project.

Graham city manager Chris Rollins gave us access to the city's historical photograph collection. The Graham Historical Museum's photographs and information were invaluable. Much of the information contained in this book was found in the museum's files, donated by Dr. Durward T. Stokes. His book *Auction and Action: Historical Highlights of Graham* documented the town's history.

Dr. William M. Vincent, curator of the Alamance County Historical Museum, shared photographs on display at the museum. He proofread pages of manuscript and gave suggestions and advice to provide historical accuracy. Don Bolden, editor emeritus of the *Times-News*, provided counsel and generously allowed the use of hard-to-find photographs from his files. Skee Johnson shared his extensive research on the Nicks family and the W.J. Nicks store. Pat Bailey provided many negatives that documented events that occurred during her career as a professional photographer. Graham fire chief Johnny Andrews shared his knowledge and stories of the fire department. Jeff Prichard, the chief of police, shared the department's scrapbooks.

Wendy Kimbro spent many evenings after work researching facts in city directories, local history books, and newspapers. Our sessions working on the book's layout and captions often lasted until the wee hours of the morning. In these few pages, we have attempted to capture a snapshot of Graham's rich history. Space does not permit us to mention everyone by name that has contributed to this endeavor. However, we would like to give special thanks to the following people: Jack Henderson, Heather Holley-Hall, Jim McClure, Ted Nelson, Mimi Saunders, Linda S. Stewart, Sue Ward, and the family of Foust Thompson. Thanks to the citizens of Graham, our friends and neighbors who make this town so special.

INTRODUCTION

The town of Graham was created in 1849 as the county seat for the new county of Alamance. Land for the town was purchased from farmers who had carved their pastures and farmland from the forests that covered the Piedmont region of North Carolina. The nearest settlement was 19 miles away at the Orange County seat, Hillsborough. When a local resident needed to attend court or conduct business, reaching the court officials could be challenging. Farmers left work for others to handle and made the two-day trip by horse or wagon. The Haw River and the many creeks and streams that feed it were obstacles between Graham and Hillsborough. There were few bridges, so residents rode miles out of the way on wagon-rut roads to cross the river. When the weather was poor or the river was high, it was dangerous to make the trip.

On reaching Hillsborough, lodging was needed for both the farmer and his horse. Weary of the expense, local residents met at mills, homes, and churches and signed petitions requesting that Orange County be divided for the formation of a new county. The petitions were submitted to the North Carolina General Assembly. Their endeavor was successful in 1849, and Alamance County was established.

Almost immediately, planning for the new county seat began. A committee was appointed to buy land in the geographical center of the new county. Farmland was purchased from John A. Holt, Joseph M. Freeland, and William Clendenin for the courthouse square and what would become the surrounding town. A total of 75 acres were purchased at a cost of $603.68. Silas M. Lane, a local surveyor, was hired to lay off the town of Graham. The exact center of the county was discovered to be a marshy area on what is now South Main Street, just south of the interstate. Since the land was too soft to build on, the site for the courthouse was moved approximately one mile uphill. Land for the courthouse and lots on seven surrounding streets were drawn off and surveyed. The streets intersecting Court Square needed to be wide so that stagecoaches and wagons could make a complete turnaround without stopping. The land auction began on August 7, 1851. Many of the lots were sold at that time, while others were purchased later. The North Carolina General Assembly chose the name Graham in honor of Gov. William A. Graham, and the town was officially incorporated in 1851.

Stores and homes sprang up quickly in the years following the auction. The 1850s saw at least eight stores built. Attorneys hung out their shingles near the courthouse. Visiting lawyers stayed at the wooden hotel of John Klapp or at the brick hotel built by John Trolinger. Other early businesses on Court Square included a saloon and a drugstore.

Shortly after the town's incorporation, news circulated that the North Carolina Railroad planned to lay tracks one block north of the courthouse. The railroad looked favorably on Graham as an ideal spot for repair and maintenance shops due to its location near the center of the Goldsboro-Charlotte line. Graham residents were concerned that the noise of the trains and the smoke and activity of the railroad would disturb court sessions as well as daily life in their peaceful town. Town officials quickly passed an ordinance that the railroad pass no closer than one mile from the courthouse. The railroad then bypassed Graham. The tracks were laid north of town, and the repair shops were built on farmland two miles to the west, which gave birth to the town of Company Shops, later renamed Burlington.

The decision to deny the railroad repair shops caused rocky times for many early Graham businesses. Competition from the newly established town of Company Shops lowered the profits of some Graham merchants. In 1857, two businesses failed: McLean & Hanner Trading Company and the Graham drugstore, run by William Michael Holt and Pleasant Allen Holt.

The Civil War caused Graham to pause, as it was focused on the course of the war and its outcome. Several schools closed, including the Graham Institute. Young men from across the county joined the Confederacy, many of them serving with Col. Charles F. Fisher's men, who left from Company Shops. By the war's end, 236 Alamance County soldiers had lost their lives.

In the years following the war, unrest spread across the South. The White Brotherhood, a secret society that also called itself the Ku Klux Klan, sought to restore white supremacy by threats and violence against blacks and white progressives. Local bands made many nighttime raids, terrorizing local citizens.

Graham briefly became the center of national attention in 1870 when Wyatt Outlaw, the town commissioner in Graham, was lynched near the courthouse by the White Brotherhood. Outlaw, an outspoken African American, had helped establish the Republican Party in North Carolina and had promoted establishing a school for African Americans. Gov. William W. Holden had recently appointed him justice of the peace. In the inquiry that followed his murder, residents stated that at least 200 members of the White Brotherhood were active in the county. The accounts suggested Outlaw's hanging might have been in response to a rumor that he had fired on Klansmen earlier in the week as they rode through Graham.

Due to the events in Graham and unrest in neighboring Caswell County, Governor Holden sent troops under the command of Union veteran George W. Kirk to restore order, beginning the short-lived Kirk-Holden War. Kirk's troops arrested 82 suspected Klansmen, 63 of whom were indicted by the Alamance County Grand Jury. Shortly after the indictments were handed down, Democrats in the legislature repealed the law that was used for the indictments, and all charges were dropped. Governor Holden was impeached and removed from office in the ensuing political backlash.

As Graham continued to grow, services also followed, including a telephone exchange in 1888 in the Simmons Drug Store. In 1892, Albright Avenue earned the distinction of being the first paved street in the city. By this time, the railroad was firmly established, and many travelers arrived at the Graham depot. Stagecoaches and hired wagons carried early passengers from the depot to town. From 1911 to 1923, streetcars provided transportation between Burlington, Graham, and Haw River.

Stores and offices on Court Square moved often, as merchants jockeyed for the best piece of real estate for their establishments. The sound of hammers was commonplace in the early 1900s. Old buildings were improved and new constructions, including that of the Wrike Drug Store, the Patterson Building, the Vestal Hotel, and the Monte White Theatre, were added to the Graham landscape.

Graham is unique in that it is one of the few communities in Alamance County that did not come into being because of textile operations. Its central location has made it a crucial part of Alamance County by continuing to provide citizens a place to trade and transact legal business through the years.

Although Graham has not grown into the big city envisioned by some, it has embraced progress without losing its small-town charm. Many of Graham's current residents are descendants of generations of Graham families. Neighbors know one another in Graham, and often know each other's parents, grandparents, and extended families as well.

One

The Early Years

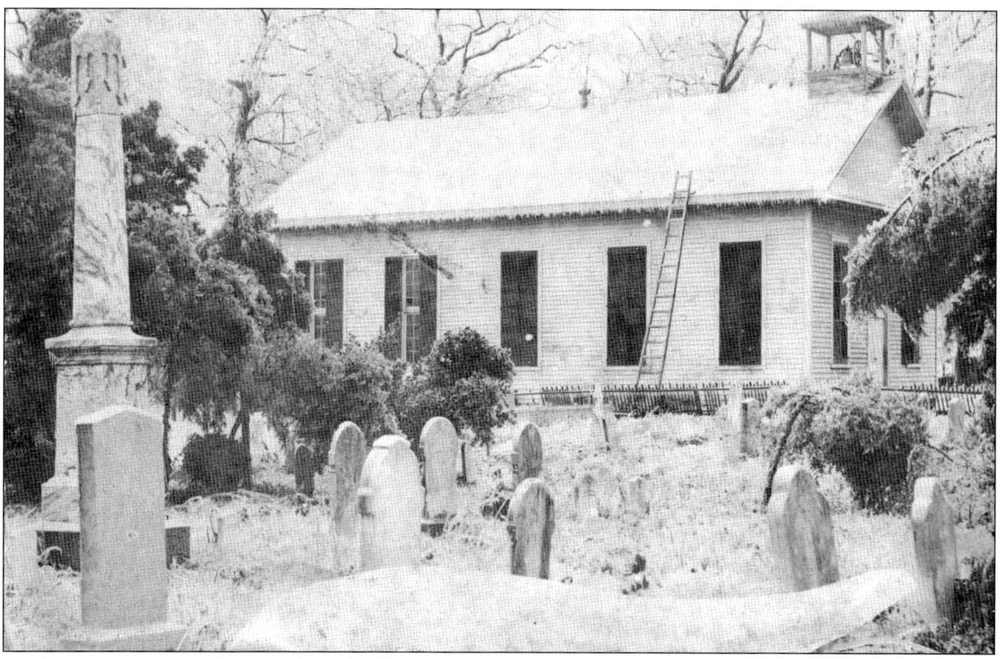

Built in 1763, Providence Church played a role in establishing the town of Graham. Located along the stagecoach line, the church was a natural gathering place for early settlers in what was then the western part of Orange County. The meeting to form Alamance County was held at the church on April 24, 1849. Providence was the center of community events, housing an early school and a public library. County court met here until 1851, when the courthouse was completed. This snowy photograph of Providence Church, located on North Main Street, was taken around 1900. (Courtesy of Historic Providence Church.)

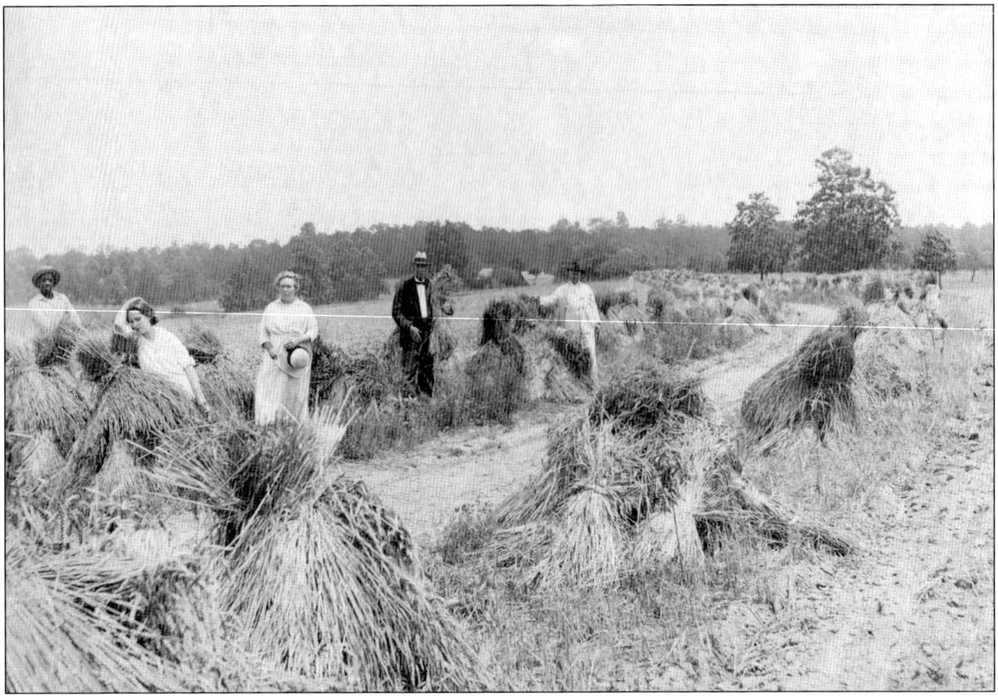

Farming was a way of life in early Alamance County. The W.J. Nicks farm, seen here in 1907, was about a mile southeast of the courthouse in what is now the Greenway Park neighborhood. The land was formerly the Freeland family property. In this photograph are, from left to right, unidentified, Enita Nicks, Minnie Nicks, unidentified, and W.J. Nicks. (Courtesy of Graham Historical Museum.)

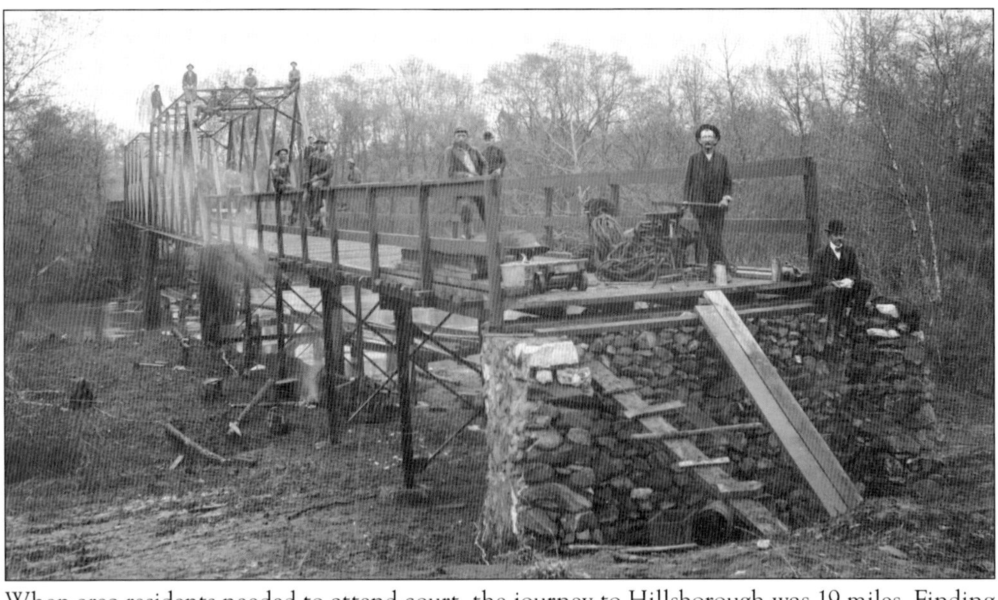

When area residents needed to attend court, the journey to Hillsborough was 19 miles. Finding a safe place to cross the Haw River meant traveling miles out of the way. This early bridge that was under construction may have crossed the river at Saxapahaw. (Courtesy of Alamance County Public Libraries.)

Several names were considered for the new county seat, including Gallatin, Vernon, Montgomery, and Berry. Representative Giles Mebane, who had been instrumental in forming Alamance County, urged the legislature to choose Graham in honor of Gov. William A. Graham of Hillsborough, who was in office at the time. (Courtesy of North Carolina State Archives.)

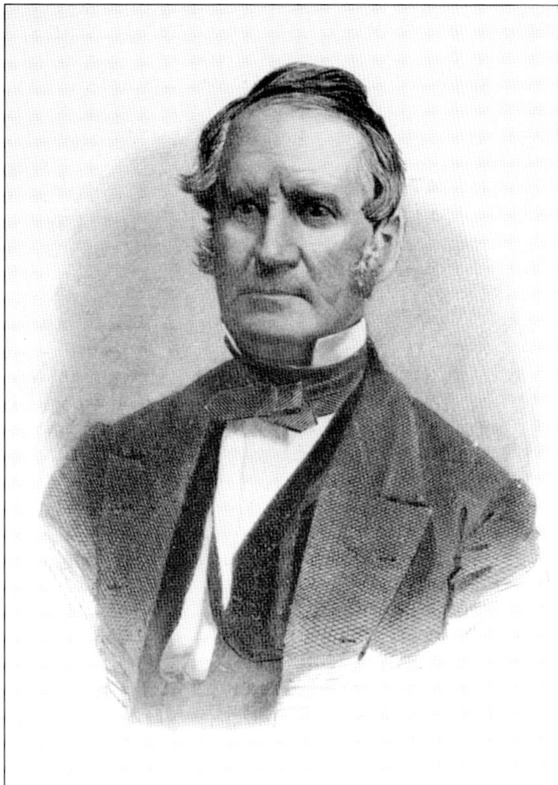
WILLIAM A. GRAHAM.

The courtroom filled the second floor of the first courthouse (below), built in 1851. The ground floor housed the clerk of superior court, the register of deeds, and the sheriff's office. East and west wings were added during extensive renovations in 1889. The fountain by the north door was presented to the county by Graham Water and Electric Company in 1906. (Courtesy of North Carolina State Archives.)

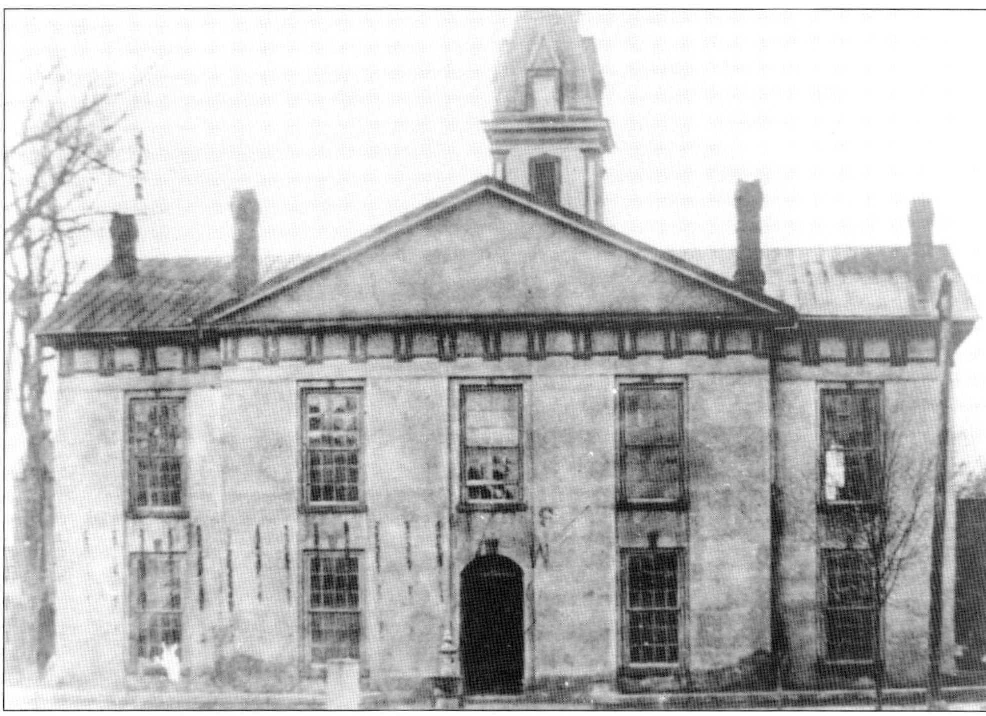

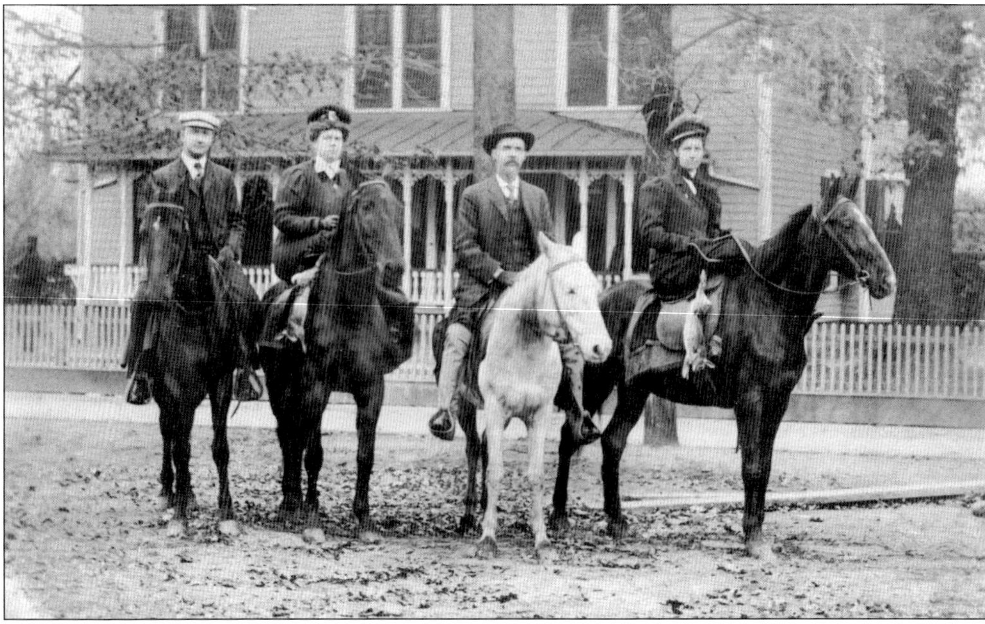

Two couples pose on horseback after a successful hunting excursion. The day's catch could have been dinner or may have been used to barter at one of the stores on Court Square. (Courtesy of Green & McClure.)

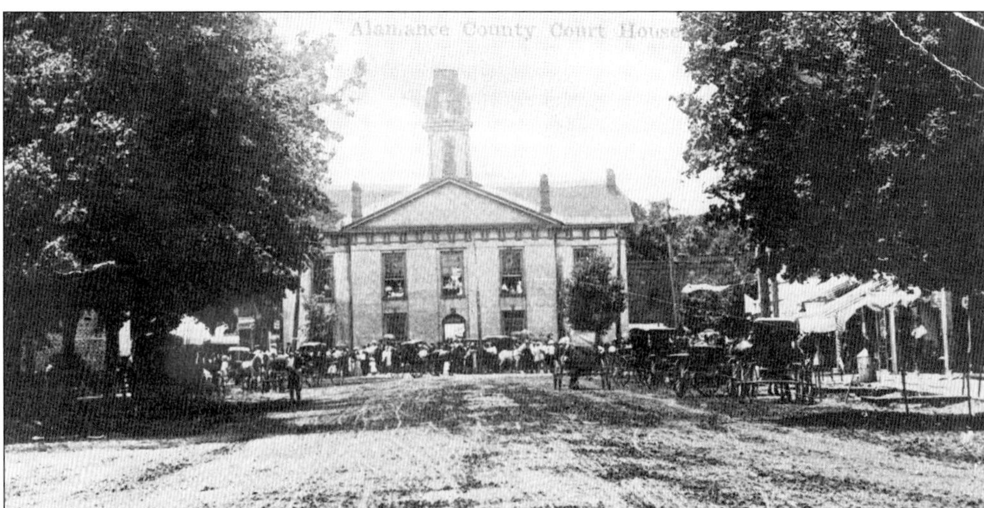

Muddy streets were an ongoing problem, as livestock roamed freely and pigs wallowed in front of businesses. The corners of Court Square were hitching lots for horses and popular places for traders to sell "plug horses" to gullible purchasers. The silver maple trees seen in this postcard of the courthouse were planted by W.C. Donnell in 1900. (Courtesy of North Carolina State Archives.)

John D. Kernodle Sr. published Graham's weekly newspaper, the *Alamance Gleaner*, from 1880 to 1944. Kernodle used the newspaper to bring attention to town issues, including the need for better streets. In doing so, he told his readers of visiting attorney William S. Ball who had been dressed in a white suit for court. As he walked down Main Street, a hog stood up, shook himself, and spattered the pristine suit. (Courtesy of City of Graham.)

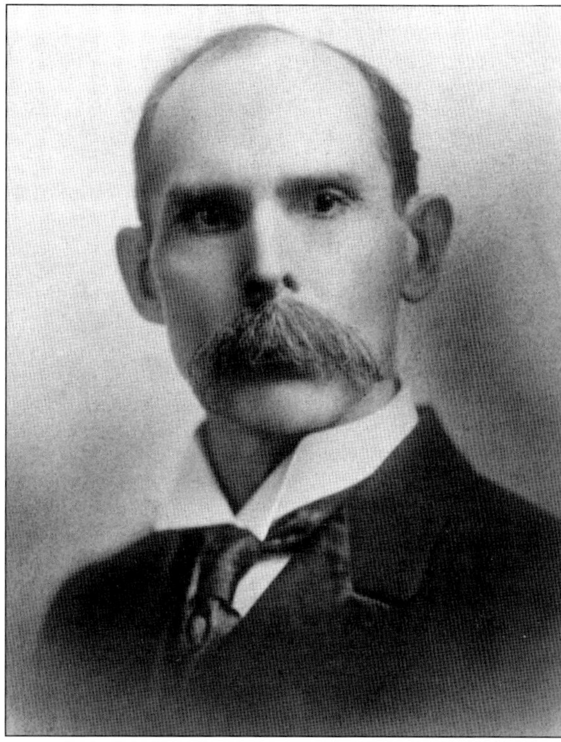

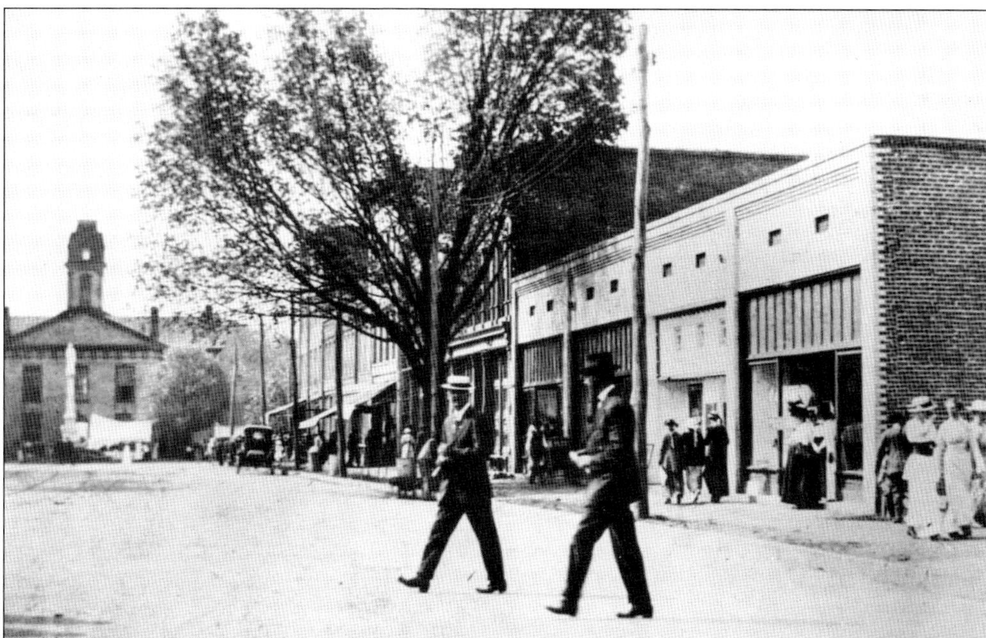

The bell in the cupola was rung to call court into session and announce services for the Presbyterian Church. These well-dressed young men may have been headed to church or to court as they crossed Stockard Street, later renamed North Main Street. The first courthouse and Confederate monument are in the background of this photograph from around 1915. (Courtesy of North Carolina State Archives.)

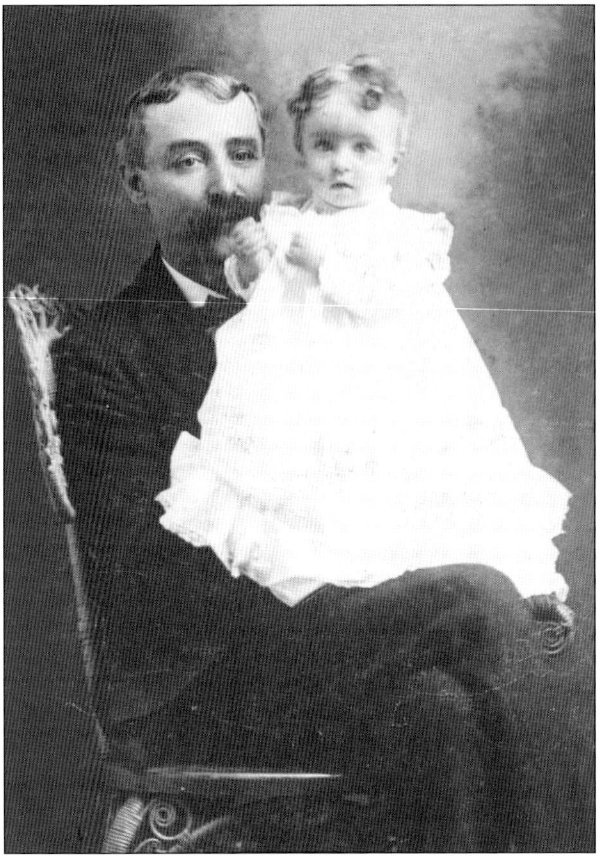

Dr. J.C. Simmons was the town's druggist. He was influential in bringing electricity to Graham. His daughter Helen pulled the switch to turn on the current for the first time. Dr. Simmons owned the first car in town, but he never learned to drive it. He served as mayor from 1903 to 1907. (Courtesy of City of Graham.)

In 1854, the town paid Daniel S. Harden $30 for two acres on Main Street (later Elm Street) to be used as a town cemetery (below). Named Linwood Cemetery in 1905, it is the resting place for citizens from all walks of life, including North Carolina governor Thomas Michael Holt. The African American section of the cemetery lies close to Pine Street. (Courtesy of Patrick G. Jordan.)

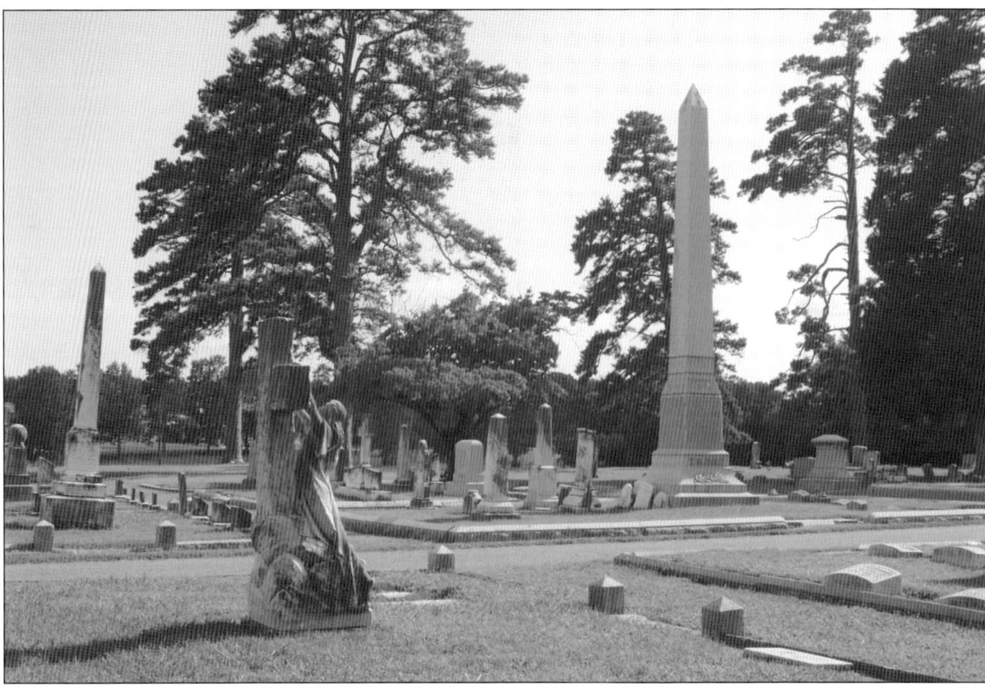

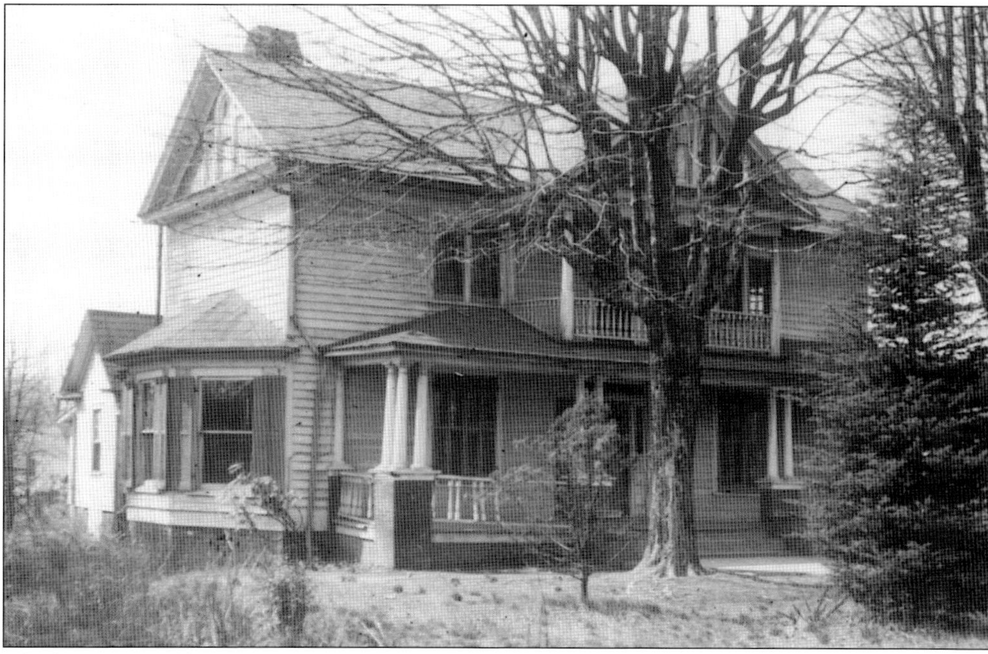

The home of William Freshwater Jones, the town coffin-maker, stood on land adjoining Linwood cemetery. In 1894, when the cemetery needed more space, Jones sold the city additional land. Later, his daughters allowed more land to be used as a cemetery but retained the title. The house, seen here, was eventually purchased by Rich & Thompson and remodeled into a funeral home. (Courtesy of Rich & Thompson.)

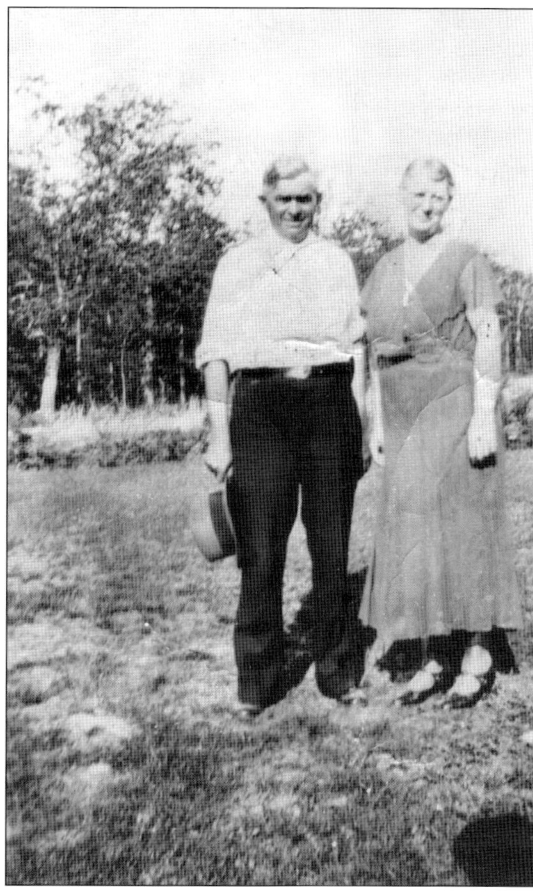

William Franklin "Frank" Dodson and his wife, Nora Ellen, lived on Marshall Street. He was the manager of the Graham Roller Shop on East Elm Street, which made roller covers for the cotton mills. He and Nora are seen here in the 1930s. (Courtesy of Carrie S. Thompson.)

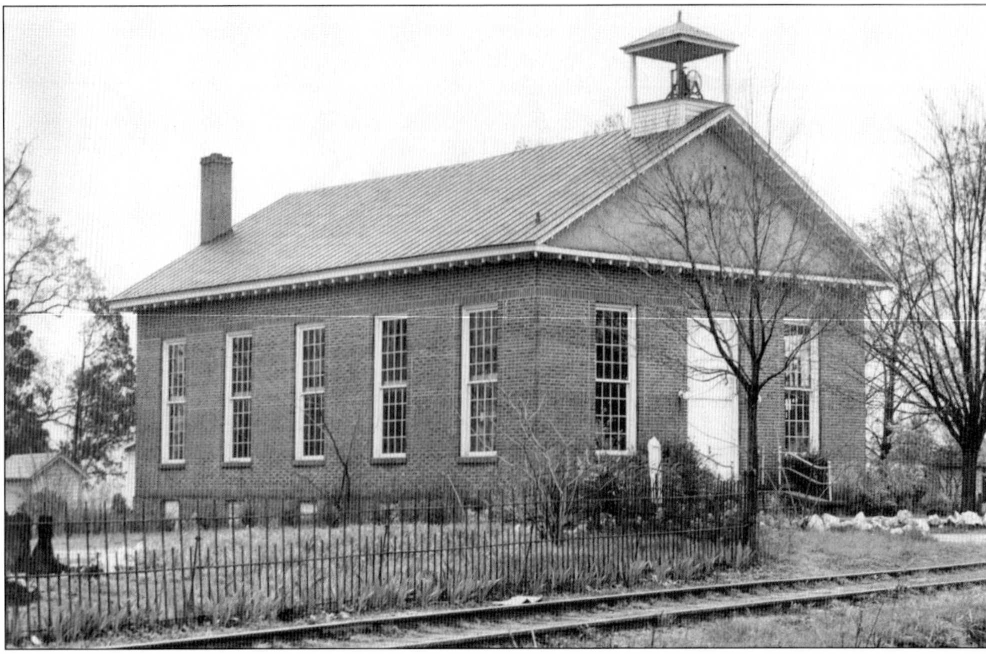

Though there had been talk of the railroad coming through the future Alamance County as early as 1828, the railroad did not arrive until 1852. The depot stood at the northern edge of town, and passengers and mail were carried by stagecoach to downtown Graham. The tracks near Providence Church on North Main Street are seen in this photograph from 1927. (Courtesy of Providence Church.)

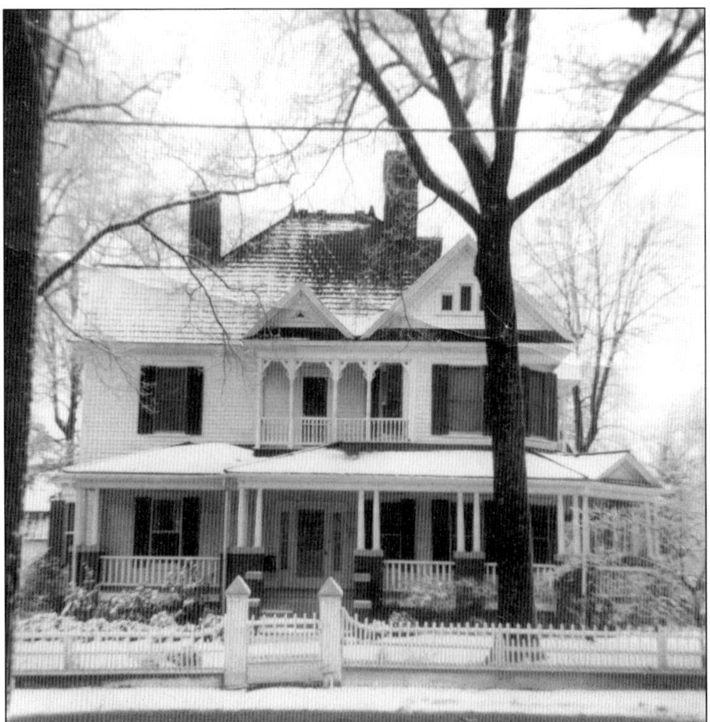

This home, built in 1904, was known as the Walker Ladies House, after three sisters who lived in the home for many years. Lucille and Mable Walker were teachers at the Graham Public School, and Eleanor Walker was a clerk in the tax department. The elegant two-story house is on Sideview Street, just off of North Main Street near Providence Church. (Courtesy of Chuck and Jennifer Talley.)

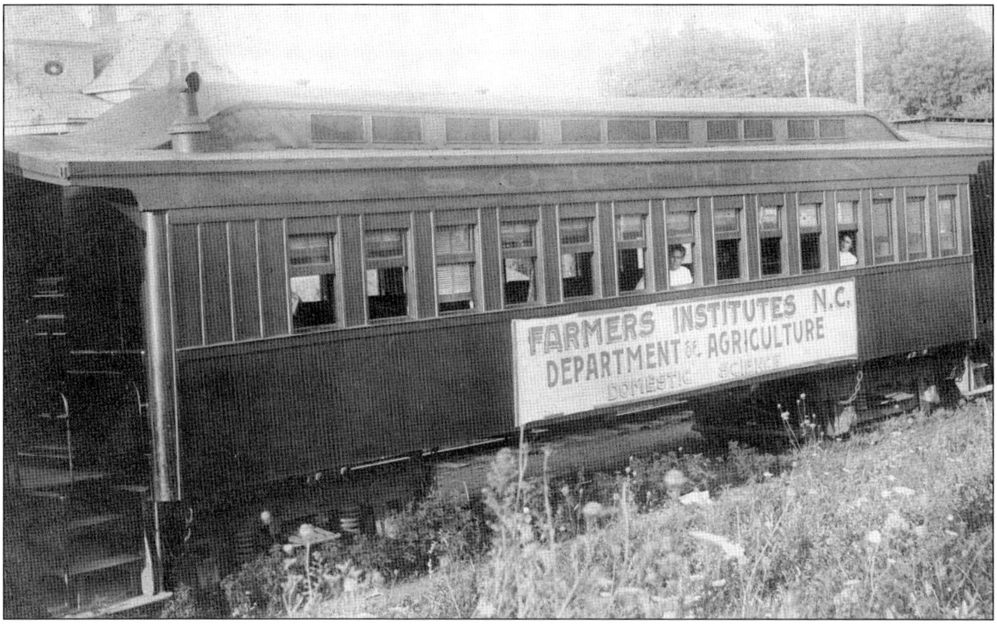

Graham prospered from the proximity of the railroad. Engineers and linemen lived and shopped in Graham, and the trains brought visitors to the hotels and stores. In 1909, the Farmers Institute in Raleigh sent demonstration trains across the state to teach the latest techniques in agriculture and homemaking. This train was visited by "progressive" Graham farmers and their families. (Both, courtesy of North Carolina State Archives.)

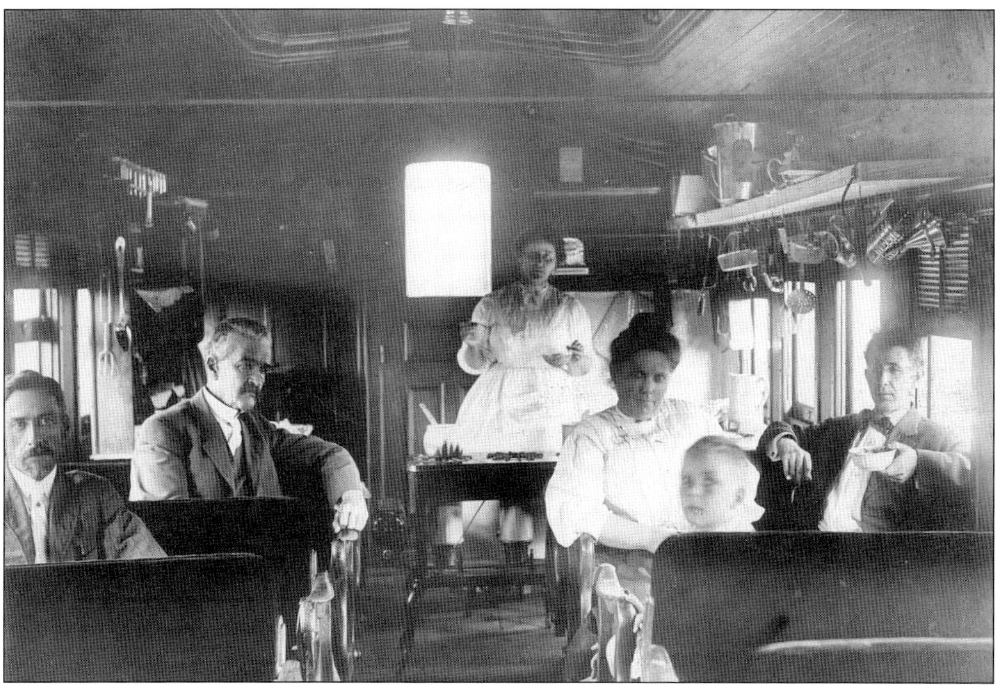

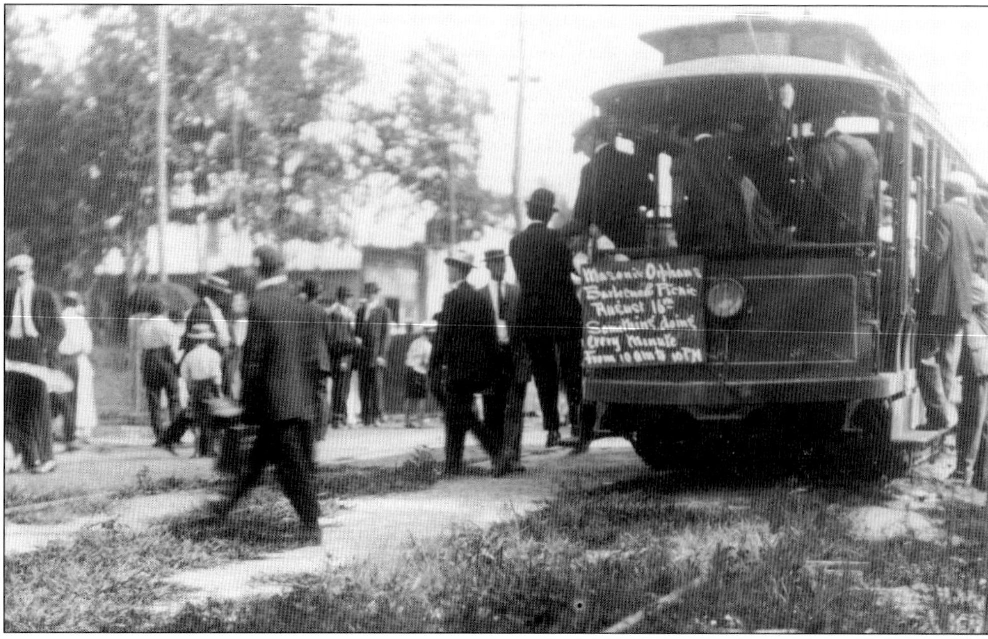

Streetcars first ran between Burlington, Graham, and Haw River in October 1911. The Piedmont Railway & Electric Company was established by a group of businessmen led by Junius H. Harden of Graham and James W. Murray of Burlington. Opening day was an exciting event, with nearly 200 passengers riding in the first two cars. The fare for the trip was only 5¢. (Courtesy of Graham Historical Museum.)

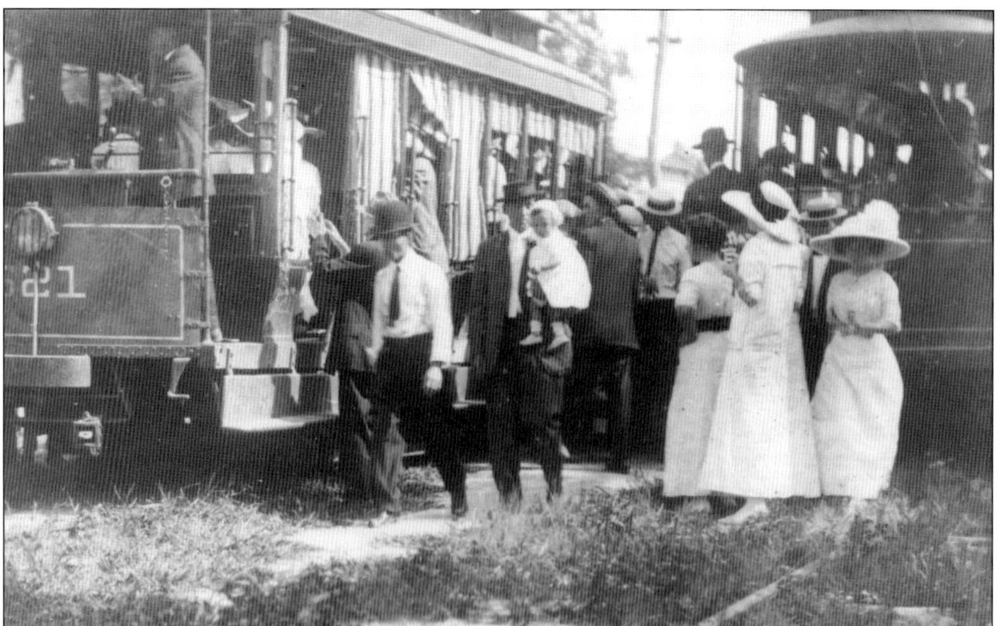

The streetcars ran seven days a week, year-round, and many people traveled by streetcar to both work and school. The cars were closed in for warmth during the winter, but in the summer, many residents rode the open-air cars and enjoyed the breeze. The streetcars' top speed was about 40 miles per hour. (Courtesy of Graham Historical Museum.)

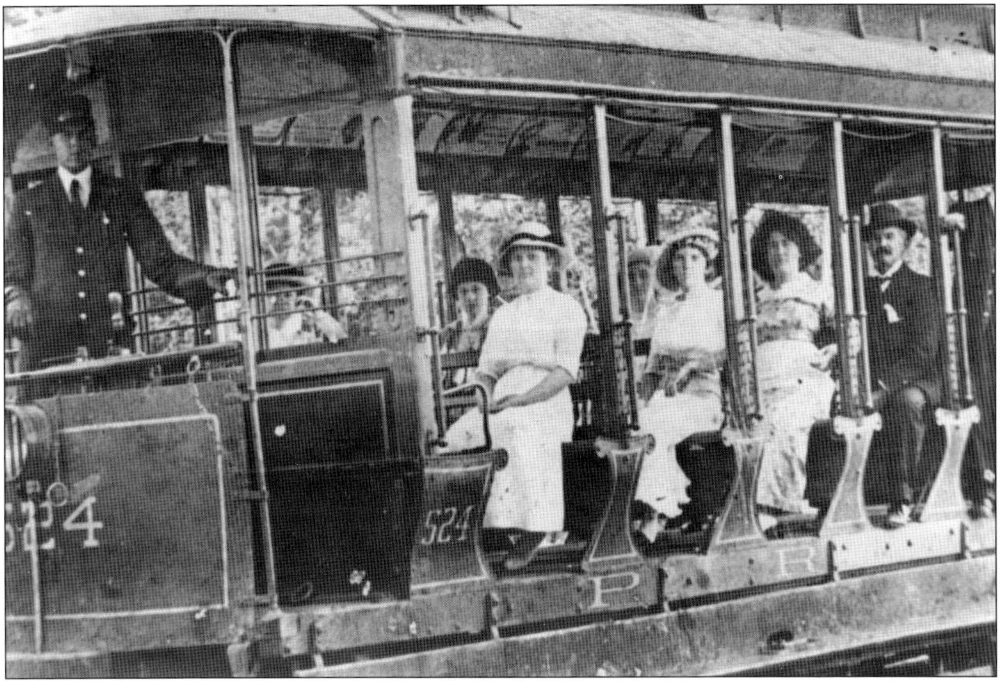

Streetcars began their daily run at 6:00 a.m. It was common for the trolleys to stop while the motormen hunted small game spotted along the tracks; the crew would then sell their catch to a local restaurant. Conductors were paid 17¢ per hour and ran the route many times each day, finally ending on Rainey Street in Burlington at 11:20 p.m. (Courtesy of Haw River Historical Museum.)

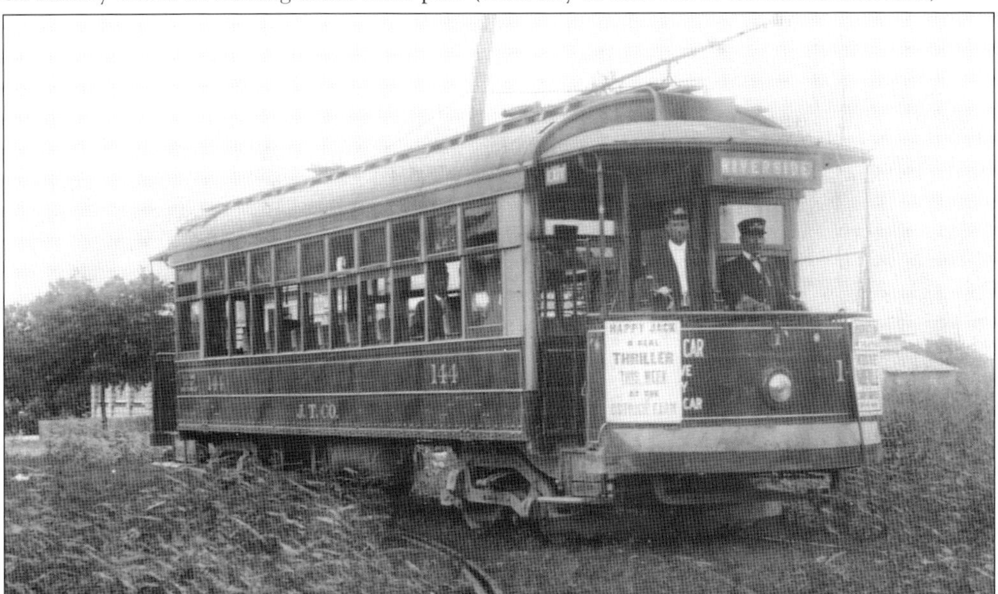

The tracks took the streetcars down North Main Street, past Graham Graded School, and to a stop near the courthouse. The arrival of automobiles contributed to the end of the streetcar service in 1923. The tracks were taken up during World War II, with the scrap metal sent to the war effort. (Courtesy of Haw River Historical Museum.)

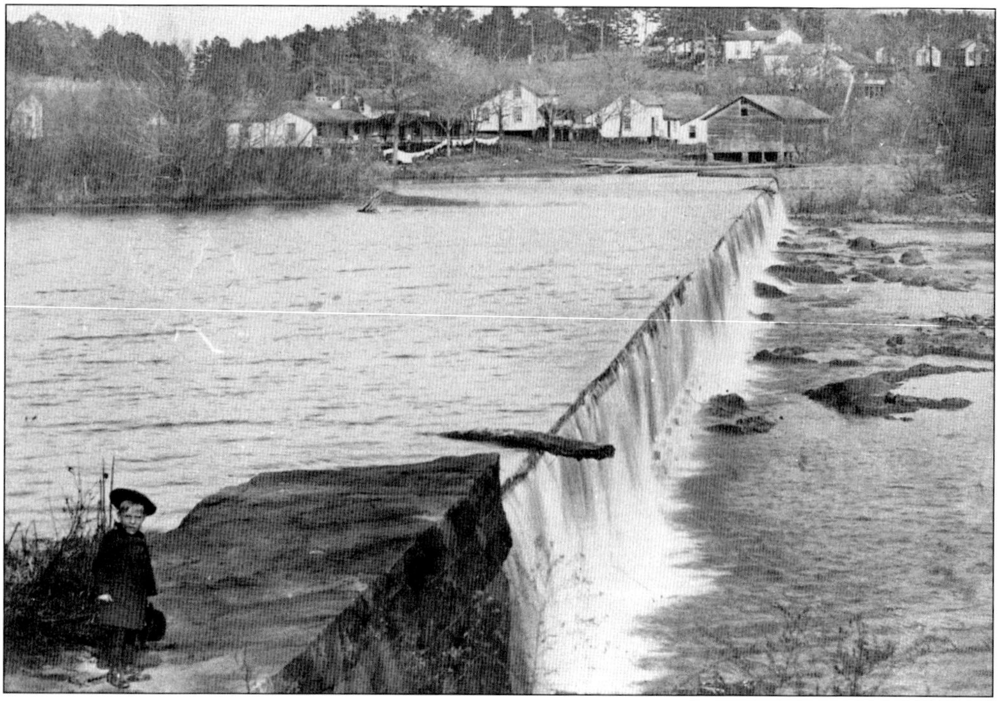

"This is a scene on the Haw River real near Graham," wrote M. Snyder on this postcard. Mills along the Haw River used water to provide power. As the mills closed, the dams were left untended, and most had eroded by the 1950s. This photograph was probably taken on the road south of Graham at the dam at Swepsonville. (Courtesy of North Carolina State Archives.)

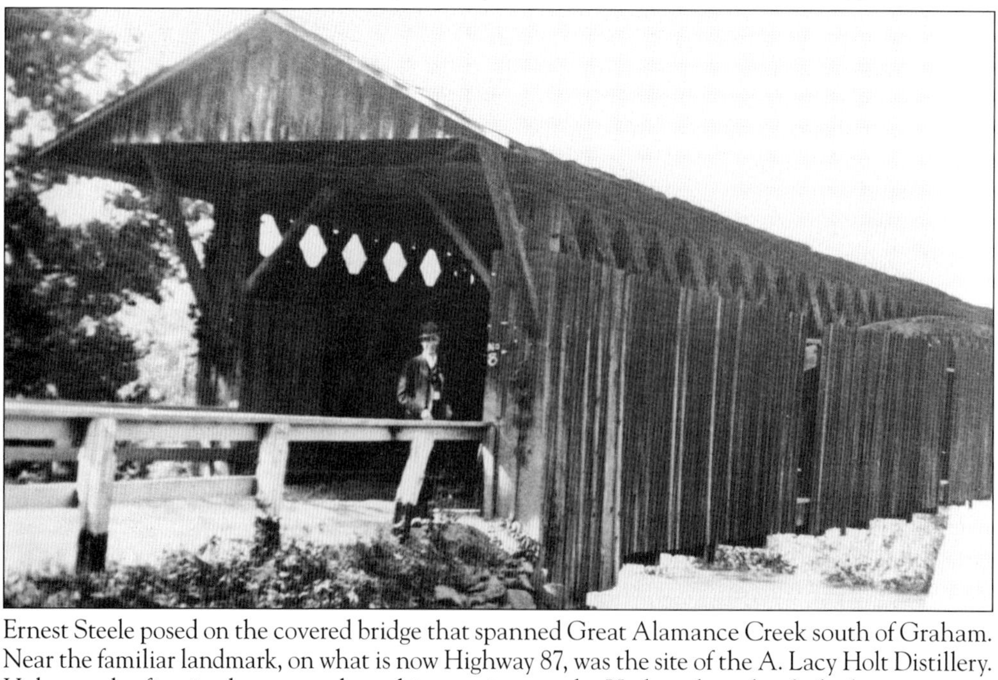

Ernest Steele posed on the covered bridge that spanned Great Alamance Creek south of Graham. Near the familiar landmark, on what is now Highway 87, was the site of the A. Lacy Holt Distillery. Holt was the first in the area to have his own jugs made. He kept barrels of whiskey sitting on shelves with tags stating the whiskey's age. (Courtesy of Wallace Steele.)

Two

The Holt Family

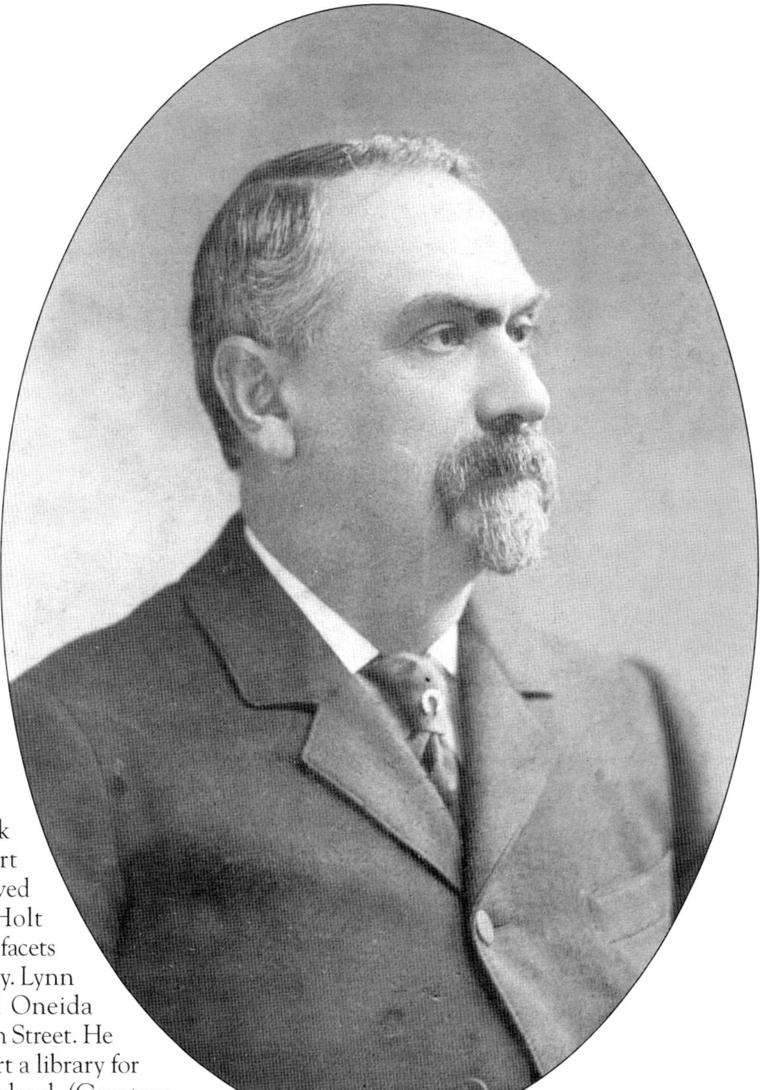

Lynn Banks Holt was born in Alamance and moved to Graham in 1886. His father, Edwin M. "E.M." Holt, bought parcels of land in Graham for four of his children. The siblings and their spouses lived within one block of each other just south of the courthouse. E.M. Holt opened the Bank of Lexington on Court Square. Though he lived in Alamance, the Holt family influenced many facets of Graham's community. Lynn Banks Holt operated Oneida Cotton Mills on Harden Street. He also gave $1,000 to start a library for the Graham Graded School. (Courtesy of Alamance County Historical Museum.)

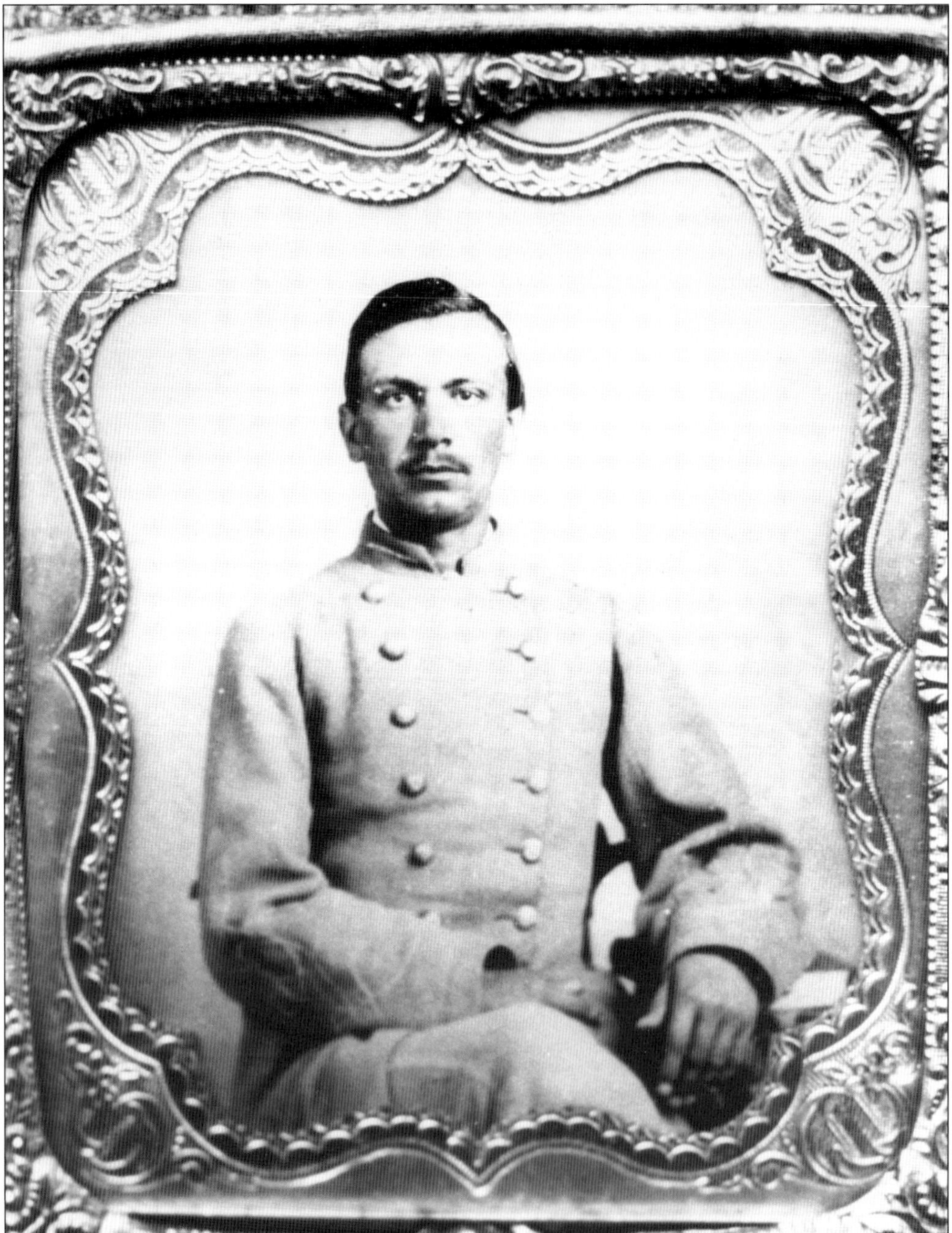

Lynn Banks Holt and his brother Alexander joined Fisher's Regiment at Company Shops on July 2, 1861. The 6th North Carolina Regiment had engaged at the Battle of Bull Run by July 21. The Confederates won the battle, but Colonel Fisher was killed. The Holt brothers survived the battle unharmed. (Courtesy of Alamance County Historical Museum.)

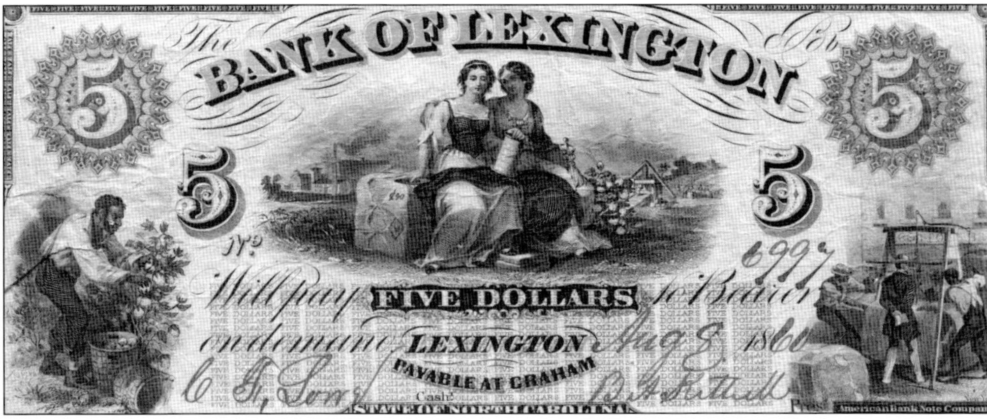

E.M. Holt organized the Bank of Lexington. The paper currency issued by the bank was payable at its Graham branch, which opened on July 25, 1859. It was located in the Holt Building, located at the corner of Court Square and South Main Street. The bank operated alongside the Alfred A. Holt & James H. Holt Store, said to be the oldest establishment in Graham. E.M. Holt's son James was the first cashier. In 1861, E.M. Holt sold his stock in the bank to George W. Swepson for $28,750. (Courtesy of City of Graham.)

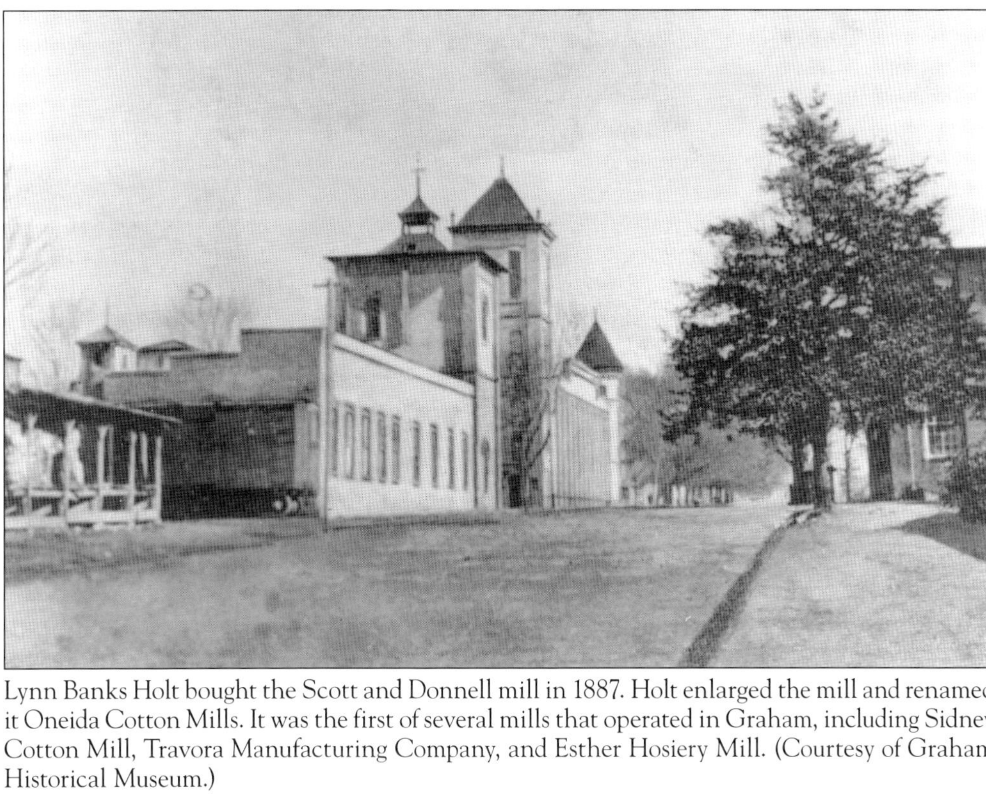

Lynn Banks Holt bought the Scott and Donnell mill in 1887. Holt enlarged the mill and renamed it Oneida Cotton Mills. It was the first of several mills that operated in Graham, including Sidney Cotton Mill, Travora Manufacturing Company, and Esther Hosiery Mill. (Courtesy of Graham Historical Museum.)

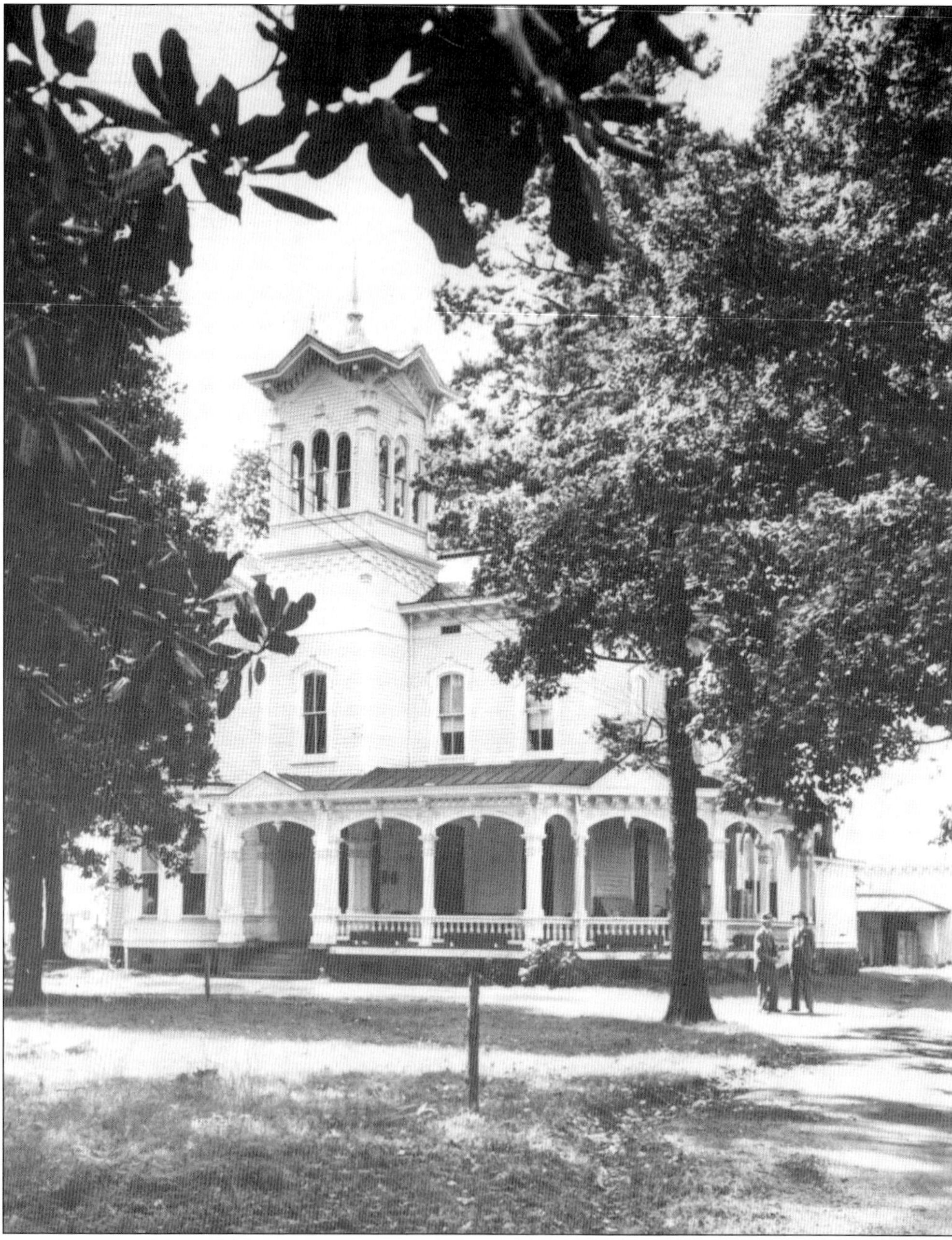

Lynn Banks Holt and his wife, Mary Catherine Mebane Holt, lived in this grand home, built in 1886 at the corner of South Maple and Banks Streets on a 470-acre tract of land known as Alamance Farm. From the cupola atop the main house, Banks could survey the estate and the racetrack. On the property were two garden areas, apple trees, and a pear orchard, as well as two barns, a greenhouse, servants' quarters, a schoolhouse, a brick gashouse, and two tenant houses. Later, a brick two-car garage was added. After Holt's death in 1920, the farm was divided, and in 1967, the house was torn down to make way for an apartment complex. (Courtesy of Alamance County Historical Museum.)

Mary Catherine Mebane, the wife of Lynn Banks Holt, was the daughter of North Carolina senator Giles Mebane of Orange County. She and Holt married in a double wedding ceremony on October 26, 1865. The other happy couple, Holt's sister Mary Elizabeth and Capt. James N. Williamson, built a home nearby. (Courtesy of Alamance County Historical Museum.)

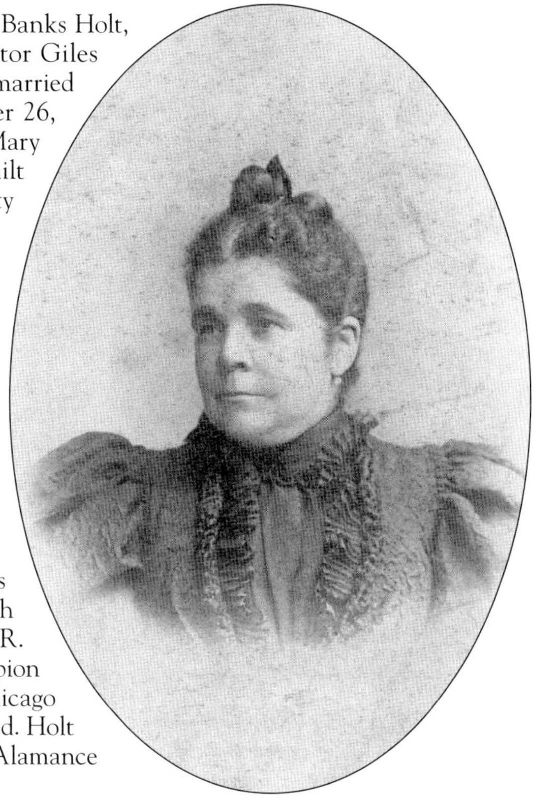

Harness racing was popular in the 1880s. Lynn Banks Holt bought his first mares in 1892 and built a barn and fenced track on his farm. In 1894, he and James F. Scott of Raleigh purchased the champion racehorse John R. Gentry, pictured here, for $10,000. The champion pacer raced in Lexington, Kentucky, and Chicago but did not perform as well as had been hoped. Holt sold his string of horses in 1896. (Courtesy of Alamance County Historical Museum.)

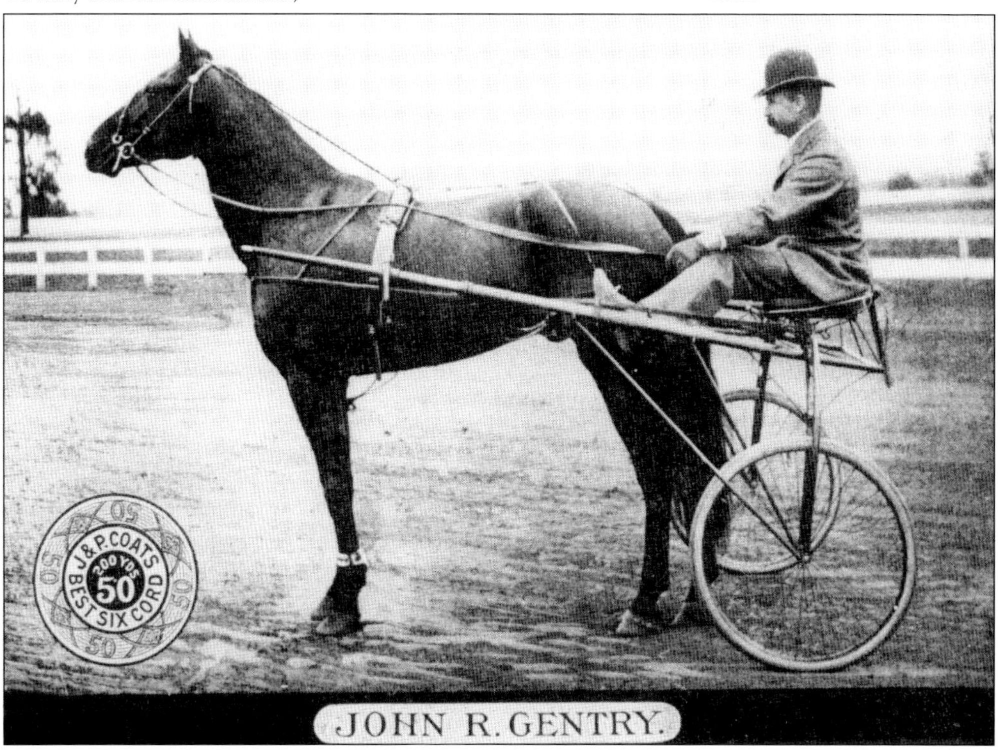

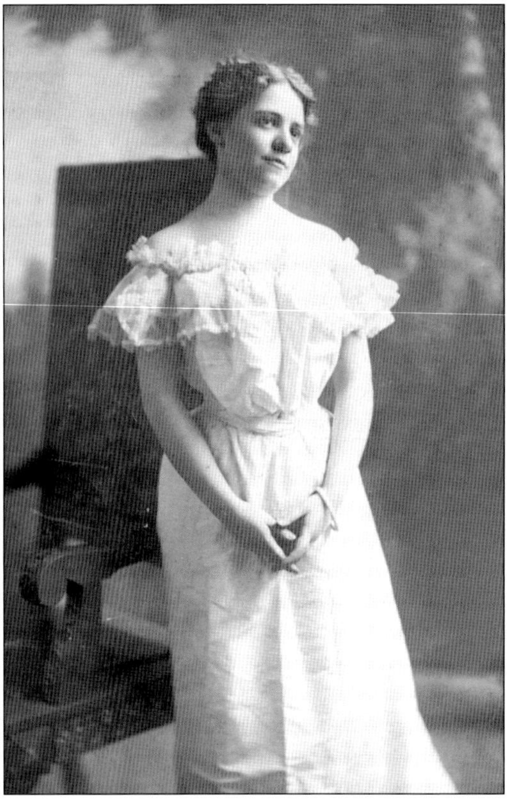

Lynn Banks Holt's daughter Mary Virginia , or "Mamie," was born on her grandfather's grain plantation in Alamance in 1867, where she and her parents lived until they moved to Graham in 1886. She married the town doctor, George Allen Mebane Jr., in 1887. (Courtesy of North Carolina State Archives.)

Frances Ann, the daughter of E.M. Holt, married John Lea Williamson of Caswell County in December 1865. The couple lived in the Victorian-style home on South Main Street pictured here, which was torn down in 1965 to make way for Graham City Hall. (Courtesy of Pat Bailey.)

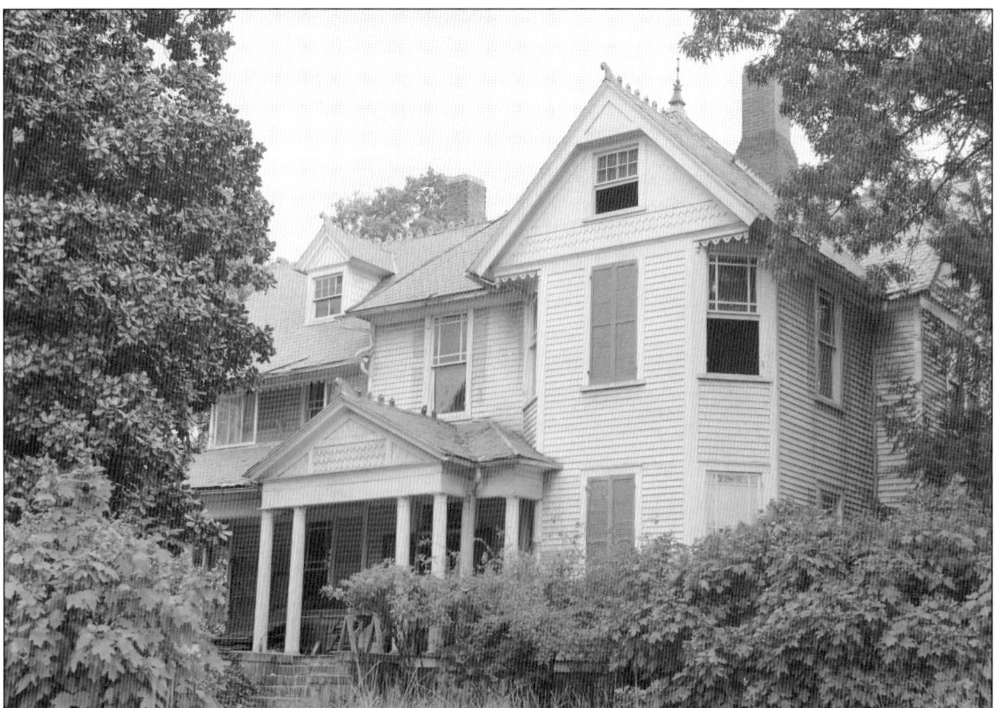

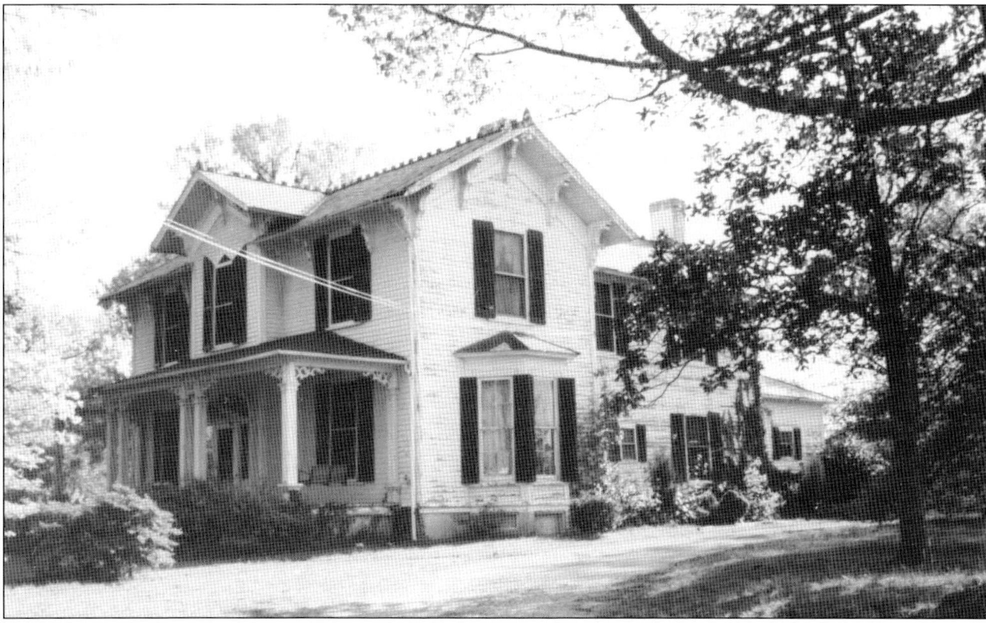

Known as the Captain White House, this two-story Victorian home was built in 1871 by Emma Virginia Holt and her new husband, Capt. James W. White of the Confederate army. The house, situated on South Main Street, was restored in 1998 and is now the home of the Alamance County Arts Council. (Courtesy of Graham Historical Museum.)

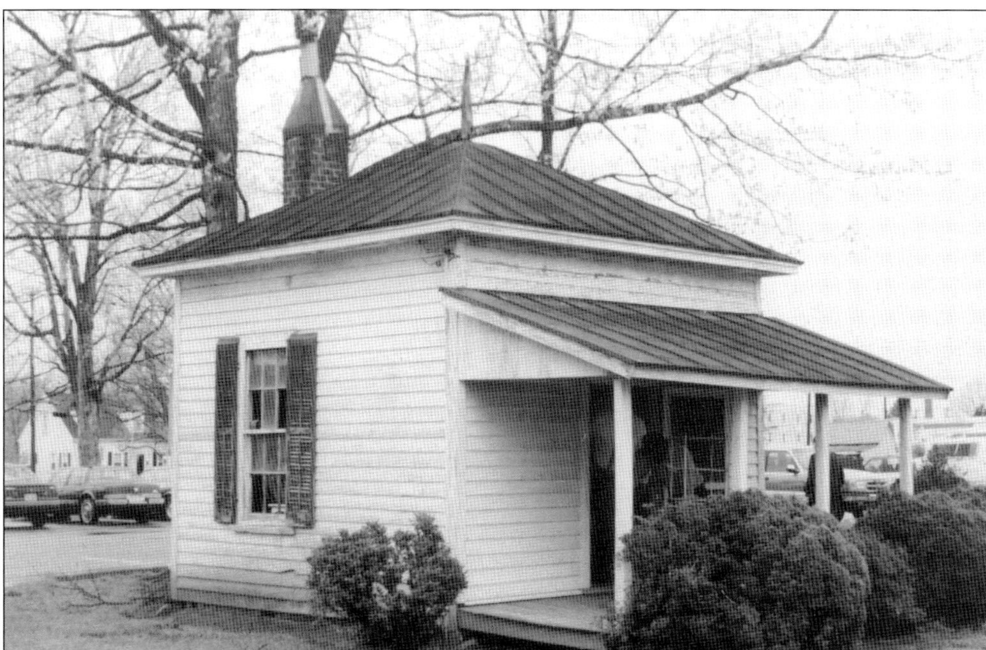

This small building stood behind the Captain White House. With only one room and a fireplace, it was probably used as servants' quarters. It was torn down in 1994 to make way for the new Graham Public Library. (Courtesy of Graham Historical Museum.)

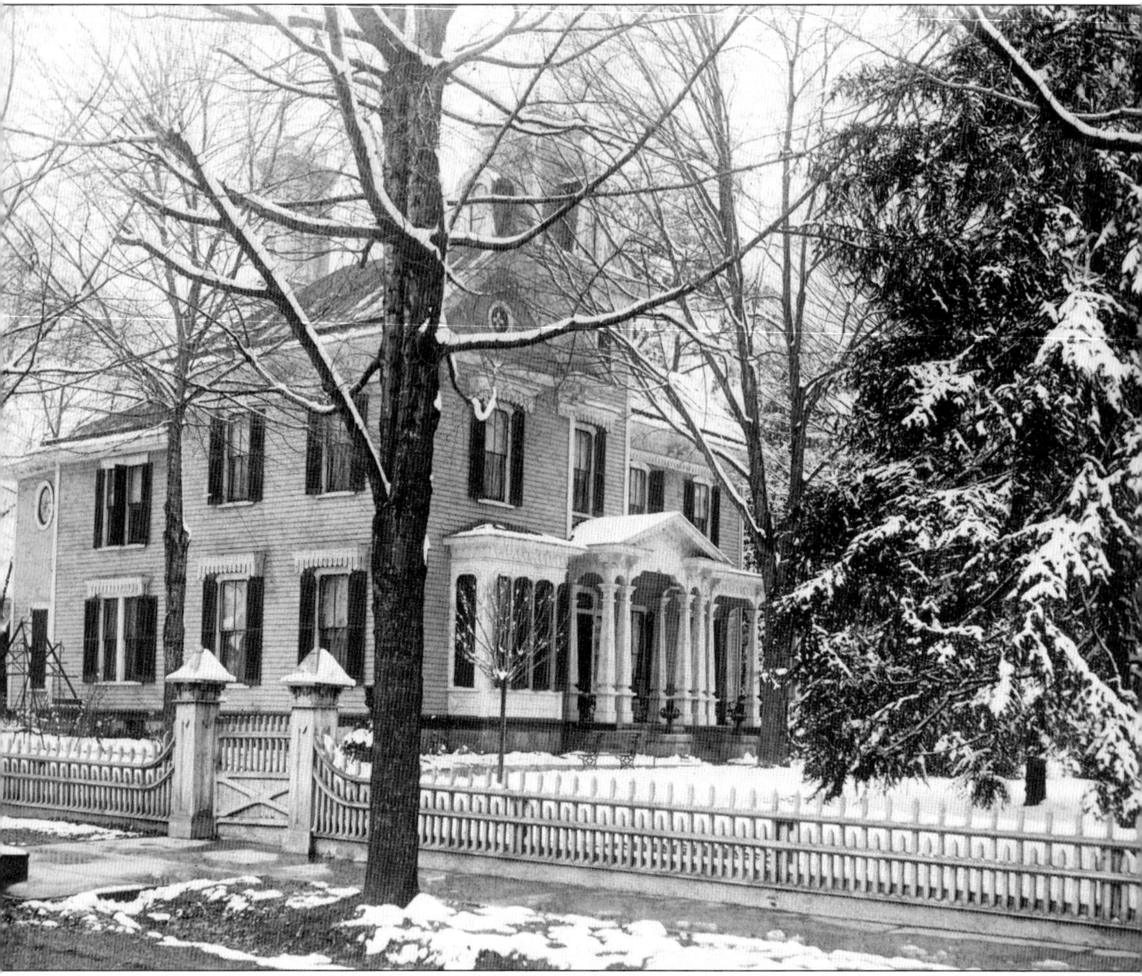

Mary Elizabeth Holt and her husband, Capt. James N. Williamson, built Elmhurst in 1869 on South Main Street. McClure Funeral Home purchased the property in 1939, and the business remained in that location until the house was acquired and renovated in 1993 by Nationsbank. It is now home to Bank of America and remains a familiar Graham landmark. (Courtesy of Alamance County Historical Museum.)

Capt. James N. Williamson of Caswell County was a commanding officer in the Confederate infantry in the Civil War. He partnered with his father-in-law, E.M. Holt, to build Carolina Cotton Mills, situated north of Company Shops. He later constructed Ossipee Cotton Mill, which opened in 1882. (Courtesy of Alamance County Historical Museum.)

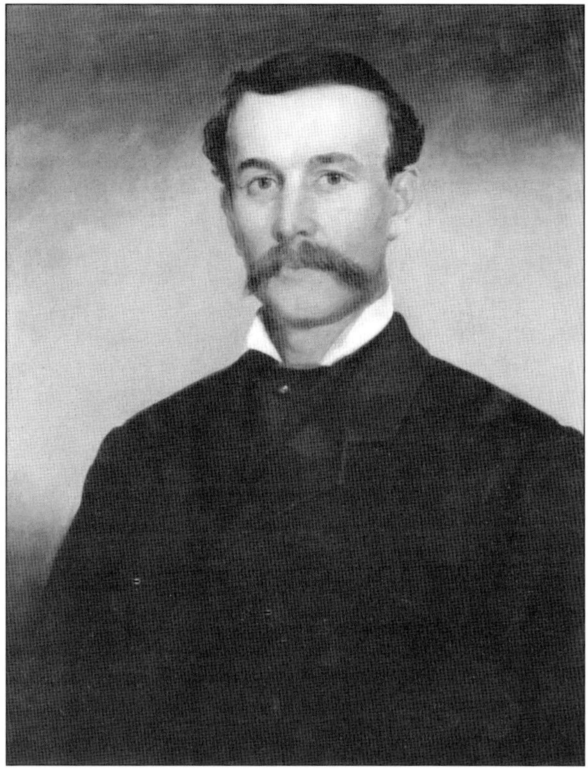

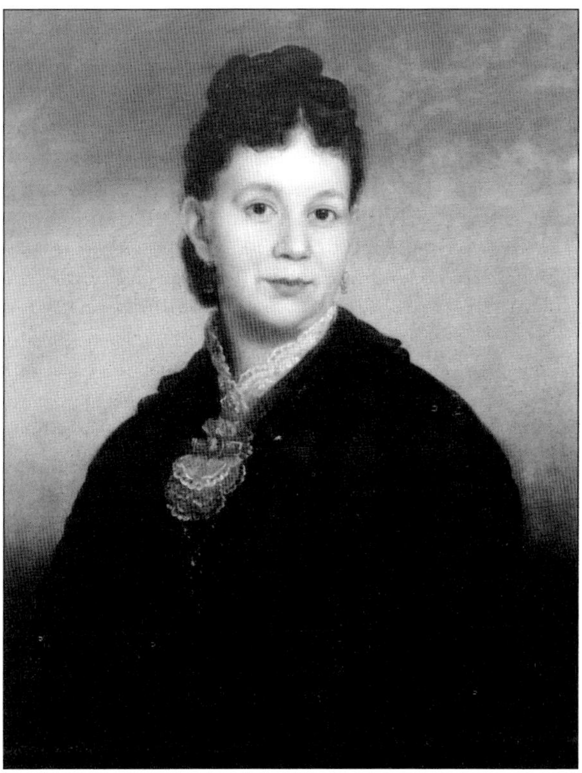

Mary Elizabeth Holt and Capt. James N. Williamson lived with her father in Alamance while Elmhurst was completed. Captain Williamson was instrumental in the construction of the railroad station known as Mill Point, which later became Elon College. The couple built one of the first homes at Mill Point. (Courtesy of Alamance County Historical Museum.)

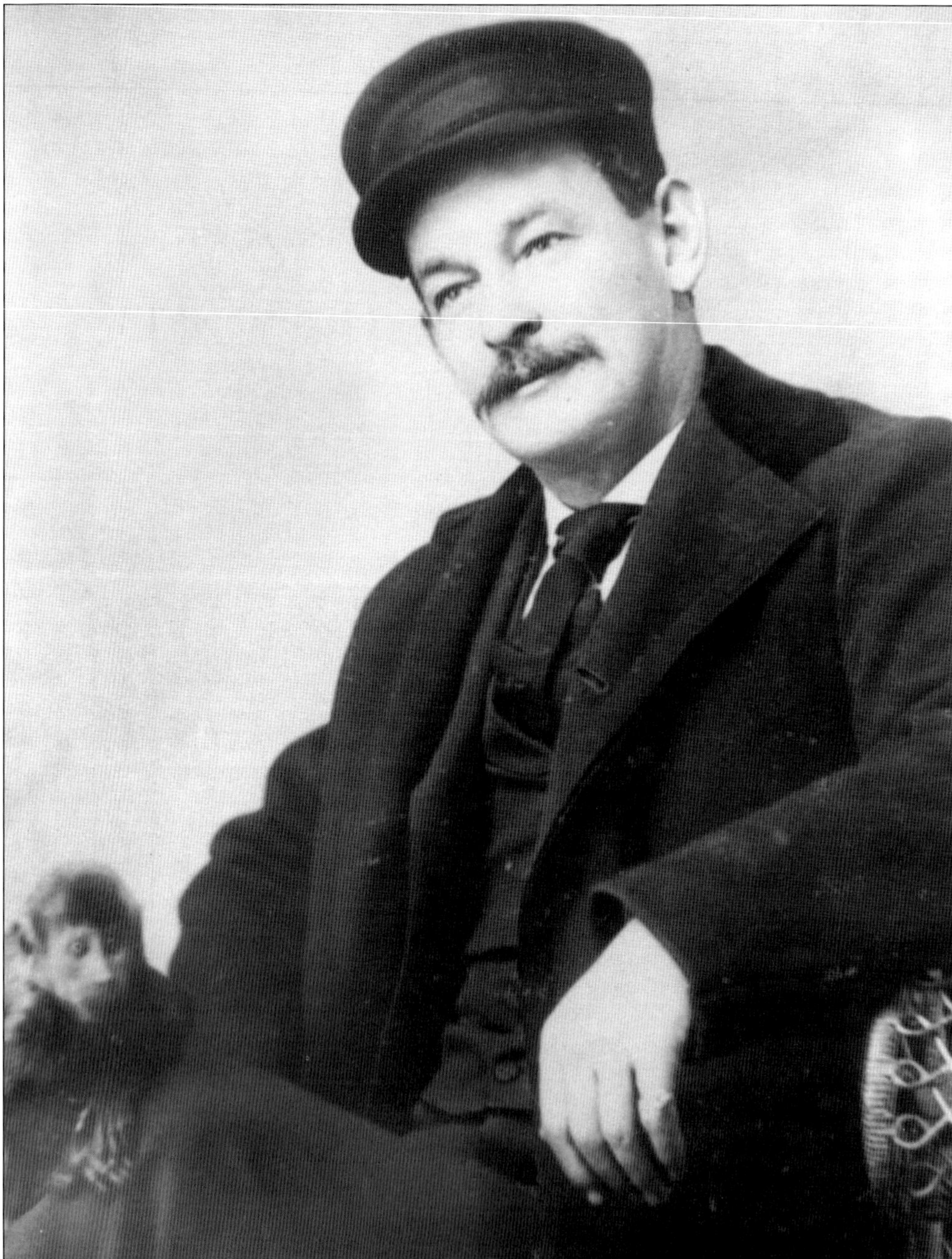

Samuel Moore Holt, a grandson of E.M. Holt, was an adventurous world traveler and sea captain. On his journeys from 1881 to 1900, he witnessed a volcanic eruption on the island of Montserrat and experienced an earthquake on St. Kitts. He acquired a parrot and a pet capuchin monkey, which he named Jocko. He also wrote travel accounts that were syndicated in many newspapers in the late 1800s and published under the pseudonym "Tropic." According to the story, when Jocko became too old to travel, he lived out his days at a local drugstore. (Courtesy of Alamance County Historical Museum.)

Three

Business and Industry

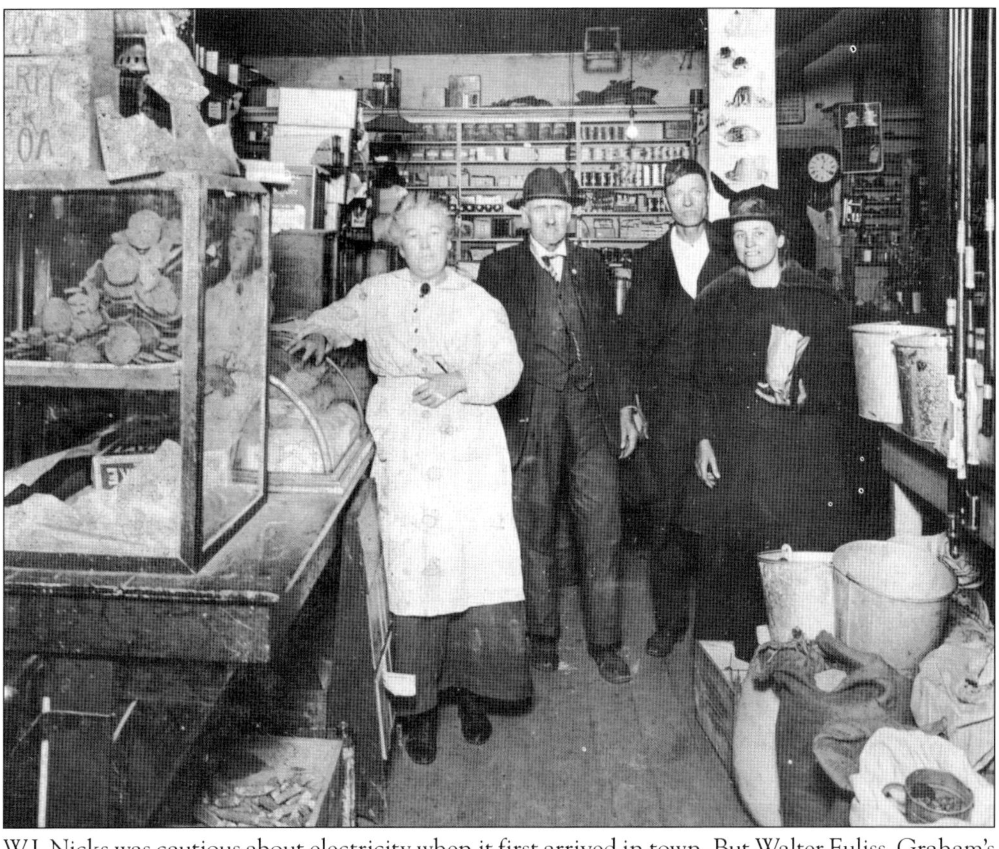

W.J. Nicks was cautious about electricity when it first arrived in town. But Walter Euliss, Graham's first electrician, who ran a shop next door, talked Nicks into adding one lightbulb to the back of his store. The bulb is seen here over Nicks's left shoulder around 1920. (Courtesy of Graham Historical Museum.)

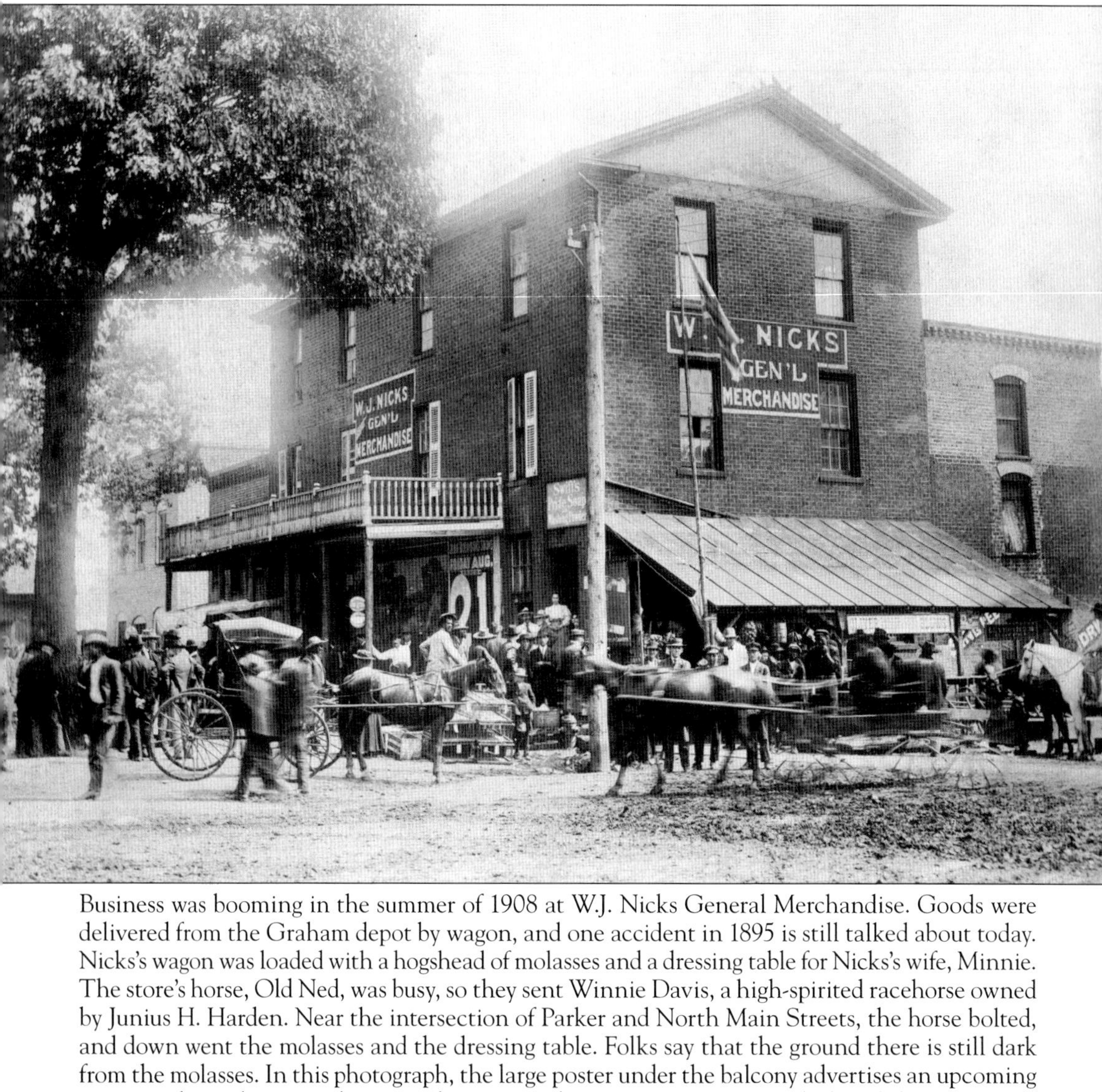

Business was booming in the summer of 1908 at W.J. Nicks General Merchandise. Goods were delivered from the Graham depot by wagon, and one accident in 1895 is still talked about today. Nicks's wagon was loaded with a hogshead of molasses and a dressing table for Nicks's wife, Minnie. The store's horse, Old Ned, was busy, so they sent Winnie Davis, a high-spirited racehorse owned by Junius H. Harden. Near the intersection of Parker and North Main Streets, the horse bolted, and down went the molasses and the dressing table. Folks say that the ground there is still dark from the molasses. In this photograph, the large poster under the balcony advertises an upcoming circus: "John Robinson's Shows, Burlington, Friday, August 21." W.J. Nicks loved the circus, and was happy to advertise in exchange for a free ticket. (Courtesy of Graham Historical Museum.)

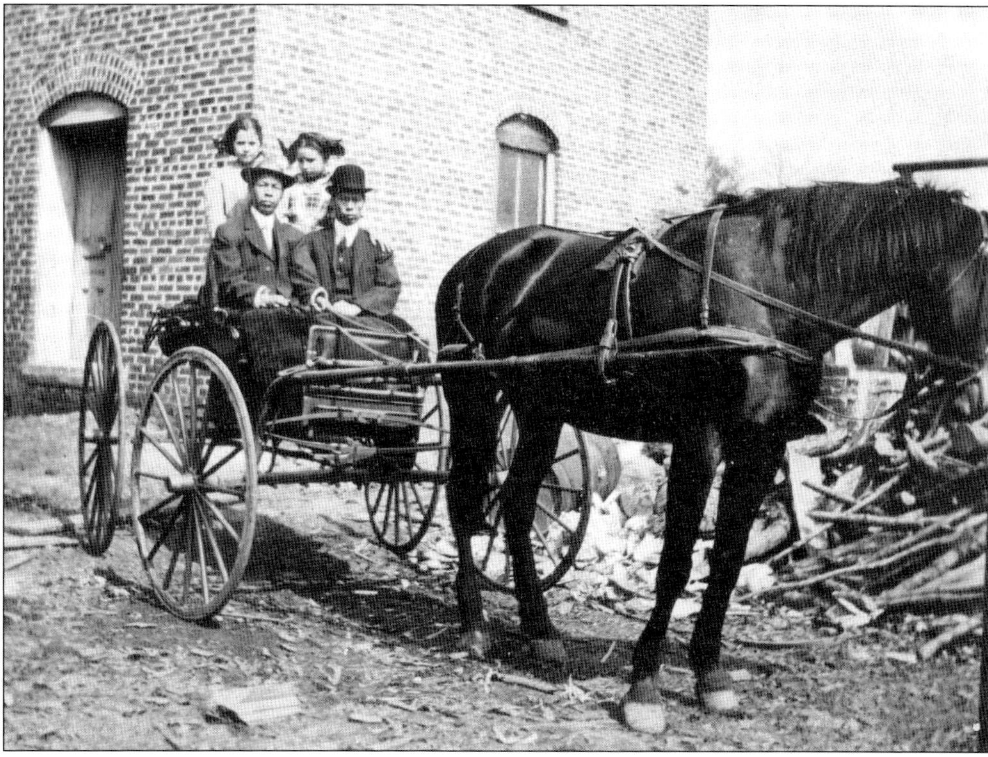

In 1902, Nicks built an addition to the store, which he rented to Sing Lee, who had immigrated to America in 1898. The Sing Lee Laundry operated until 1927 and was the only establishment of its kind in Graham. Seen here are two of the Chinese men who operated the laundry. (Courtesy of Graham Historical Museum.)

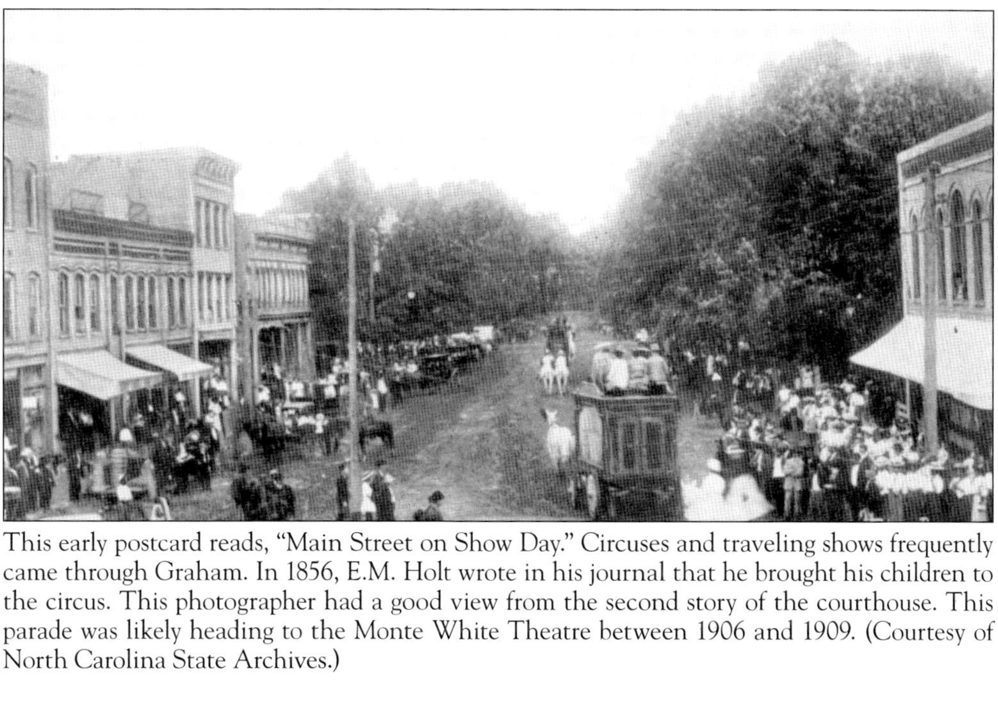

This early postcard reads, "Main Street on Show Day." Circuses and traveling shows frequently came through Graham. In 1856, E.M. Holt wrote in his journal that he brought his children to the circus. This photographer had a good view from the second story of the courthouse. This parade was likely heading to the Monte White Theatre between 1906 and 1909. (Courtesy of North Carolina State Archives.)

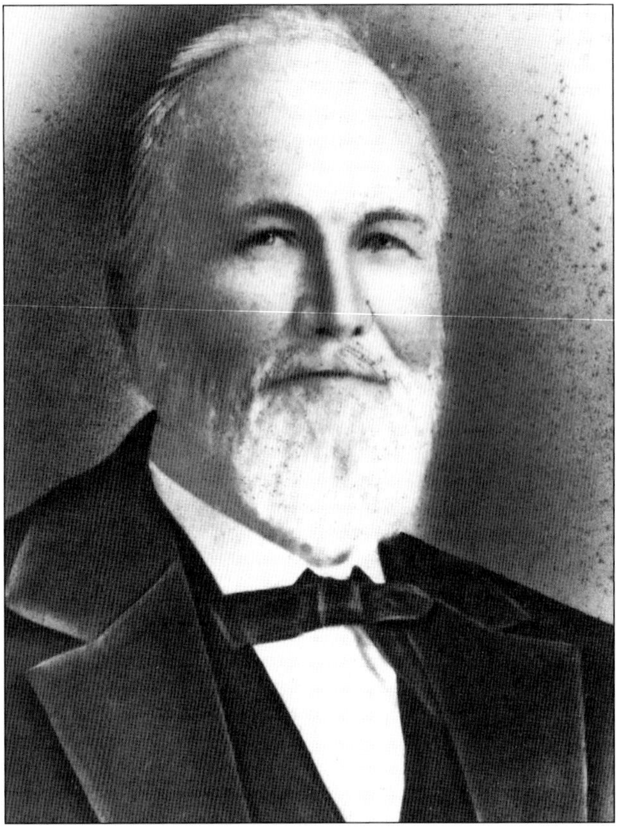

In 1876, J.W. Harden, known around town as "Mr. Billy," built the establishment seen below on the southwest corner of Court Square. The Harden store also housed the post office, with a Mr. Billy as postmaster. (Courtesy of Graham Historical Museum.)

When Harden retired to his farm south of town, he sold the store, pictured here, to Abraham Rancher Flintom and Flintom's brother-in-law John Edward Cole, who ran the successful general merchandise store. The second floor was used as a roller-skating rink in 1908. (Courtesy of Graham Historical Museum.)

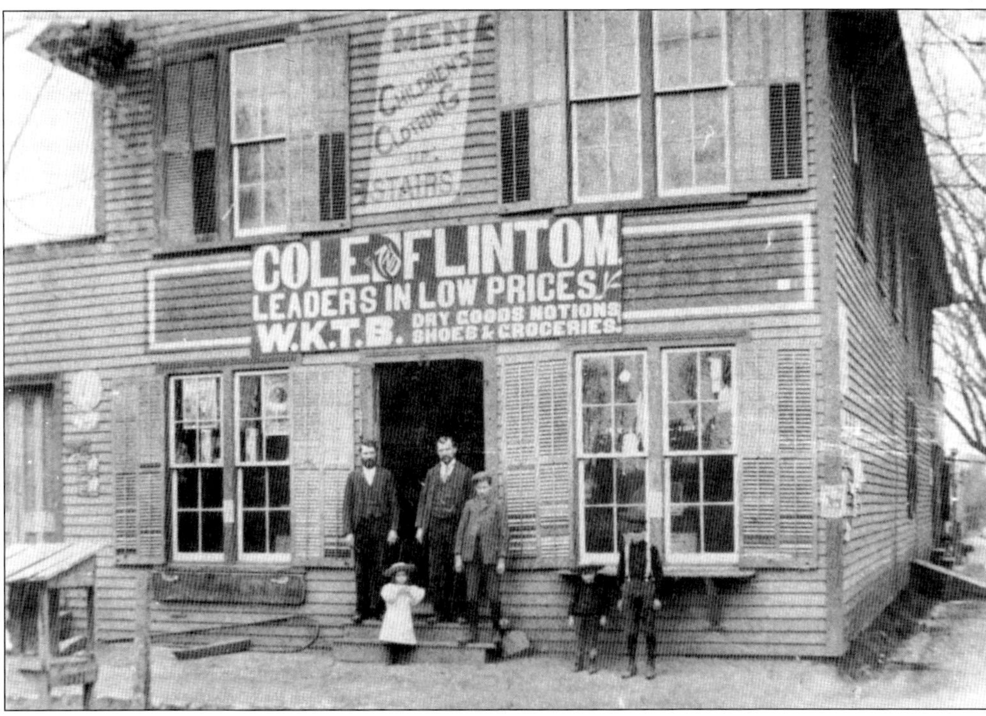

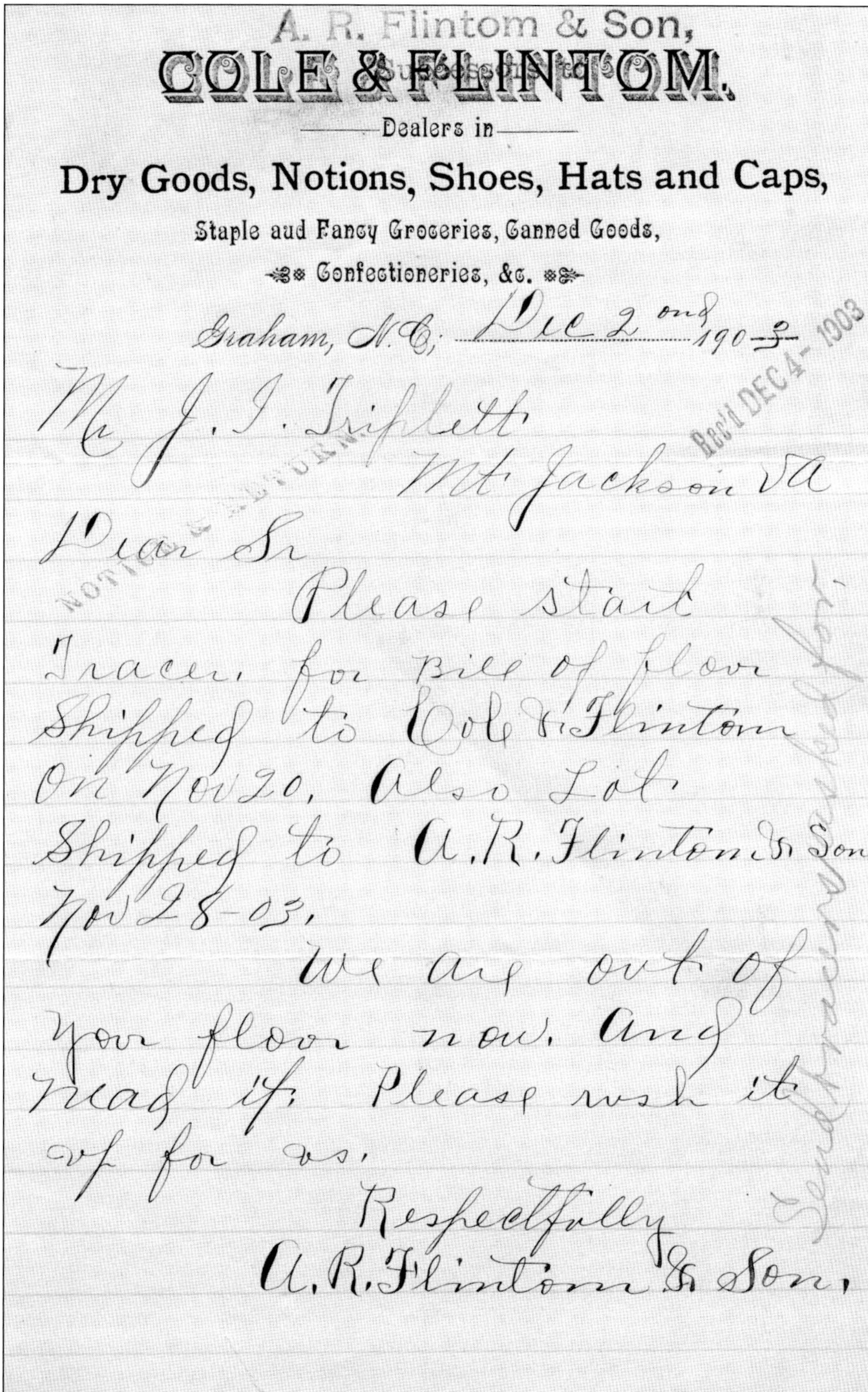

A. R. Flintom & Son,
COLE & FLINTOM.
Successors to
Dealers in
Dry Goods, Notions, Shoes, Hats and Caps,
Staple aud Fancy Groceries, Canned Goods,
Confectioneries, &c.

Graham, N.C.; Dec 2nd 1903

Rec'd DEC 4- 1903

Mr J. T. Triplett
Mt Jackson VA

Dear Sir
Please start Tracer for Bill of flour Shipped to Cole & Flintom On Nov 20. Also Lot Shipped to A.R. Flintom & Son Nov 28-03.
We are out of your flour now. And need it. Please rush it up for us.

Respectfully
A.R. Flintom & Son.

Send tracer for

By November 1903, Cole and Flintom had become A.R. Flintom & Son. The father-and-son team managed the store as a branch of W.K.T.B., one of the largest grocery stores across the South. They touted fresh, naturally grown produce. (Courtesy of Alamance County Public Libraries.)

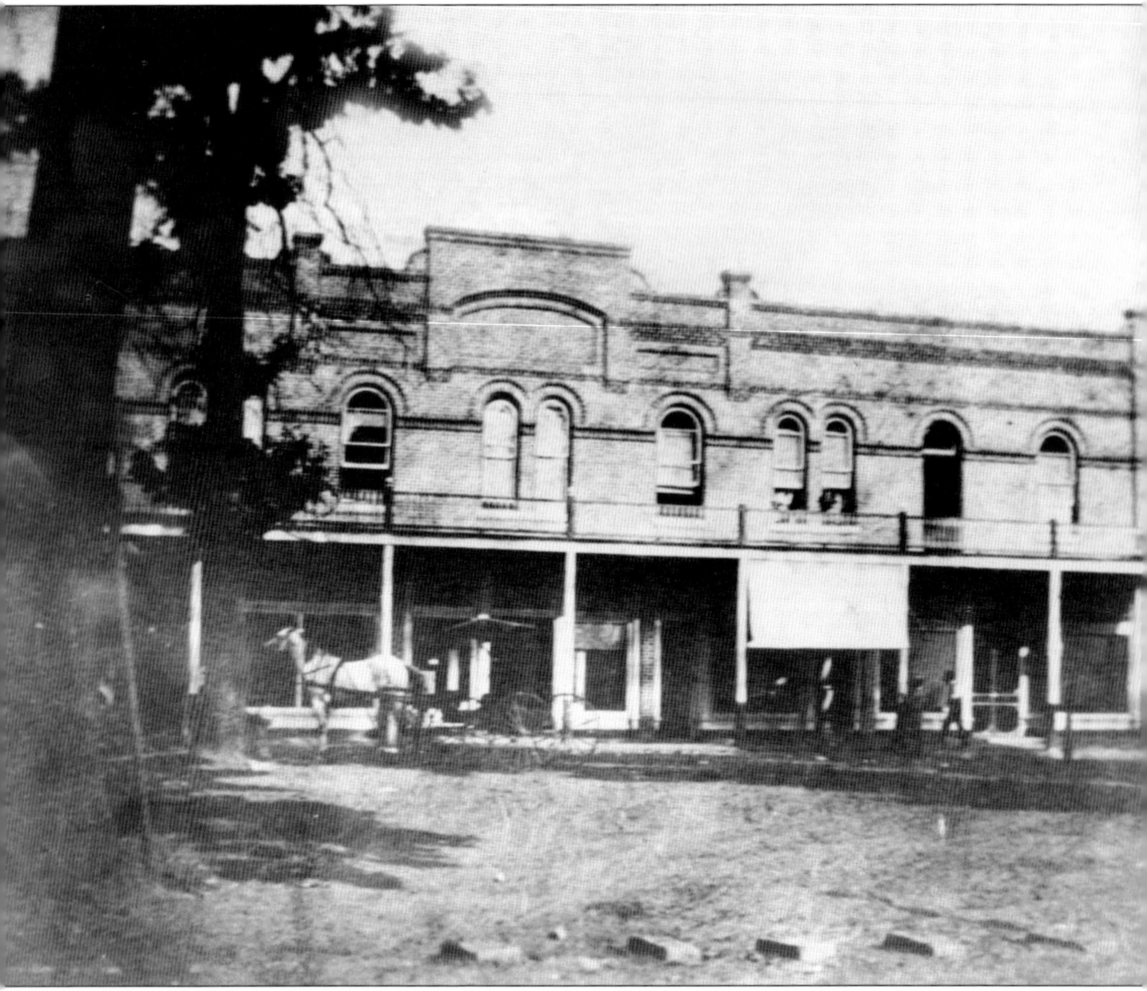

The Vestal Hotel, seen here in an early photograph, was built by William Sherman Vestal on Court Square. The hotel opened on New Year's Day, 1903, and burned to the ground seven months later. Vestal immediately rebuilt, and the hotel opened again in 1904. The new manager, W.C. Tripp, lived at the hotel with his family, and Vestal was a young widower at the time. Graham residents talked about a romance that made the newspaper in 1908, when Vestal eloped with Mildred Tripp, the innkeeper's daughter. The *Alamance Gleaner* gave a detailed description of the events that evening: a dance at the hotel had broken up about midnight, after which the elopers carried out their plans. The young lady made her escape on a ladder placed at her window. They drove through the countryside all night, and at 7:00 a.m., they were married in Reidsville. (Courtesy of Skee and Virginia Johnson.)

Henry William "Buck" Scott stood up to one of Graham's most famous visitors, Carrie Nation, a national prohibitionist who traveled the country denouncing alcohol use. She visited Graham in July 1907, setting her sights on three downtown businesses. Scott politely informed her that any disturbance would be frowned upon and could potentially land her in jail. Nation opted to lecture the patrons of the barrooms before moving on. (Courtesy of City of Graham.)

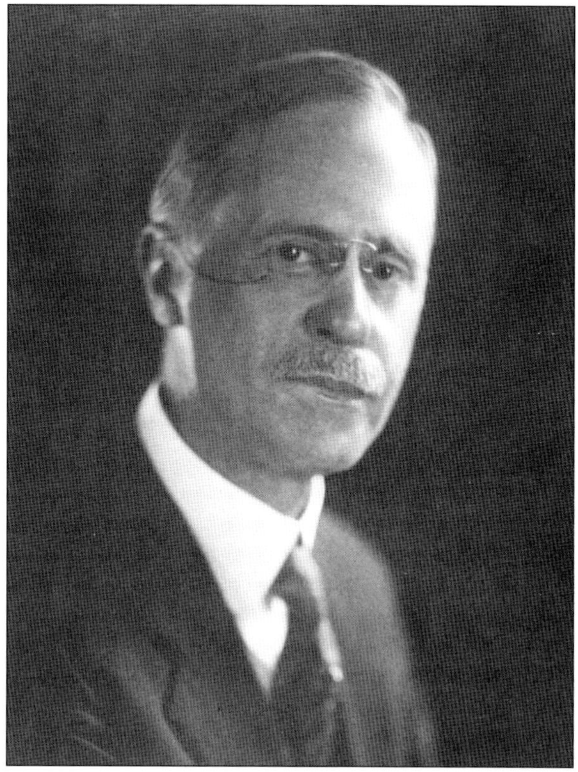

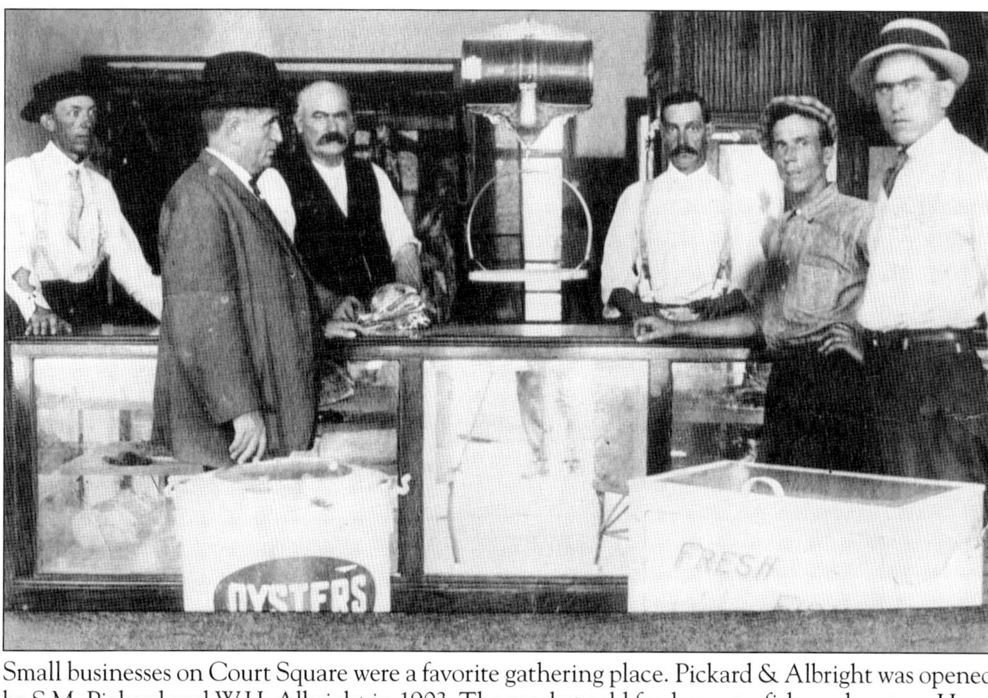

Small businesses on Court Square were a favorite gathering place. Pickard & Albright was opened by S.M. Pickard and W.H. Albright in 1903. The market sold fresh meats, fish, and oysters. Here, Sam Johnston (far left), James A. Ray (third from left), and others gather at the seafood market around 1914. (Courtesy of Charles Whittemore.)

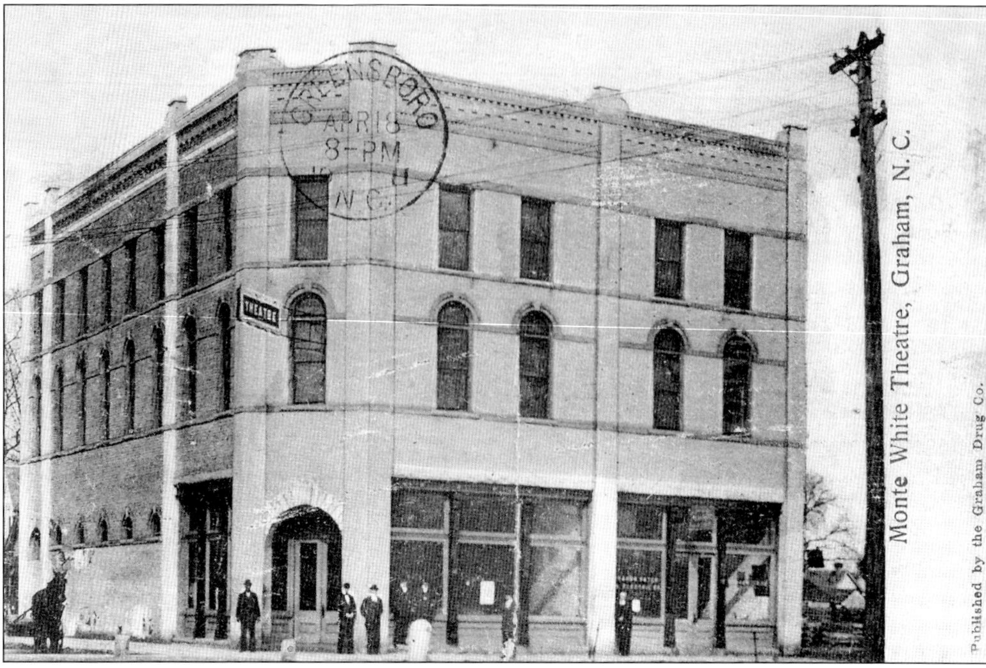

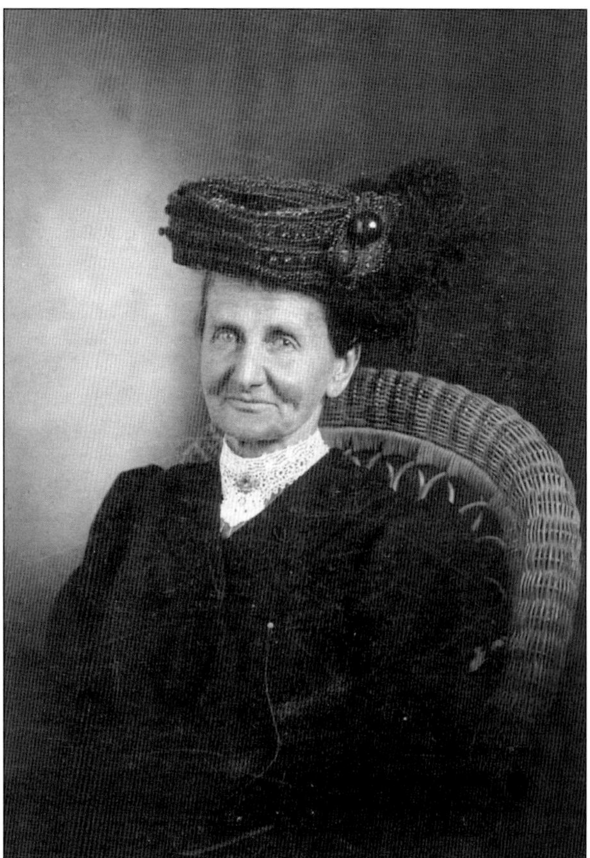

The first play at Monte White Theatre (seen here in an early postcard) opened in 1907 to a packed house. Ticket prices ranged from 50¢ to $1. The first floor was used by several stores, including Crack & Joe, which sold dry goods, fabric, clothing, and other accessories. The second floor held the stage and orchestra seats, and a balcony was on the third floor. Built by Edwin H. White and Thomas Montgomery, the elaborate theater operated until 1921. (Courtesy of Don Bolden.)

A night at the Monte White was an occasion to remember. Ladies certainly wore their best dresses and fancy hats. Here, Dora Harden of Graham looks ready to go to the opera or a play. (Courtesy of Graham Historical Museum.)

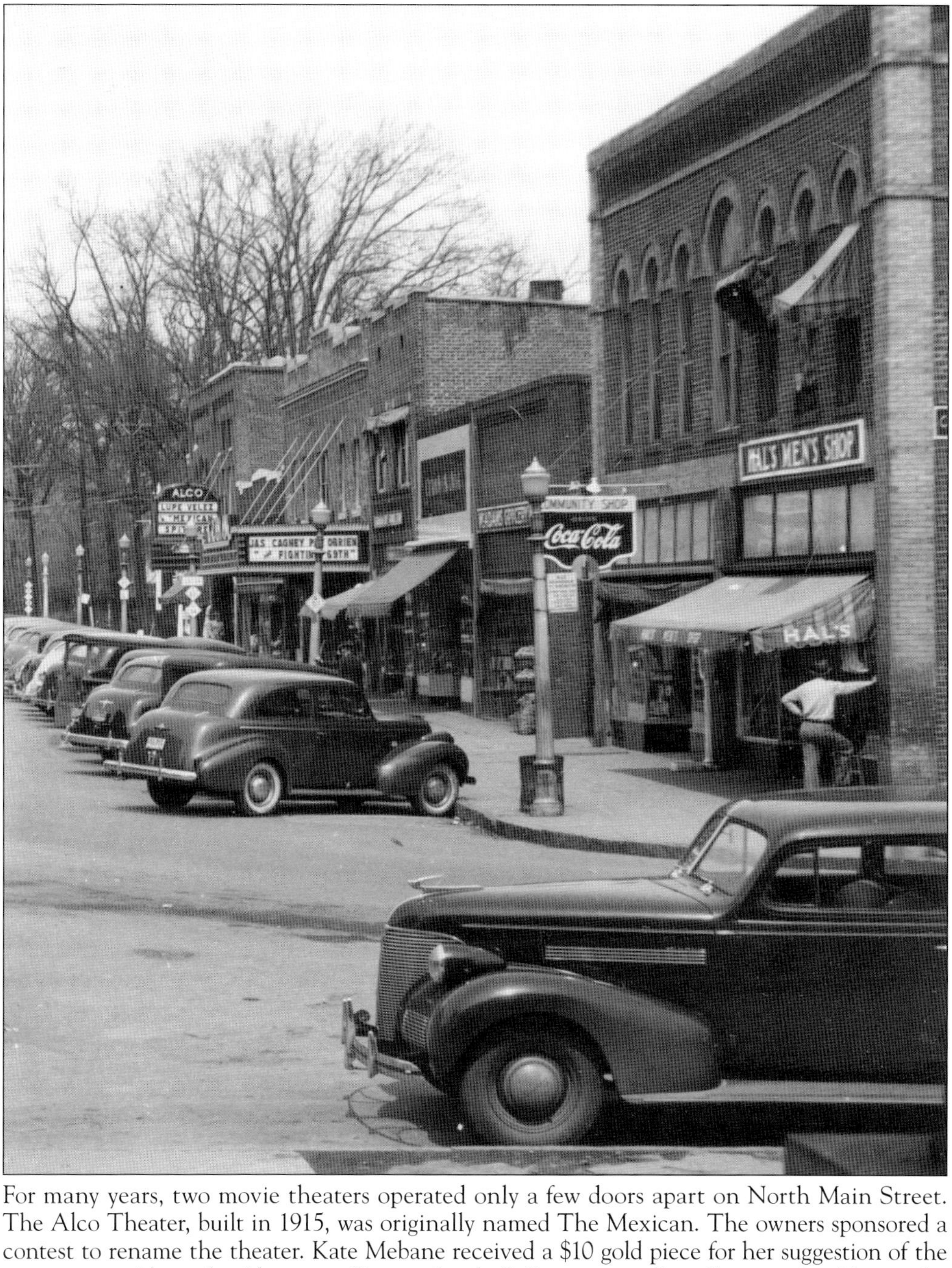

For many years, two movie theaters operated only a few doors apart on North Main Street. The Alco Theater, built in 1915, was originally named The Mexican. The owners sponsored a contest to rename the theater. Kate Mebane received a $10 gold piece for her suggestion of the new name—Alco—for Alamance County. Linda S. Stewart recalls walking to the Alco in the early 1950s, usually to see a Western. It cost 9¢ to get into the movie and 1¢ for a Tootsie Pop, a lollipop with a chocolate center. The Graham Cinema was built in 1928 and is still in operation today. (Courtesy of Skee and Virginia Johnson.)

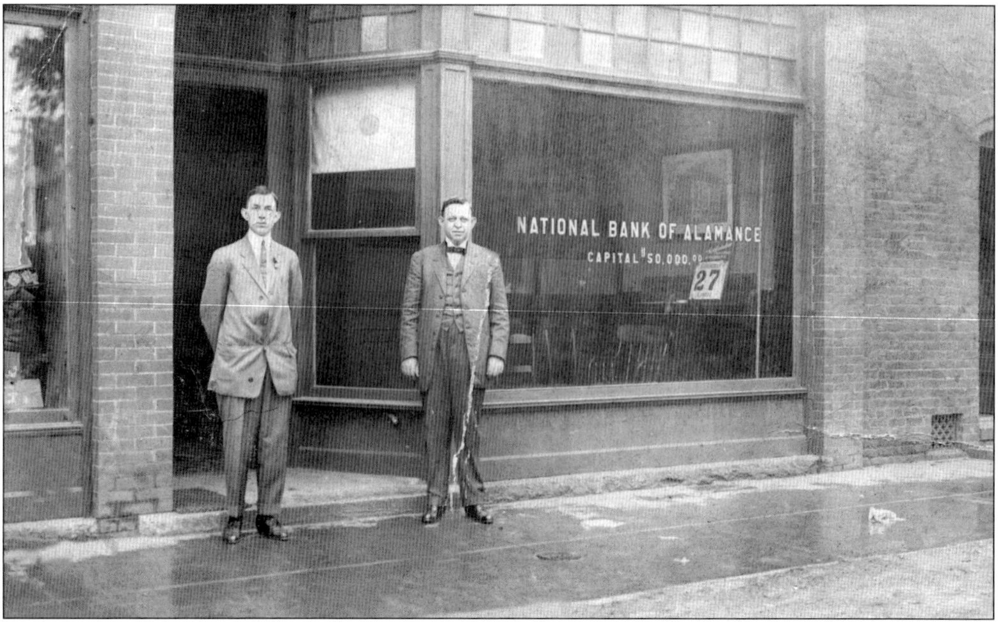

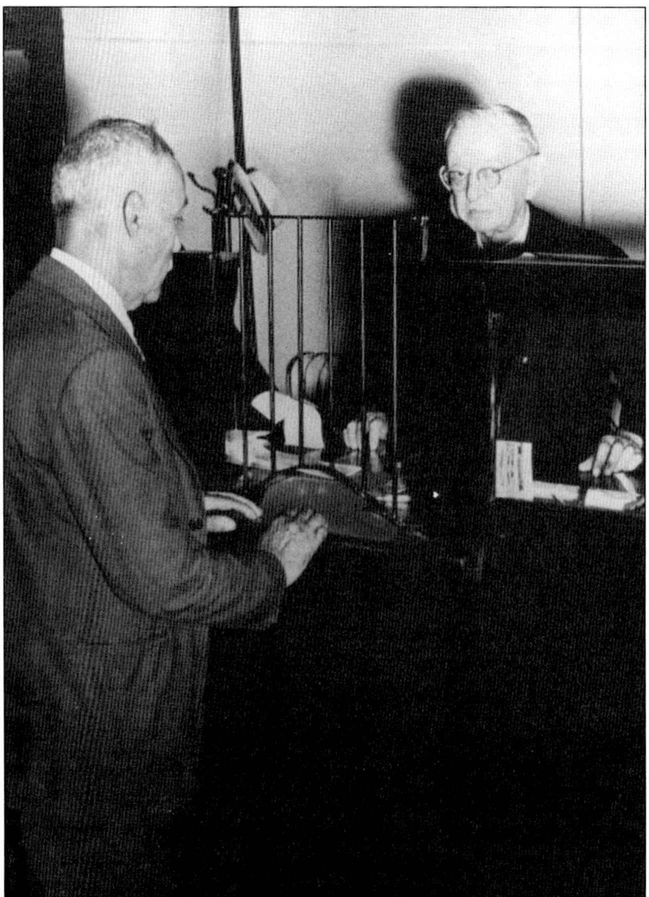

The Bank of Alamance opened in 1899 with Eugene M. Armfield as president and J.L. Scott Jr. as vice president. The first cashier was Charles A. Scott. This photograph was taken in 1907, when the bank became the National Bank of Alamance. Sound business practices enabled the bank to remain open throughout the Great Depression of the 1930s. (Courtesy of Graham Historical Museum.)

When the Bank of Alamance opened, the first deposit was made by Color "Cola" Russell, an African American tinsmith. This photograph was taken on August 4, 1951, the bank's 52nd anniversary, as Russell (left) again makes the first deposit of the day. (Courtesy of Graham Historical Museum.)

Edward S. "Ned" Parker Jr. ran a law office beside the Bank of Alamance. When the first courthouse was torn down in 1923, there was talk of rebuilding it on Harden Street. Parker spoke passionately for keeping the courthouse at the center of Graham. He went on to serve as mayor several times and was president of Graham Water, Ice & Electric Company. (Courtesy of Alamance County Public Libraries.)

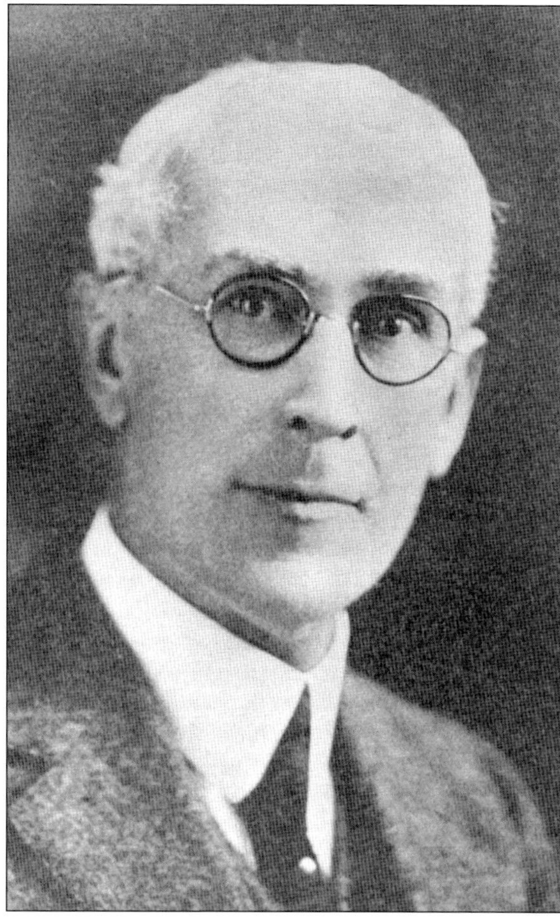

Thomas Store Company, run by James Thomas, was at the southwest corner of Court Square and South Main Street. The man in the center is Will P. "Billy" Smith, who operated the store prior to World War I. The store closed in 1920, and the building is presently used as a law office. (Courtesy of Graham Historical Museum.)

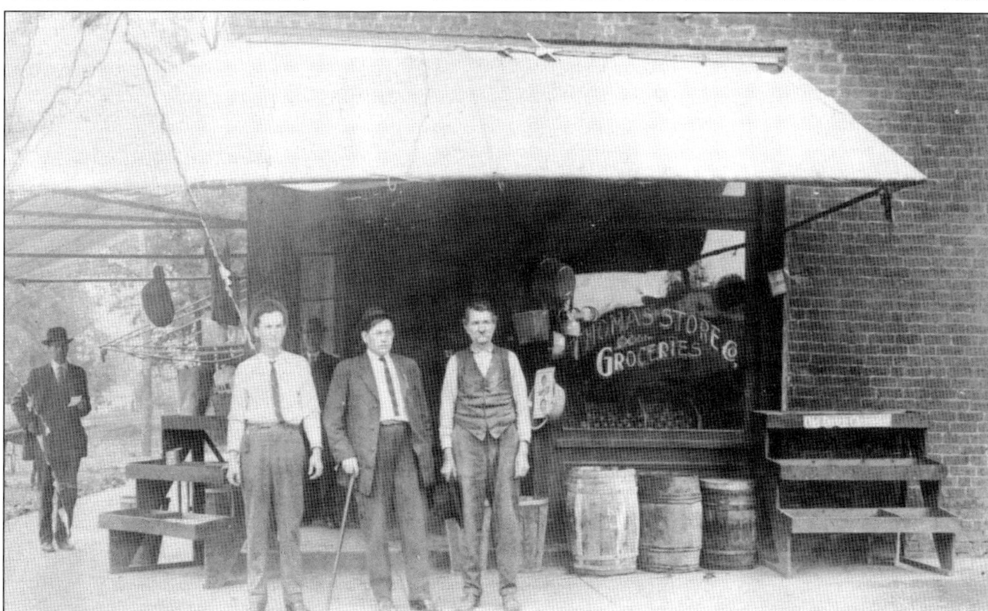

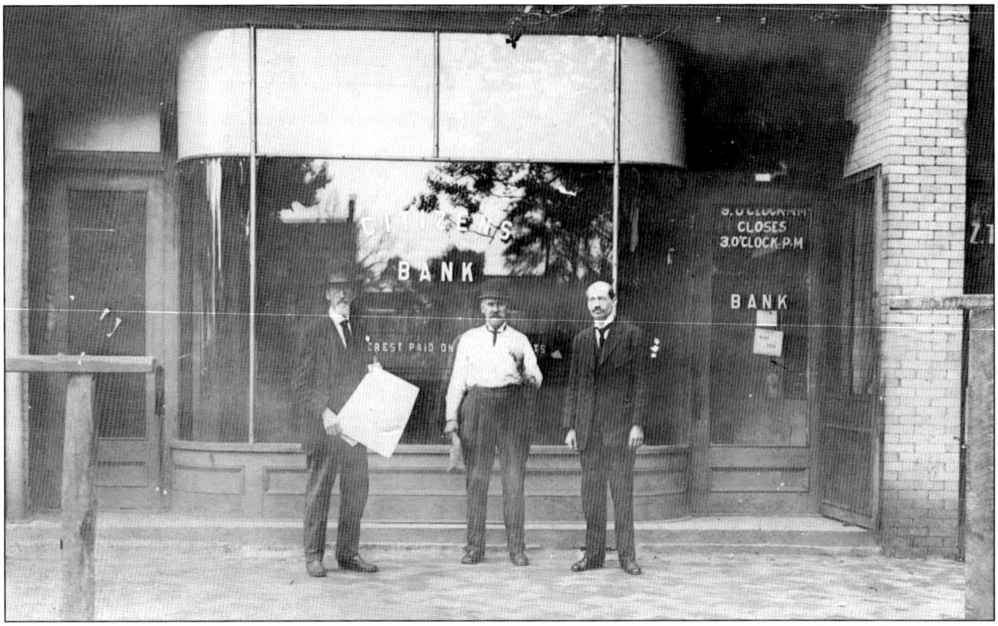

Citizens Bank opened in 1905 on the northeast corner of Court Square. Seen here, from left to right, are J.N.H. Clendenin, director; W.J. Nicks, president; and Charles S. Thompson, cashier. In 1915, the bank advertised a Christmas Savings Club with more than 500 members. The bank changed locations along the square several times and closed in 1933 due to the Great Depression. (Courtesy of Graham Historical Museum.)

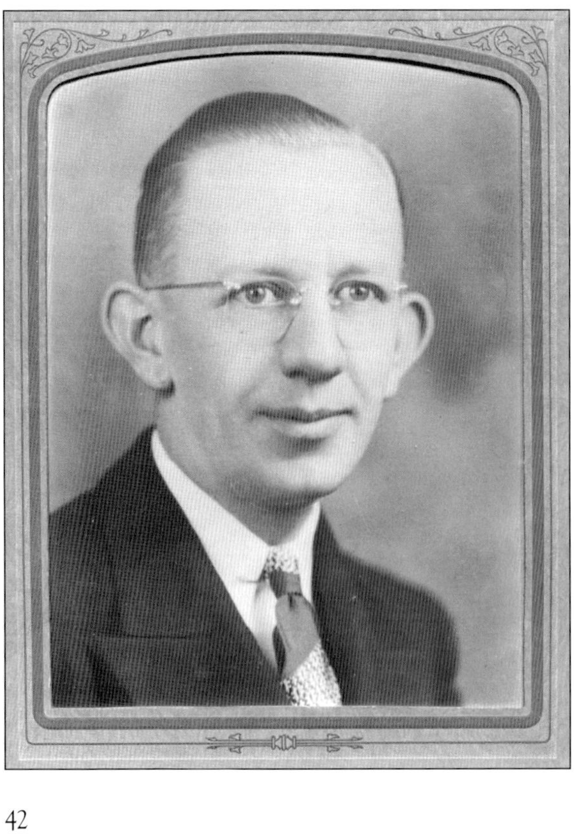
William "Bill" Hadley lived on Harden Street not far from Court Square, where he ran the family business, Hadley's Jewelry, with his father, Z.T. Hadley. The store was beside Citizen's Bank. (Courtesy of Chuck and Jennifer Talley.)

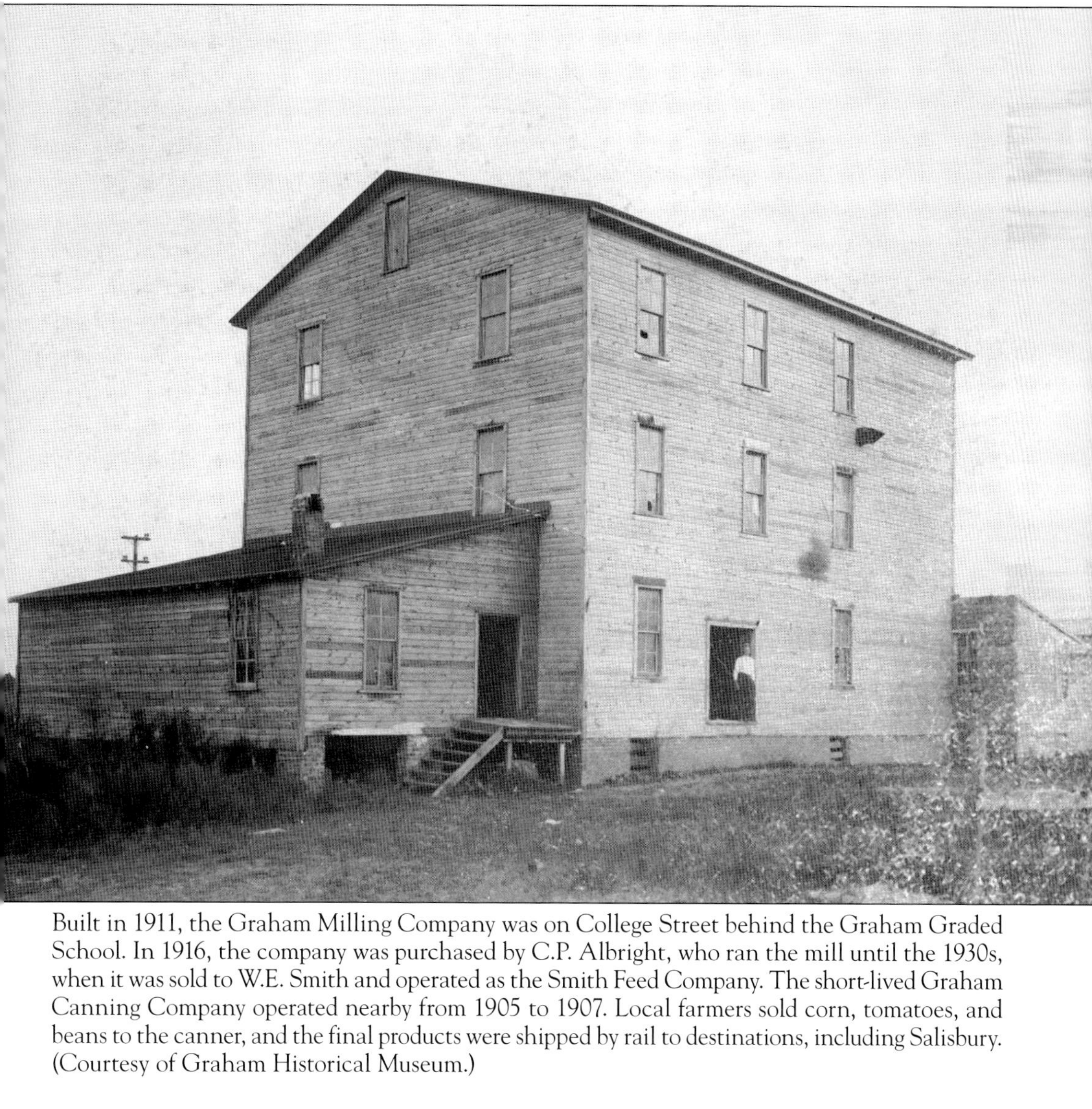

Built in 1911, the Graham Milling Company was on College Street behind the Graham Graded School. In 1916, the company was purchased by C.P. Albright, who ran the mill until the 1930s, when it was sold to W.E. Smith and operated as the Smith Feed Company. The short-lived Graham Canning Company operated nearby from 1905 to 1907. Local farmers sold corn, tomatoes, and beans to the canner, and the final products were shipped by rail to destinations, including Salisbury. (Courtesy of Graham Historical Museum.)

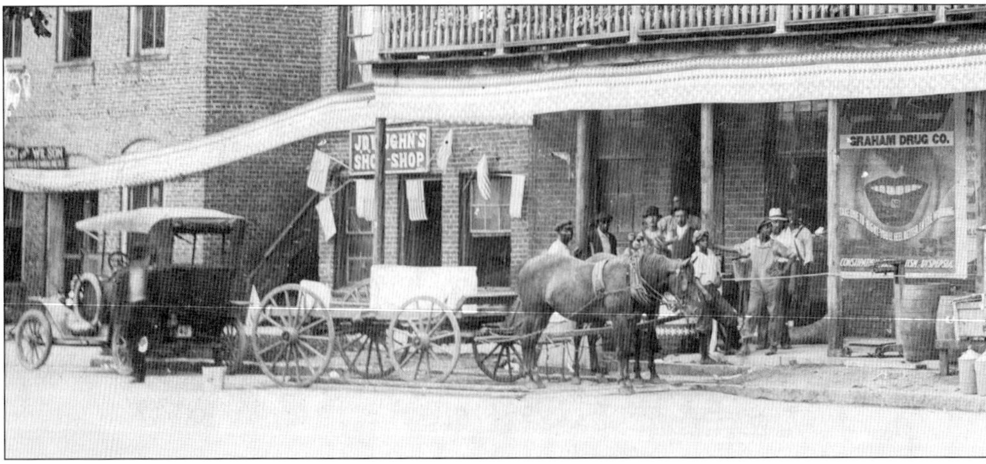

Wagons and automobiles shared the roads in 1915. Here, John Vaughn's car sits in front of his shoe shop, which was next to W.J. Nicks General Merchandise. (Courtesy of Graham Historical Museum.)

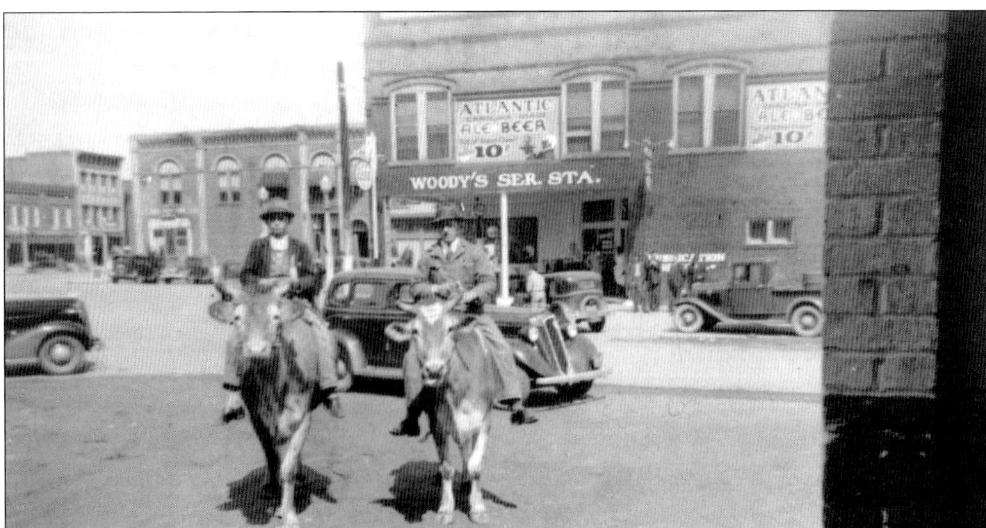

In this 1940s photograph, two gentlemen pose on steers in front of Woody's Service Station on Court Square. This creative form of travel likely occurred during the gasoline rations of World War II. (Courtesy of the family of Foust Thompson.)

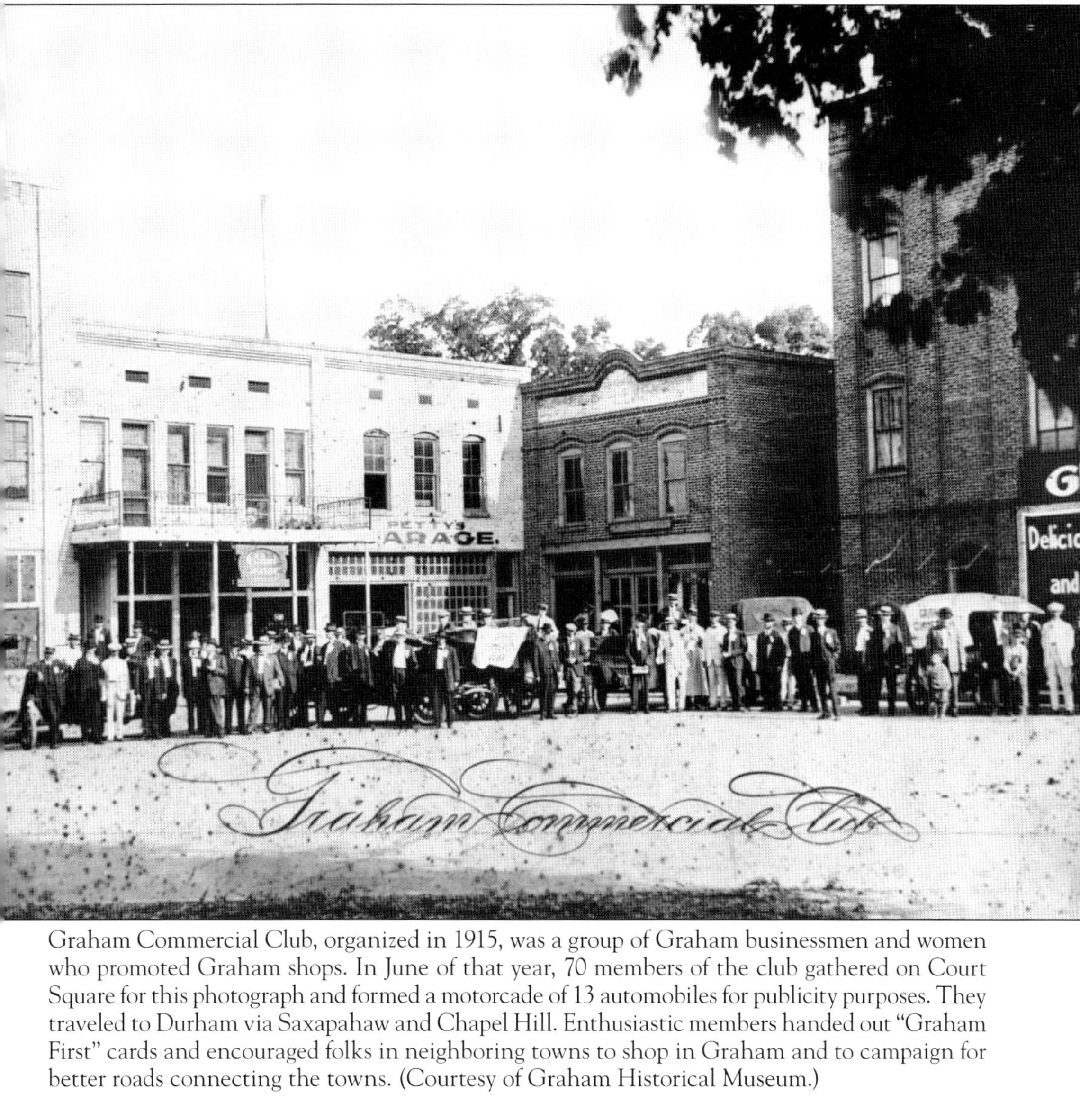

Graham Commercial Club, organized in 1915, was a group of Graham businessmen and women who promoted Graham shops. In June of that year, 70 members of the club gathered on Court Square for this photograph and formed a motorcade of 13 automobiles for publicity purposes. They traveled to Durham via Saxapahaw and Chapel Hill. Enthusiastic members handed out "Graham First" cards and encouraged folks in neighboring towns to shop in Graham and to campaign for better roads connecting the towns. (Courtesy of Graham Historical Museum.)

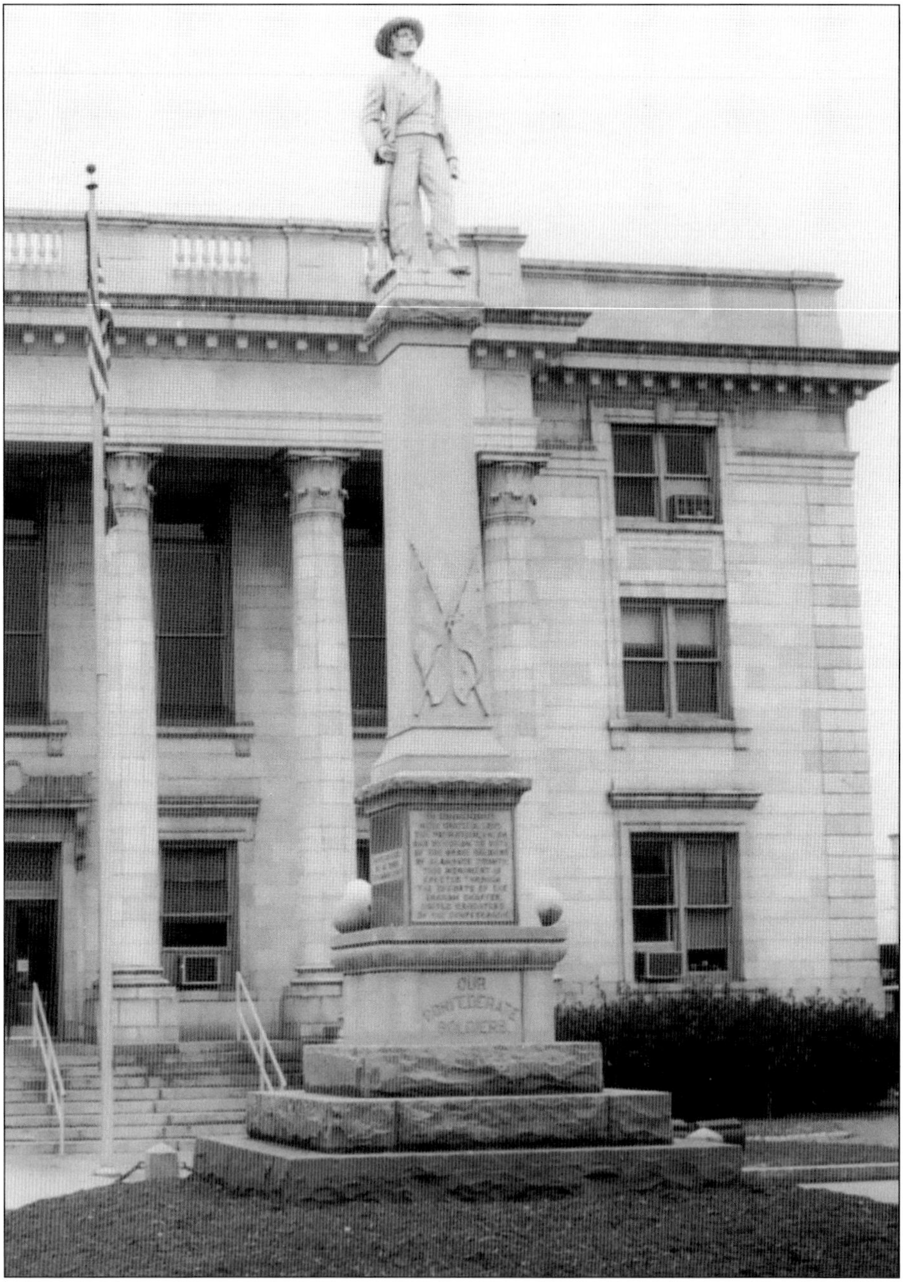

The Graham chapter of the United Daughters of the Confederacy raised money for a fitting memorial for Civil War veterans. The ladies held fundraisers, including ice cream suppers and a recital at the opera house, and even worked as "lady conductors" on the streetcars. The Confederate monument was unveiled on May 21, 1914, and placed on the north side of the courthouse, where the town scales had stood for many years. Before the monument was raised, a box was buried beneath it. No records exist about its contents, but Durward T. Stokes remembered that he put in a small Confederate flag given to him by his grandfather, Capt. James A. Turrentine. The Confederate soldier on the statue, sometimes known as "Conrad," stands at rest but faces the enemy to the north. The origin of the name Conrad is no longer known. (Courtesy of Pat Bailey.)

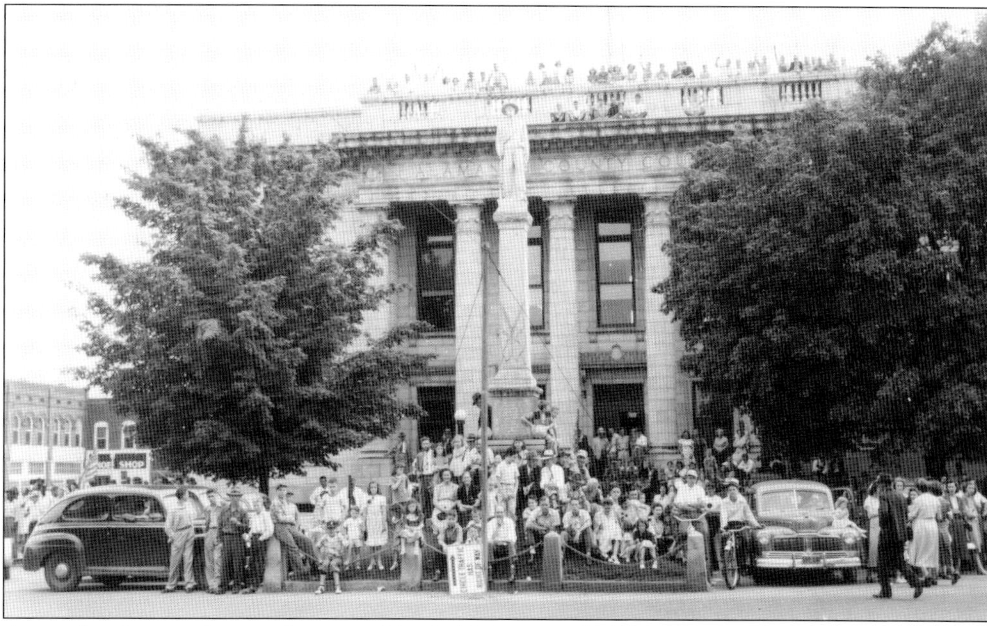

A crowd gathers at the courthouse on May 9, 1949, to watch Alamance County's centennial parade. Part of a weeklong celebration, the parade began in Graham, where 10,000 spectators perched atop buildings and in trees to get a better view. Gov. W. Kerr Scott was given the place of honor in the parade. In Burlington, another 65,000 spectators lined the streets, many wearing Robin Hood hats purchased for the occasion. (Courtesy Alamance County Chamber of Commerce.)

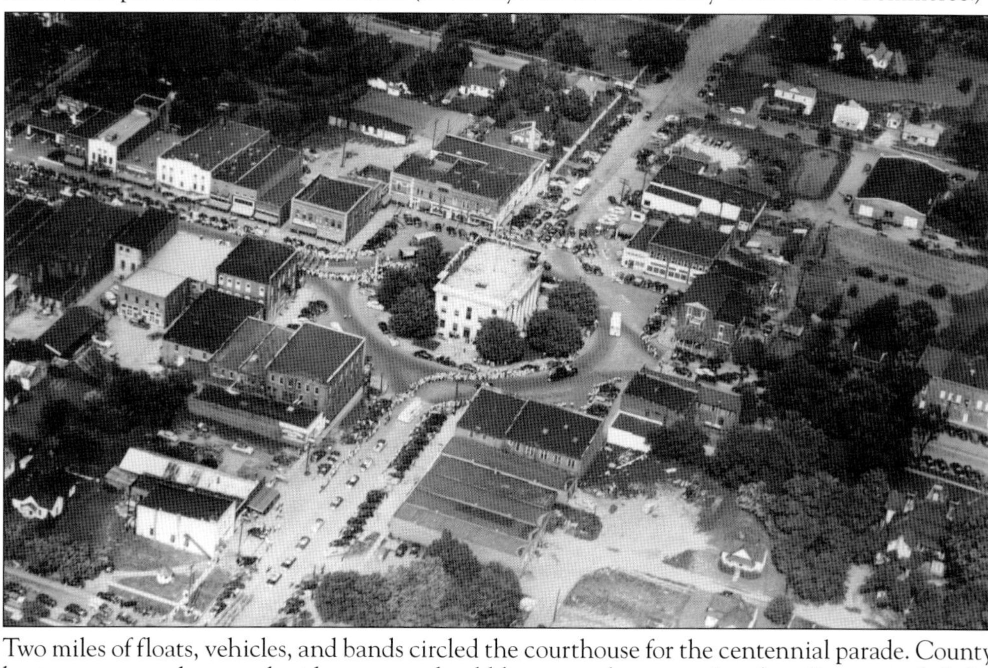

Two miles of floats, vehicles, and bands circled the courthouse for the centennial parade. County businesses were decorated with green and gold banners, the county's colors. Events included a banquet, a beard contest, and the play *Alamance Heritage*. A cast of 600 residents performed the historical drama at the Burlington High School stadium. The *Times-News* published a 168-page centennial edition. (Courtesy of Graham Historical Museum.)

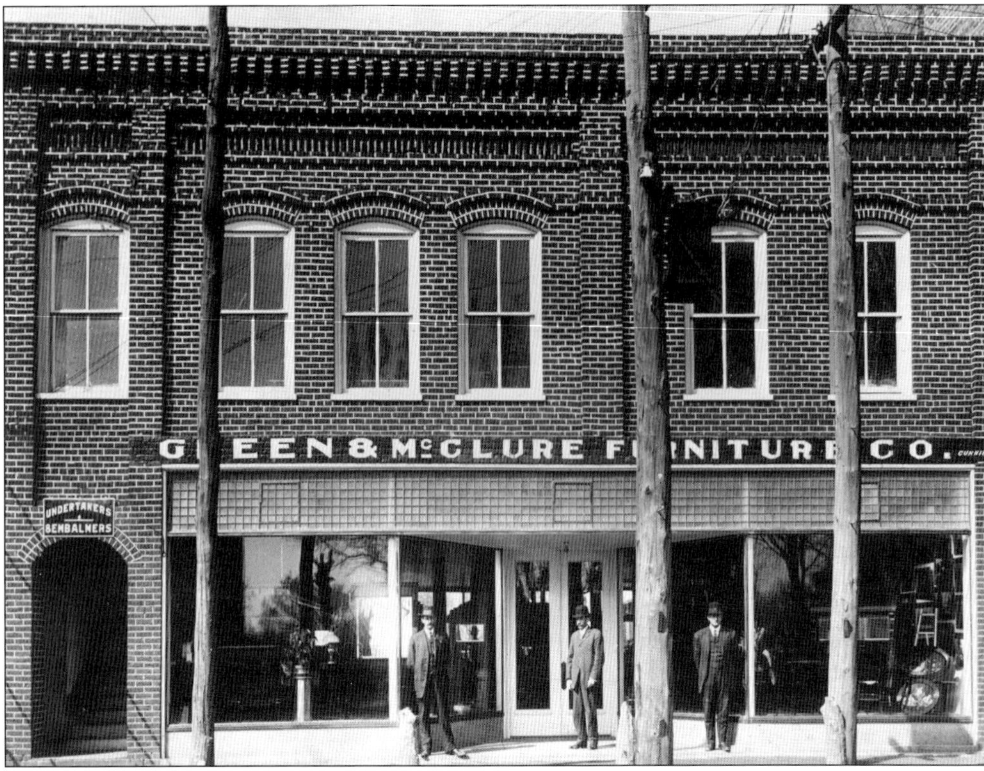

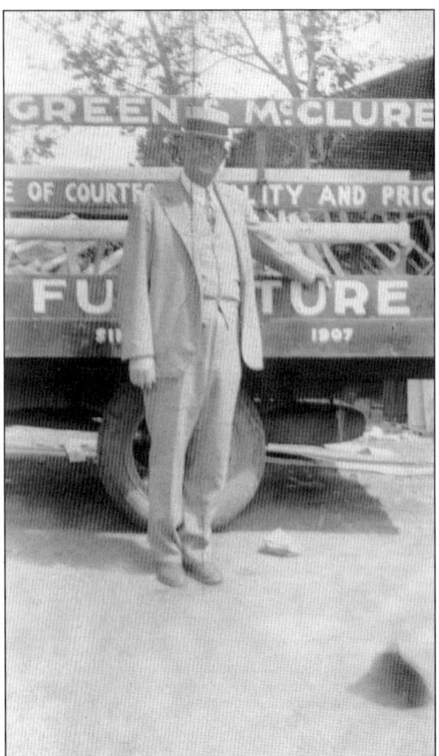

Green & McClure Furniture Company opened in 1907 on North Main Street. Previously, Rev. William Barringer Green had lost his voice and left his ministry. He then went into business with E.P. McClure. One side of the 4,000-square-foot store sold home furnishings. The other side provided for the funeral needs of the community. From left to right, Reverend Green, Thomas J. Griffin, and E.P. McClure are pictured in front of the store in 1912. (Courtesy of Green & McClure.)

Eponetius Pearce "Epp" McClure is seen here around 1939. His hand-painted logo on the delivery truck emphasizes the importance of "courtesy, quality and price." Like many of Graham's businessmen, he was a member of the volunteer fire department, serving as fire chief from 1912 to 1915. (Courtesy of Green & McClure.)

Ernest Truitt was a well-known member of the community and a longtime employee of Green & McClure Furniture Company. This photograph was taken during the big snow of January 1940. (Courtesy of Green & McClure.)

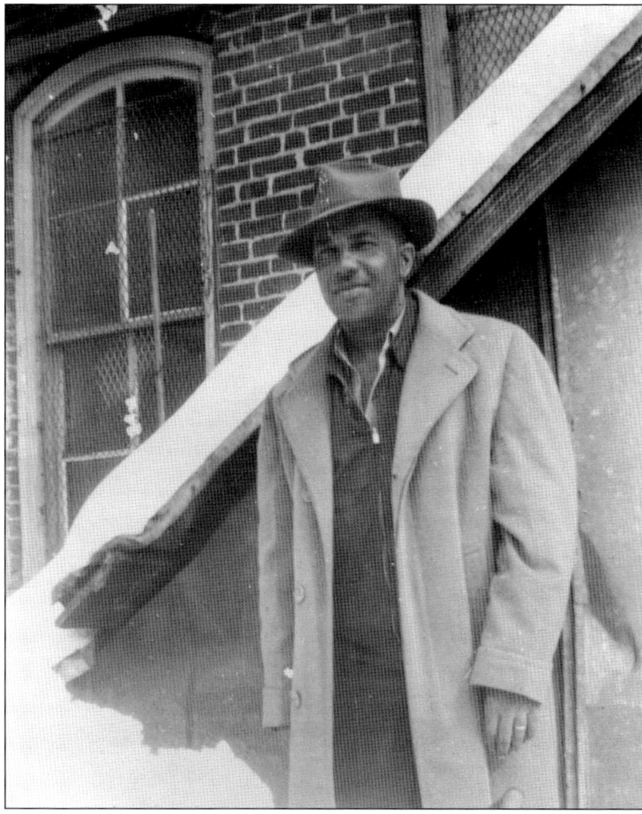

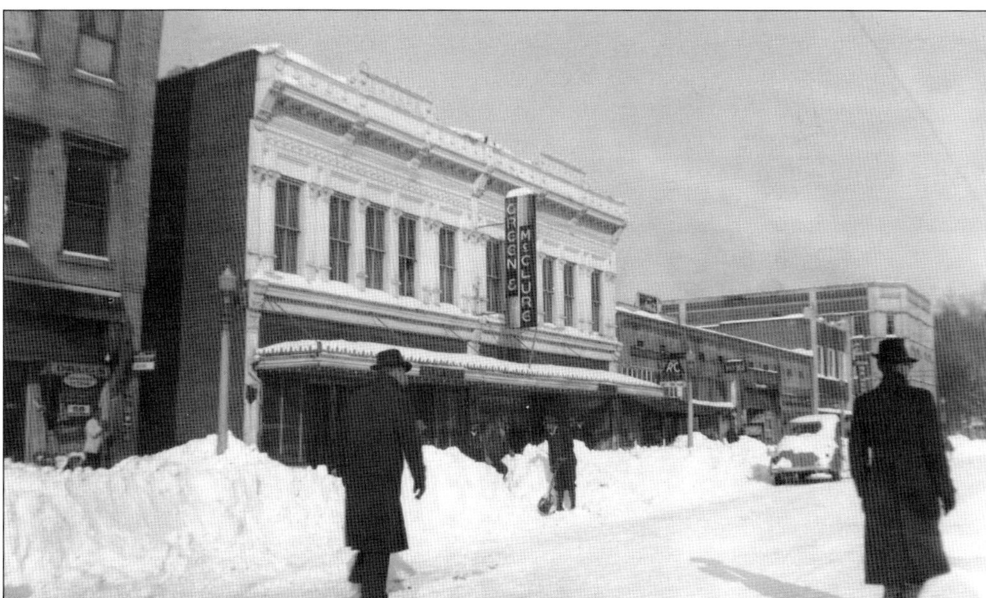

Green & McClure moved to its current location on North Main Street in 1919. On January 24, 1940, everything stopped for a time after the big snow. Residents shoveled snow from sidewalks and storefronts. A storage shed behind Green & McClure Furniture Company collapsed from the weight of the snow. (Courtesy of Don Bolden.)

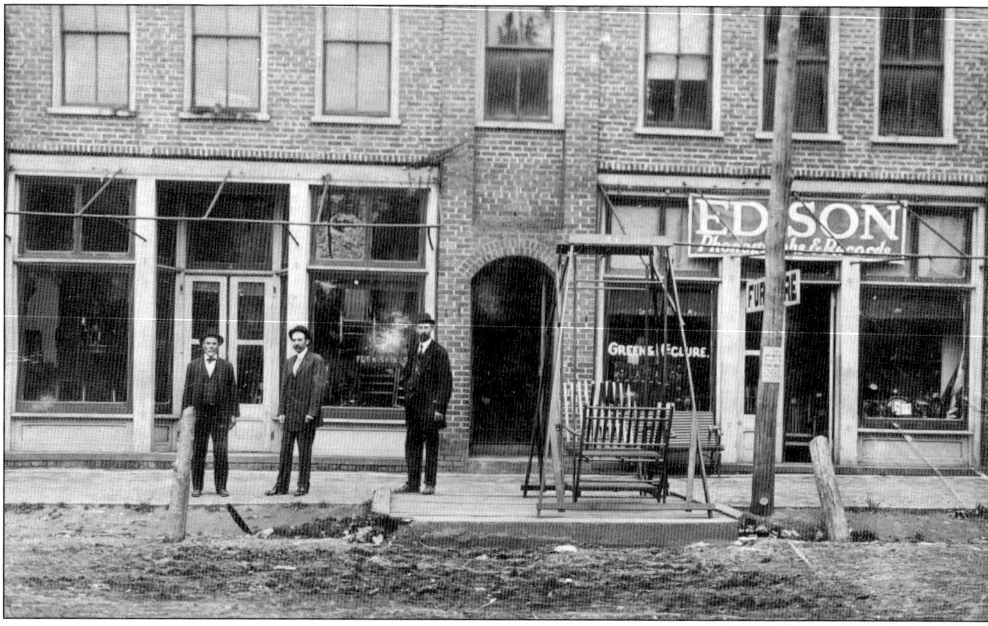

Green & McClure Furniture Company was one of the first in the area to sell Edison phonographs and records. The store would later offer the first Frigidaire refrigerators and televisions. Seen here from left to right are Thomas J. Griffin, William Barringer Green, and William Alvis Rich. (Courtesy of Green & McClure.)

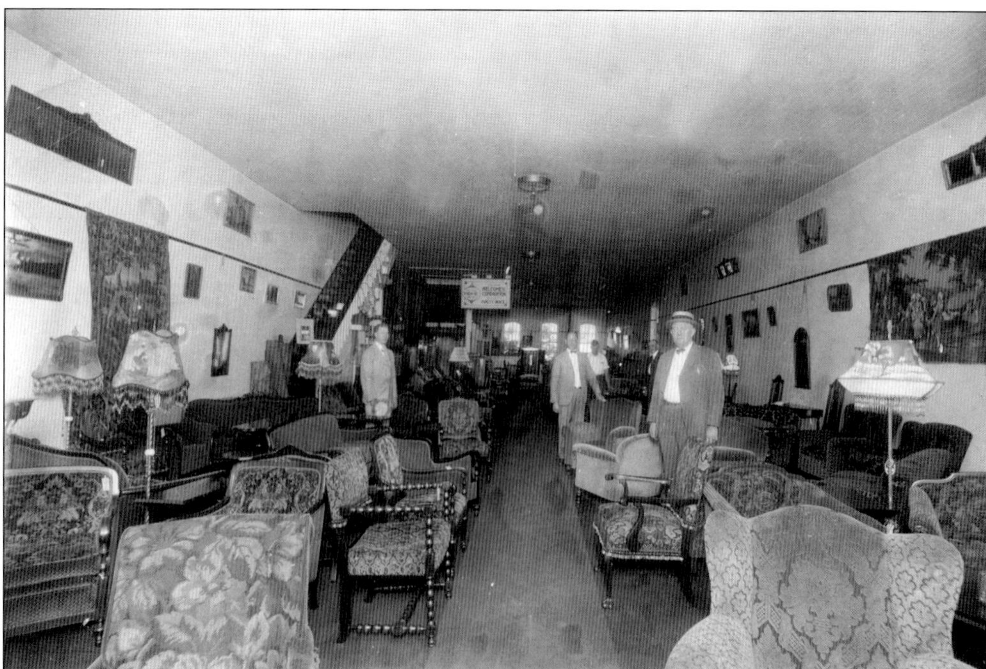

Father and son, E.P. McClure (right foreground) and James Griffin McClure Sr. (left background), are ready for customers in the showroom of Green & McClure Furniture Company around 1939. (Courtesy of Green & McClure.)

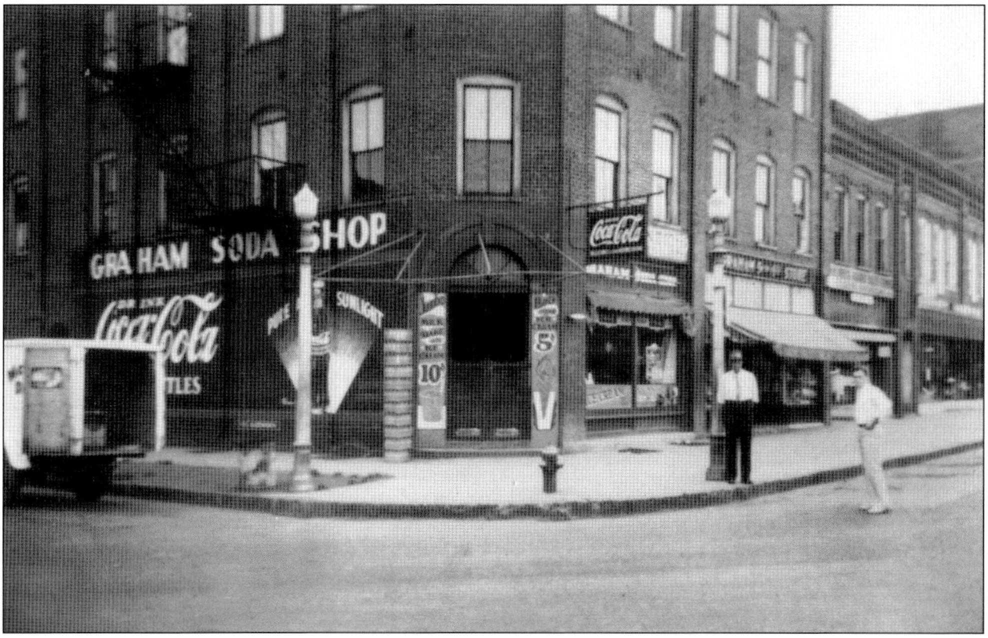

Built in 1902, the Patterson Building was originally rented to Graham Hardware Company and was home to many businesses through the years, including Graham Drug Company and the original Graham Soda Shop. The third story, known as Patterson Hall, was used for social gatherings and performances. (Courtesy of the family of Foust Thompson.)

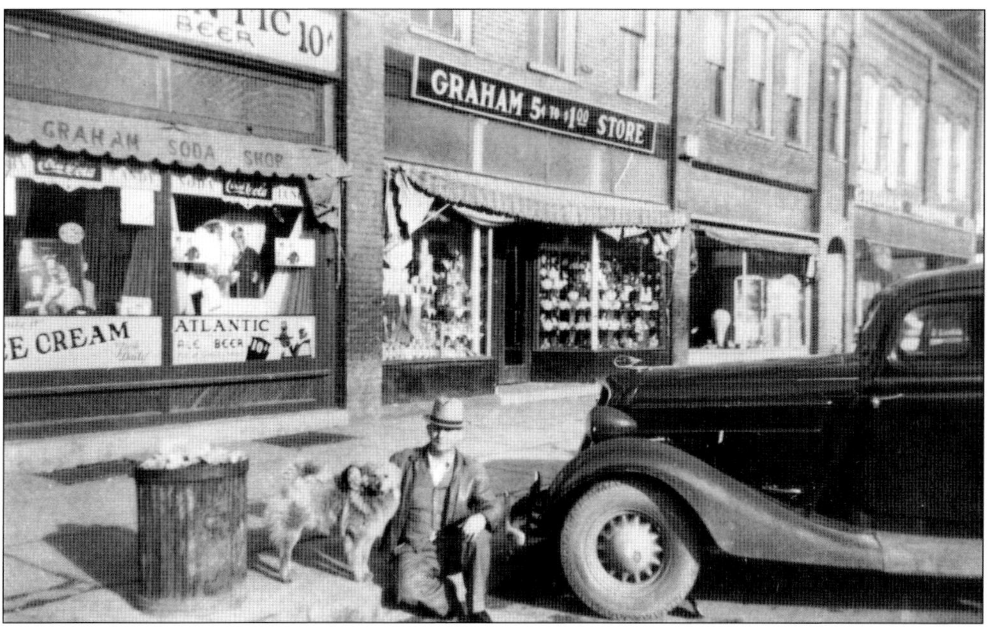

A man poses with his dog in front of the Graham Soda Shop. Graham 5¢ to $1 Store is on the right. (Courtesy of the family of Foust Thompson.)

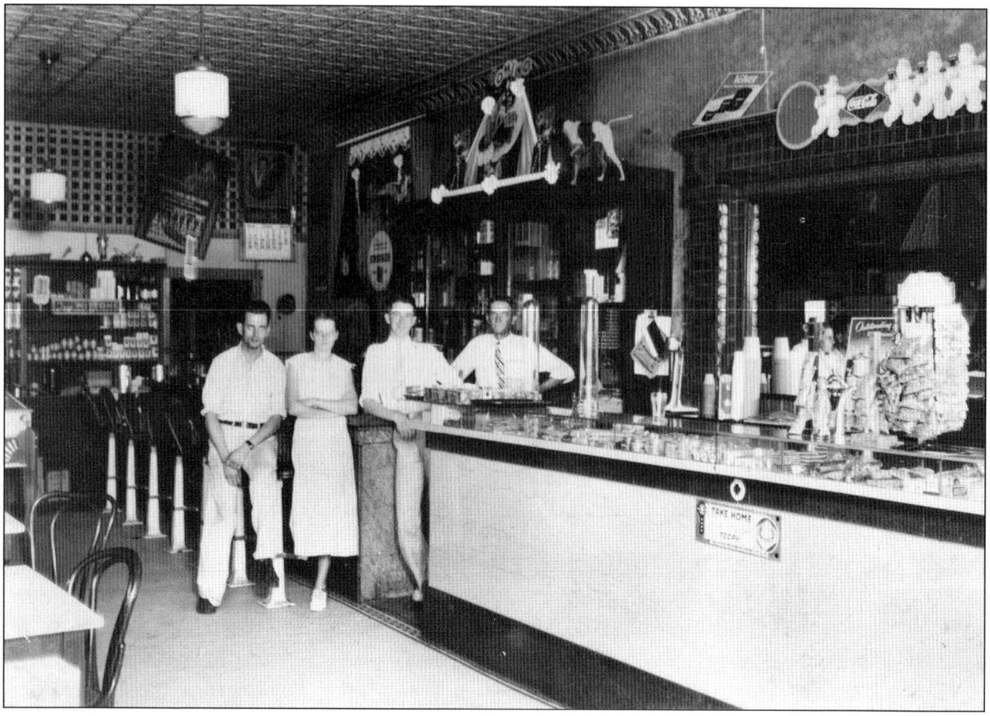

The Graham Soda Shop opened in 1933 on the northwest corner of Court Square. The owner and the staff of the classic soda shop pose by the counter in July 1937. From left to right, they are Morris Burke; his wife, Elizabeth; Raymond Puckett; and S. Foust Thompson, the owner. (Courtesy of the family of Foust Thompson.)

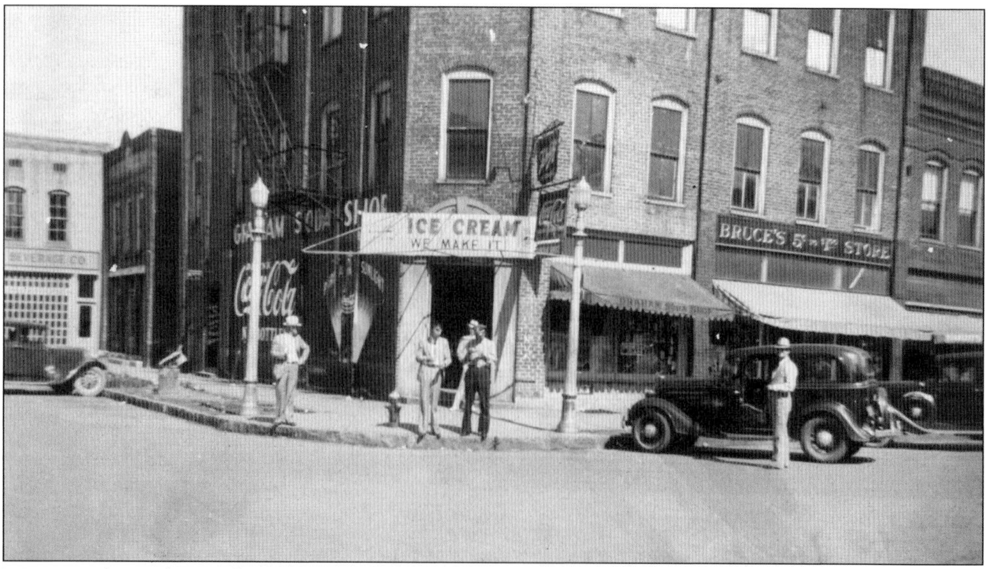

Men confer with a policeman in the 1940s in front of the Graham Soda Shop. The building was damaged by fire in 1977. During renovations in 1978, a load-bearing beam was removed. The building fell during the night and was damaged beyond repair. The lot is now the site of Sesquicentennial Park. The new Graham Soda Shop is across the square. (Courtesy of the family of Foust Thompson.)

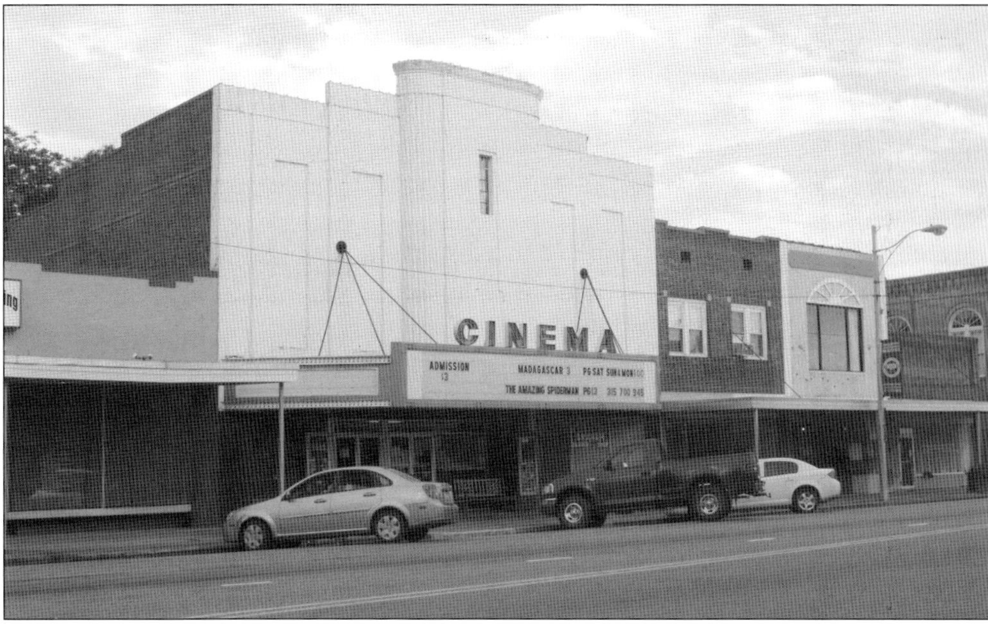

The Graham Theater opened on North Main Street in 1929 and is still in operation as the Graham Cinema. It features a large balcony and old-style charm. Tim Bob Matthews managed it for many years and was known for his movie reviews, as well as the jokes he left on the cinema's answering machine. The Graham Cinema is the oldest movie theater operating in Alamance County. (Courtesy of Patrick Jordan.)

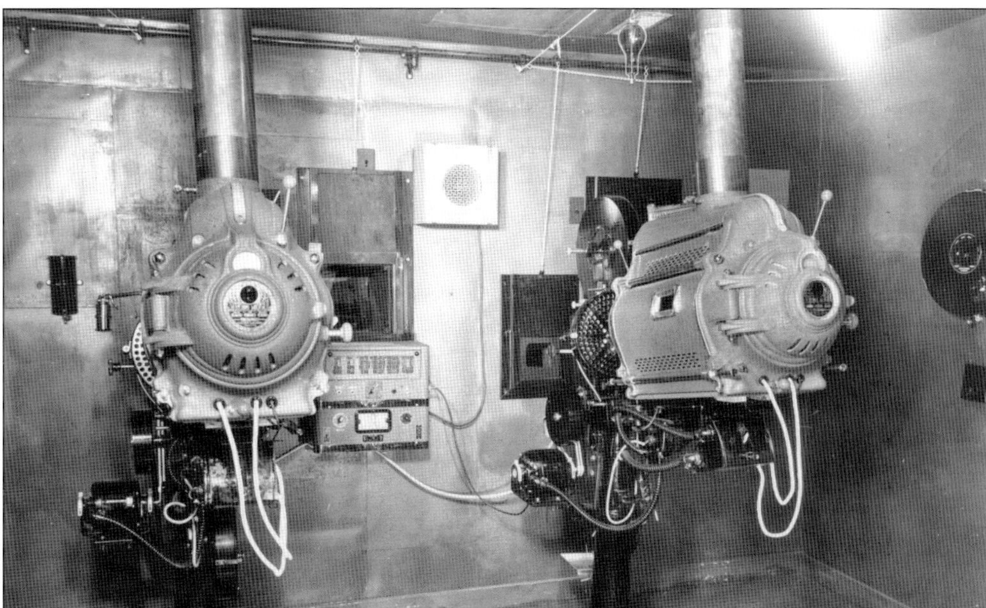
The projection booth in the Graham Cinema is high on the back wall. Most theaters had dual projectors, as seen here. As one reel ended, the next was prepped, allowing seamless viewing for the audience. Historically, the projectors contained carbon arc lamps, which made the fireproof metal room a hot place to work. The projectionist watched the cellulose film carefully, as it was flammable and broke often. (Courtesy of Graham Historical Museum.)

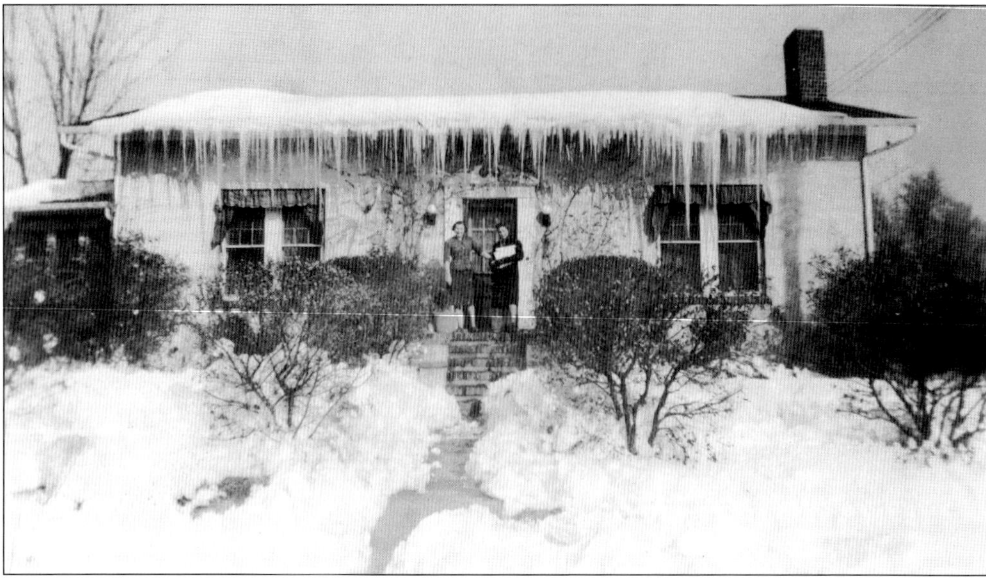

Built in 1851, this house at the corner of East Elm and Marshall Streets is the only surviving section of John Trollinger's Orange Hotel. The hotel originally extended to Court Square. In 1903, it was converted to a dwelling by Lynn Banks Holt. It has been named the Trollinger Hotel, the Orange Hotel, the Union Hotel, and the Brick Hotel at various times. (Courtesy of the family of Foust Thompson.)

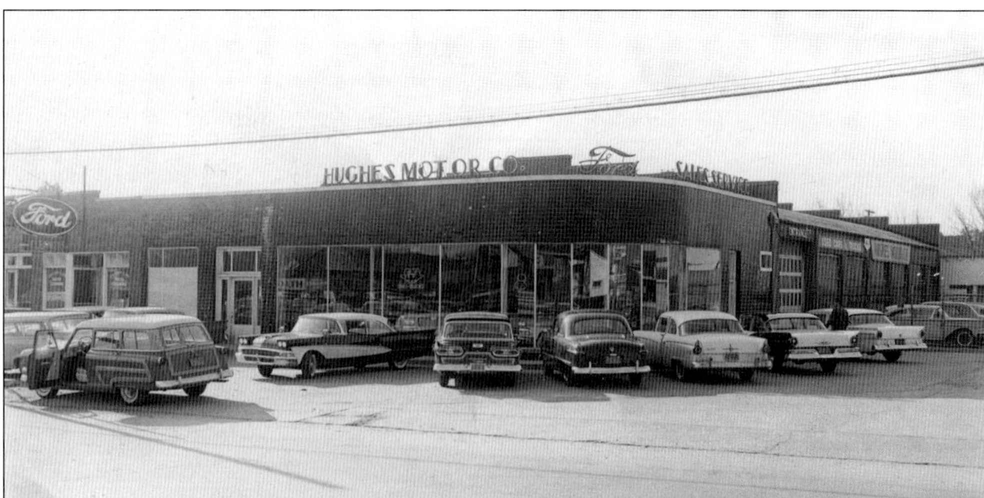

Foster Hughes owned Hughes Motor Company on West Harden Street from the 1940s to the 1960s. This 1957 photograph was taken on the day Ford's new 1958 models arrived. (Courtesy of Jack Henderson.)

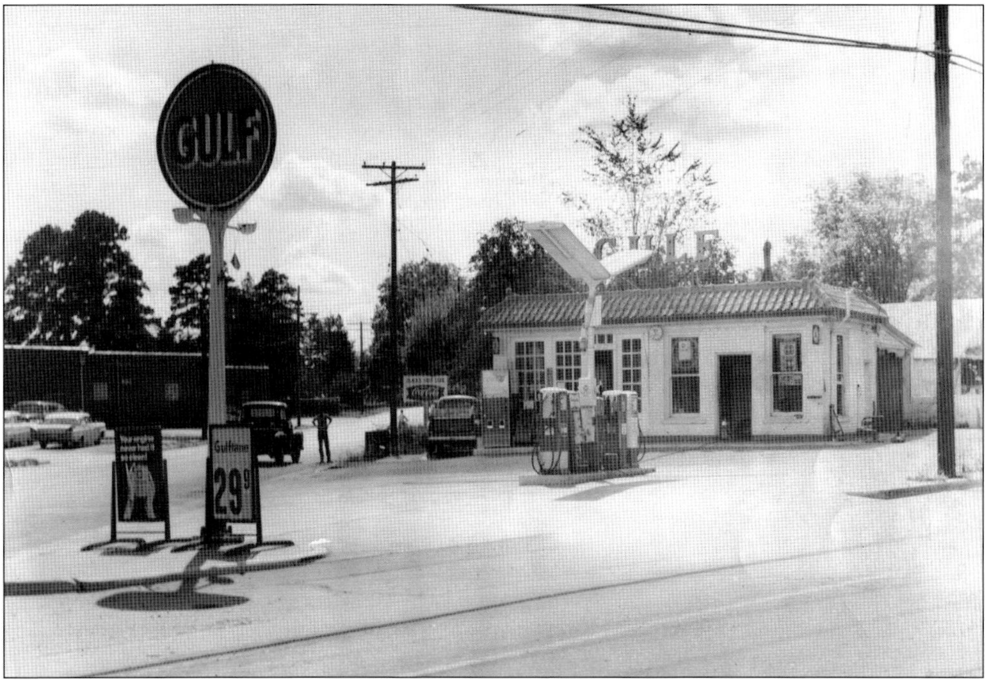

This Gulf service station, located at the intersection of East Harden and East Elm Streets, has been a Graham landmark for decades. It has seen many names through the years. When this photograph was taken, gasoline was 29¢ per gallon at Burke's Gulf Station, owned by Roby L. Burke. (Courtesy of Alamance County Historical Museum.)

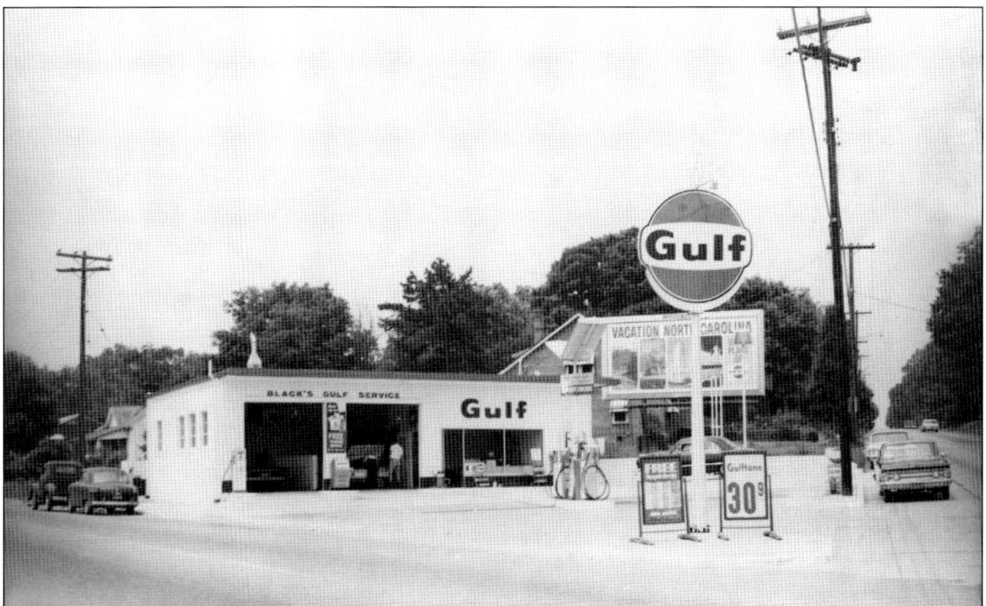

The 1960s saw Edwards Gulf Service and then Bob and Jim's Gulf Service inhabit the station. This photograph was taken about 1969, when Robert P. Black operated it as Black's Gulf Service. The two photographs on this page were taken about a decade apart, but gas prices had only risen by 1¢, to 30¢ per gallon. (Courtesy of Alamance County Historical Museum.)

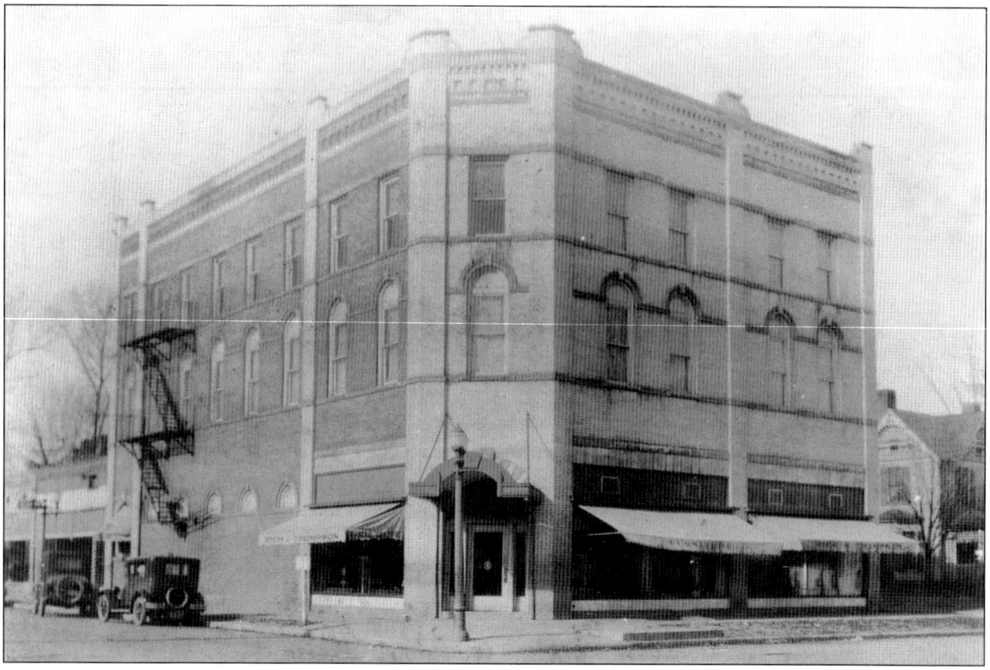

In 1902, Will Rich opened Rich Furniture Company with his brother-in-law Heenan Hawks. The store also included mortuary service. Their advertising motto, "From the cradle to the grave," indicated that the company could supply furnishing needs throughout a customer's life. Monte White Theatre housed the furniture store for many years. After Rich's death in 1913, his brother James partnered with W. Ernest Thompson to form Rich & Thompson Furniture. (Courtesy of Rich & Thompson.)

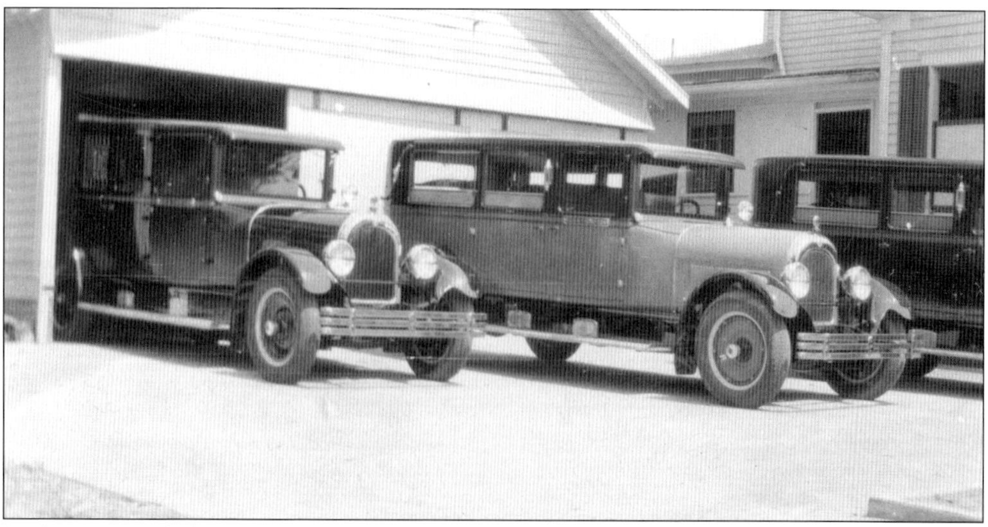

By the 1930s, ambulance services were added to funeral home operations. This began because funeral homes had hearses that could be converted easily for ambulance use. Members of the staff at Rich & Thompson were trained by local doctors and the Red Cross. (Courtesy of Rich & Thompson.)

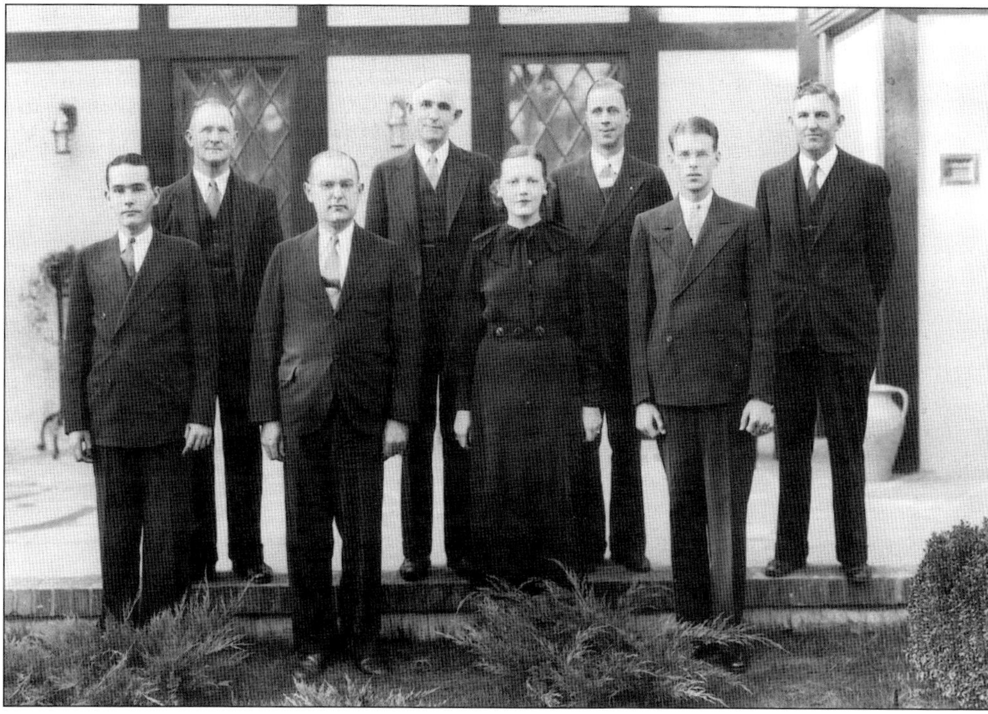

Owners and staff of Rich & Thompson Funeral Service are seen here in 1935. The firm had opened a second funeral home in Burlington in 1926, continuing their Graham funeral business on the second floor of the furniture store. From left to right, they are Buddy Linens, James H. Rich, A. Ray Reitzel, Charles A. Thompson, Helen Rich, Alvis M. Rich, Frank Rich, and W. Ernest Thompson. (Courtesy of Rich & Thompson.)

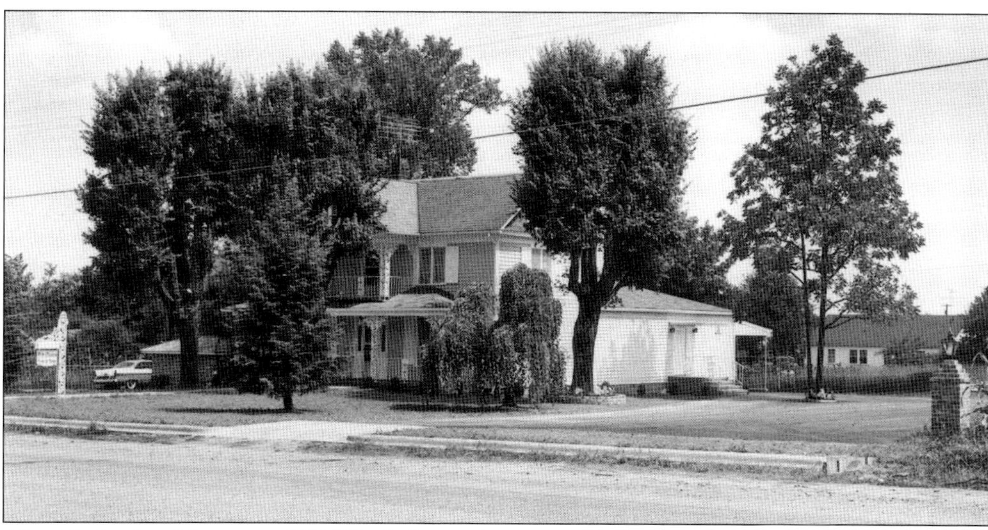

Alvis Rich, the eldest son of Will Rich, began his career in the firm during the epidemic of 1919. In 1957, Rich & Thompson passed to the next generation, with two sons of Will's brother James partnering with Alvis to expand the Graham mortuary. They remodeled the William F. Jones home place on East Elm Street, seen here. Several rooms were added, including a chapel and an ambulance dormitory. (Courtesy of Rich & Thompson.)

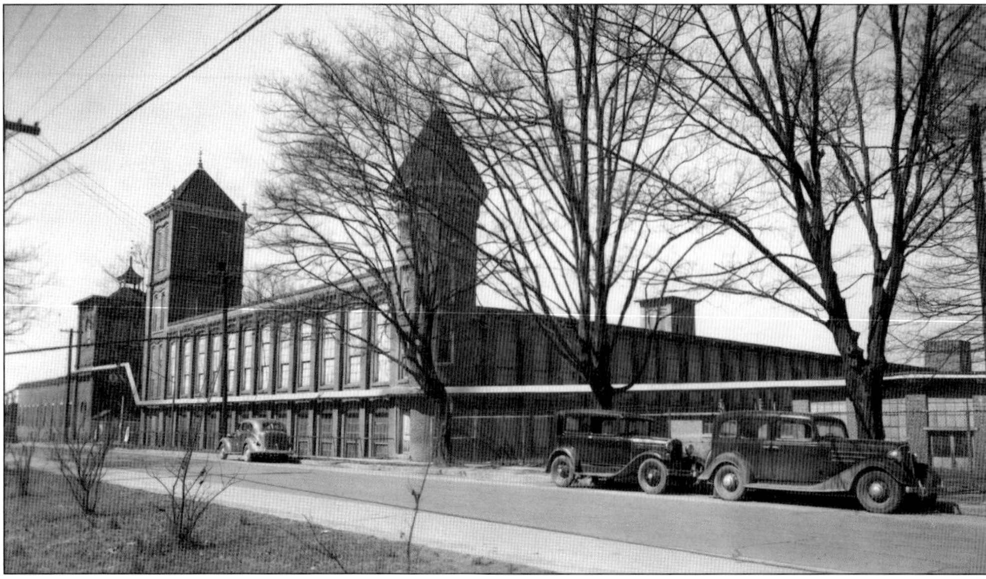

Oneida Cotton Mills on Harden Street is pictured here in 1928. The cotton mill was built in 1882 by brothers-in-law James Sidney Scott and W.C. "Uncle Cal" Donnell. Lynn Banks Holt doubled its size in the 1890s. (Courtesy of Alamance County Public Libraries.)

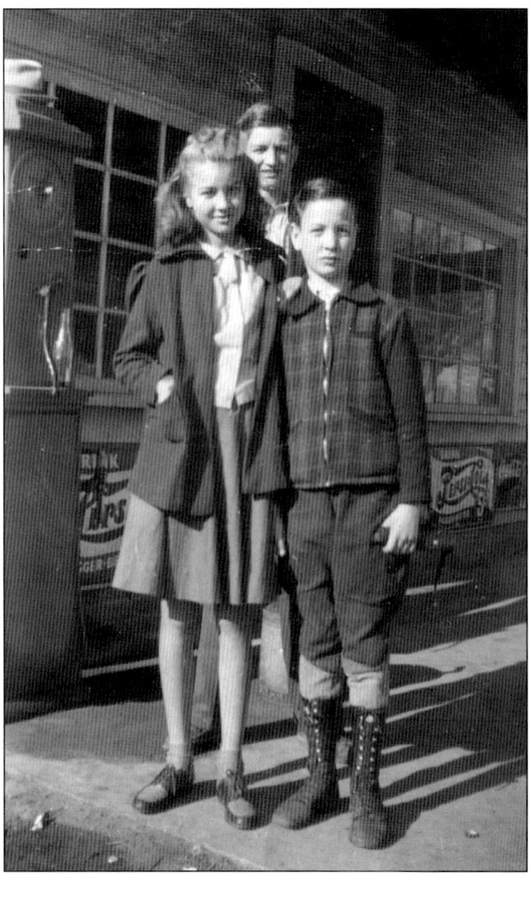

Grace Rich, James Rich, and Bradley Rich Jr. stand on the porch at Poplar Street Grocery. Mary Satterfield ran the small neighborhood store in the 1950s. Her son Thomas remembers that they lived next-door and would sometimes hear a knock at the door after supper or even on Sunday. If a neighbor needed bread, someone would run over and get it for them. (Courtesy of Suzanne Rich.)

Ernest F. Jones was the superintendant at Oneida Cotton Mills for many years. His two-story home on North Street, seen below, was typical of mill houses at the time. To the west of the mills, Harden Street and the side streets were lined with houses belonging to the company and rented to employees. (Courtesy of Linda S. Stewart.)

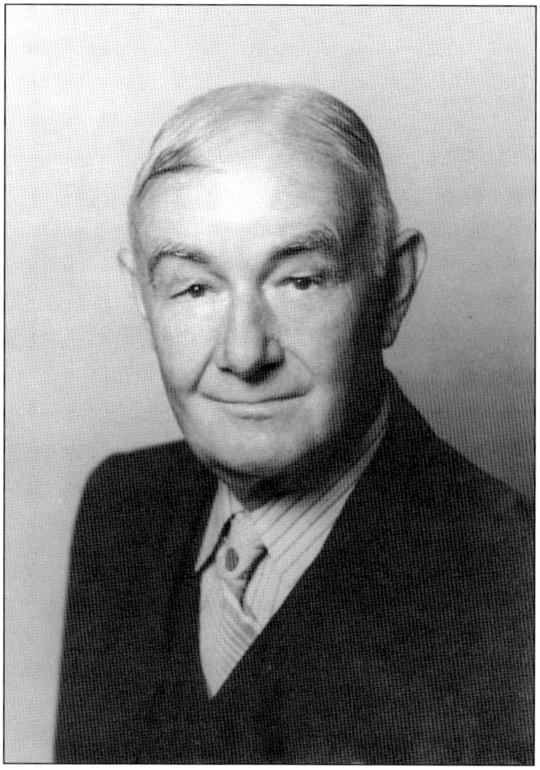

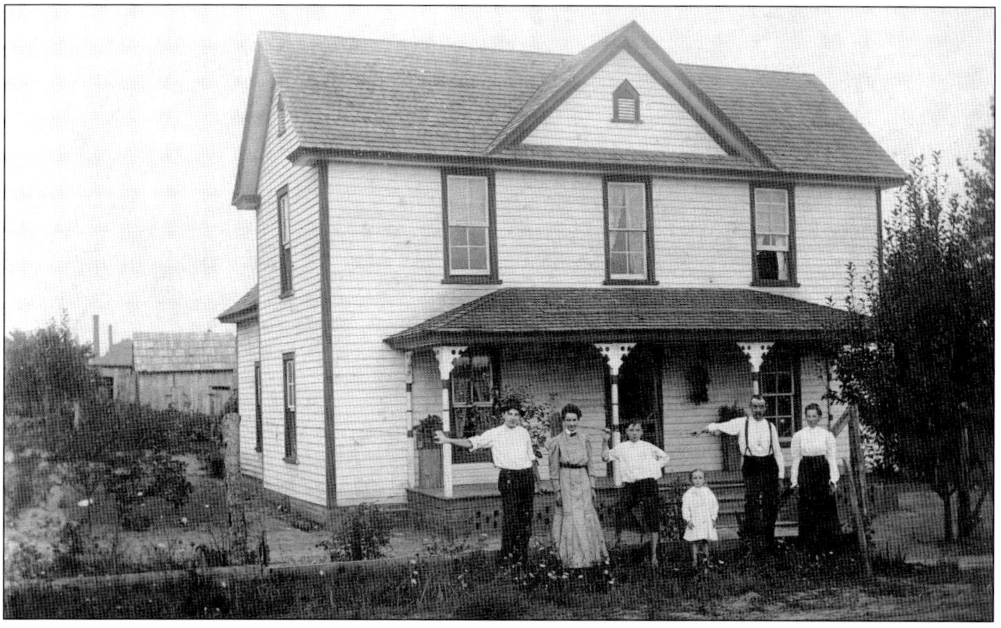

The Jones family stands in front of their home on North Street. Following World War I, a small neighborhood on nearby North Court was known as Pumpkin Hill. Older residents enjoy telling the story of a paint shortage caused by the war. Resourceful residents combined their paint, resulting in a muddy-orange brown color that was used to paint their homes, hence the name Pumpkin Hill. (Courtesy of Linda S. Stewart.)

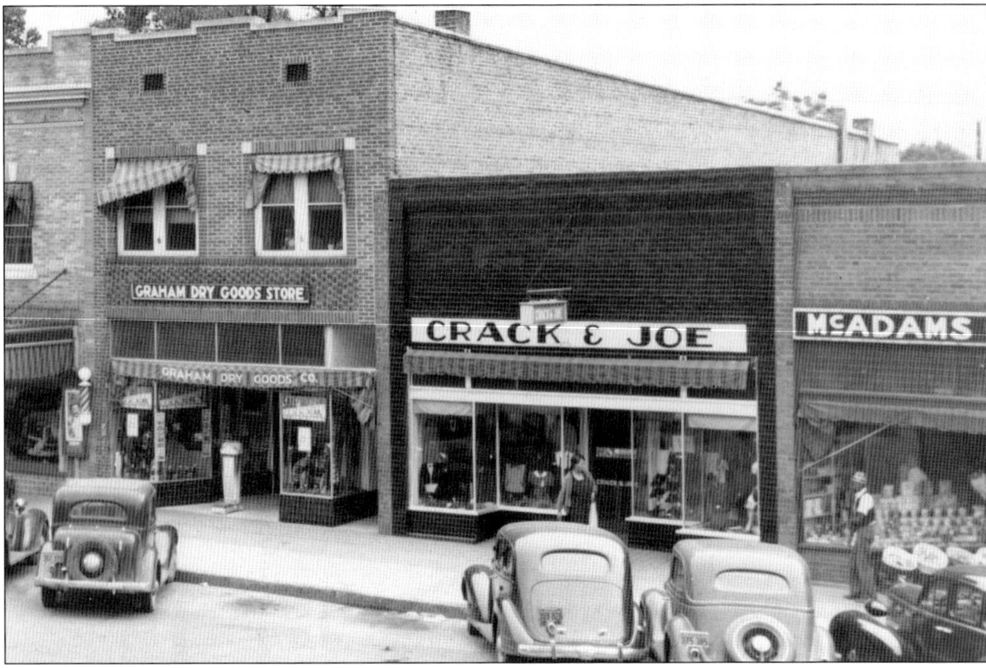

Crack & Joe moved from the Monte White Theatre to this location on North Main Street. The clothing store was open for more than 40 years and operated by J.D. "Crack" Albright and Joseph S. Holt—and later Holt's widow, Annie Holt. The store held a contest in 1907 to drum up business. Mildred Tripp, whose family ran the Vestal Hotel, won a silk dress for her poem praising Crack & Joe. (Courtesy of Skee and Virginia Johnson.)

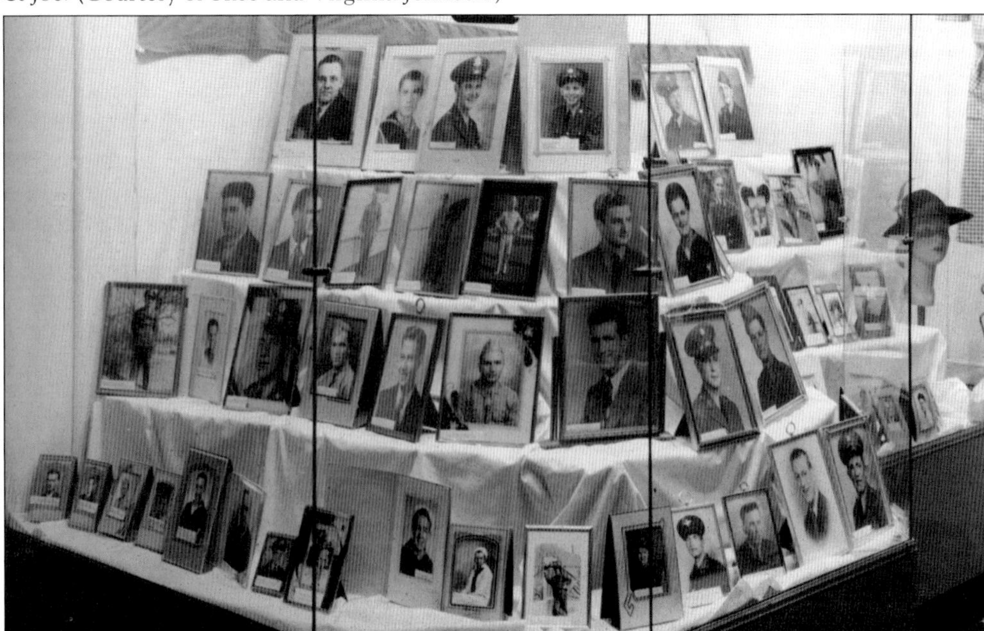

During World War II, the window at Crack & Joe was filled with photographs of Graham soldiers. The patriotic display was a tribute to the young men who were actively serving our country in the armed forces. (Courtesy of Graham Historical Museum.)

Talmadge P. Nelson Sr. joined the National Guard and later served in the Army during World War II, in North Africa and Italy. As a young man, he painted signs for the Coca-Cola Bottling Company in Burlington. In 1929, he climbed to the roof of Travora Mills and painted "Graham, N.C." in 12-foot letters, with the thought that the city's name would be seen from passing airplanes. (Courtesy of Ted Nelson.)

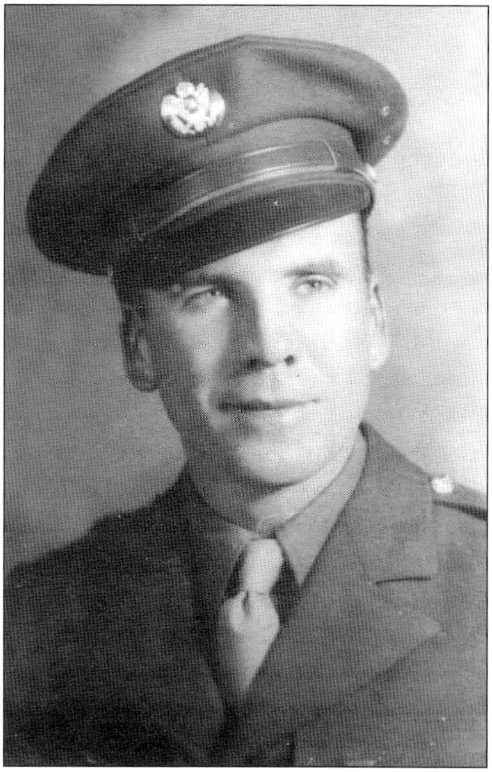

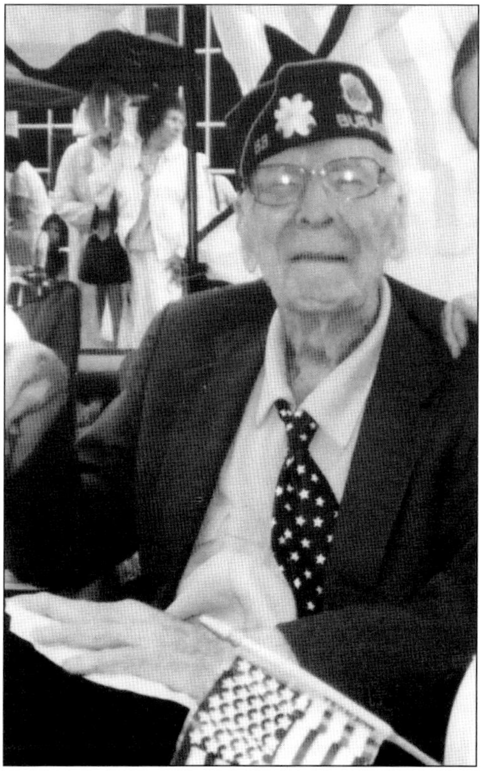

Talmadge Nelson saw a century of Graham's history. He played baseball for Graham High School and lived through the Great Depression and two World Wars. For his 100th birthday, the city gave him Talmadge Nelson Day. At age 102, he served as grand marshal of the Christmas parade and received a key to the city. He passed away in 2011 at the age of 105. (Courtesy of Delbert and Pauline Bean.)

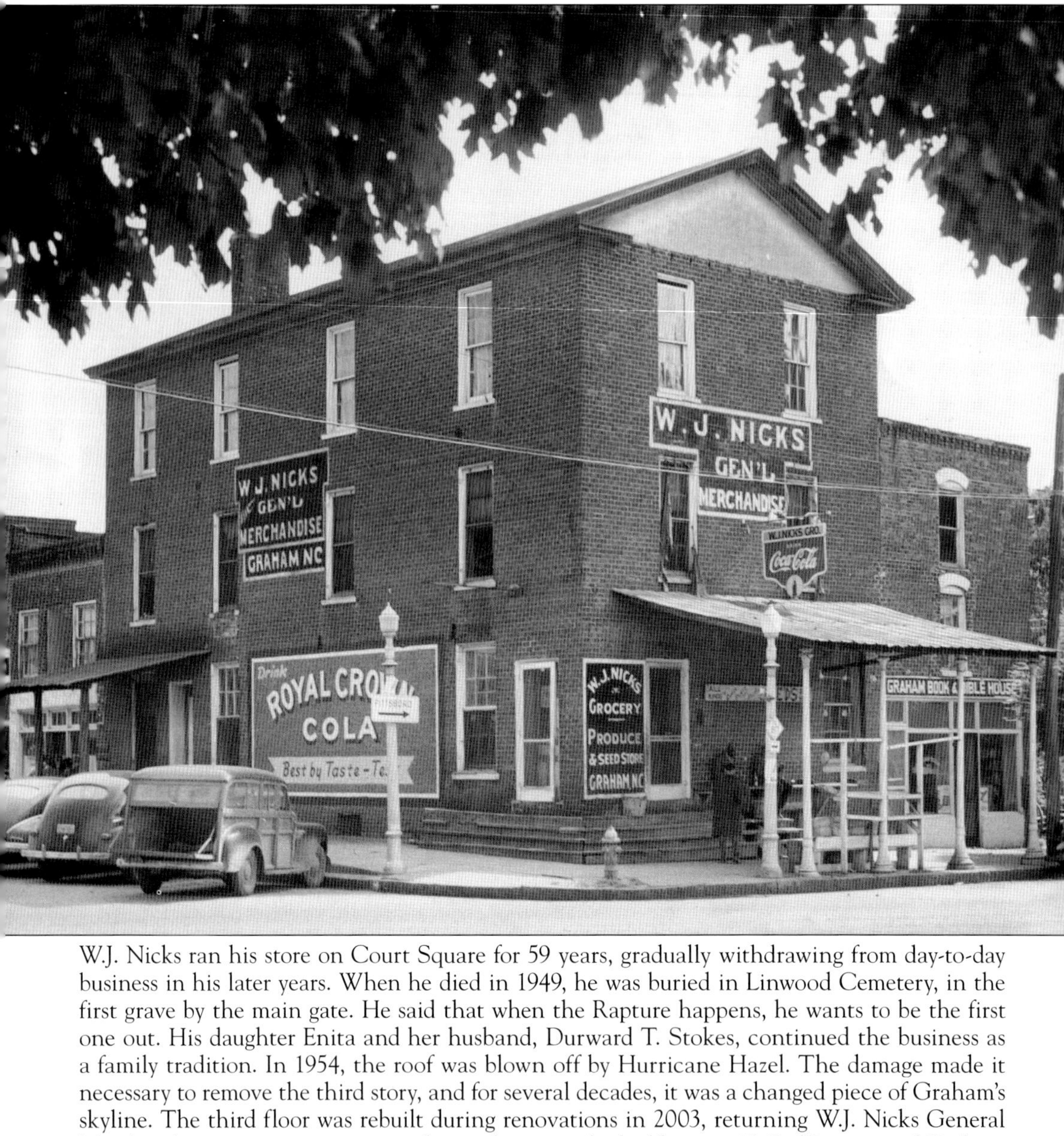

W.J. Nicks ran his store on Court Square for 59 years, gradually withdrawing from day-to-day business in his later years. When he died in 1949, he was buried in Linwood Cemetery, in the first grave by the main gate. He said that when the Rapture happens, he wants to be the first one out. His daughter Enita and her husband, Durward T. Stokes, continued the business as a family tradition. In 1954, the roof was blown off by Hurricane Hazel. The damage made it necessary to remove the third story, and for several decades, it was a changed piece of Graham's skyline. The third floor was rebuilt during renovations in 2003, returning W.J. Nicks General Merchandise to an appearance similar to the way it looked here in 1942. (Courtesy of Graham Historical Museum.)

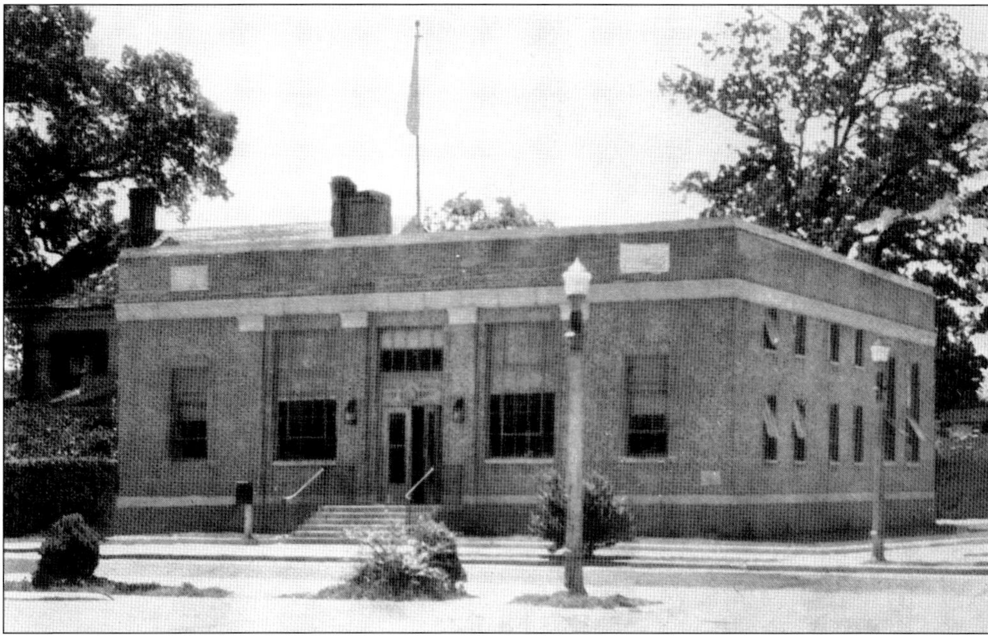

In 1934, Walter R. Harden sold the lot on the corner of Harden and Maple Streets to the US government for a new post office. The brick building has a full basement, constructed to serve as a fallout shelter. The structure housed the post office until 1977, when a new post office was opened on Marshall Street. Shamrock Jewelry and Pawn operated in the old building for many years. (Courtesy of North Carolina State Archives.)

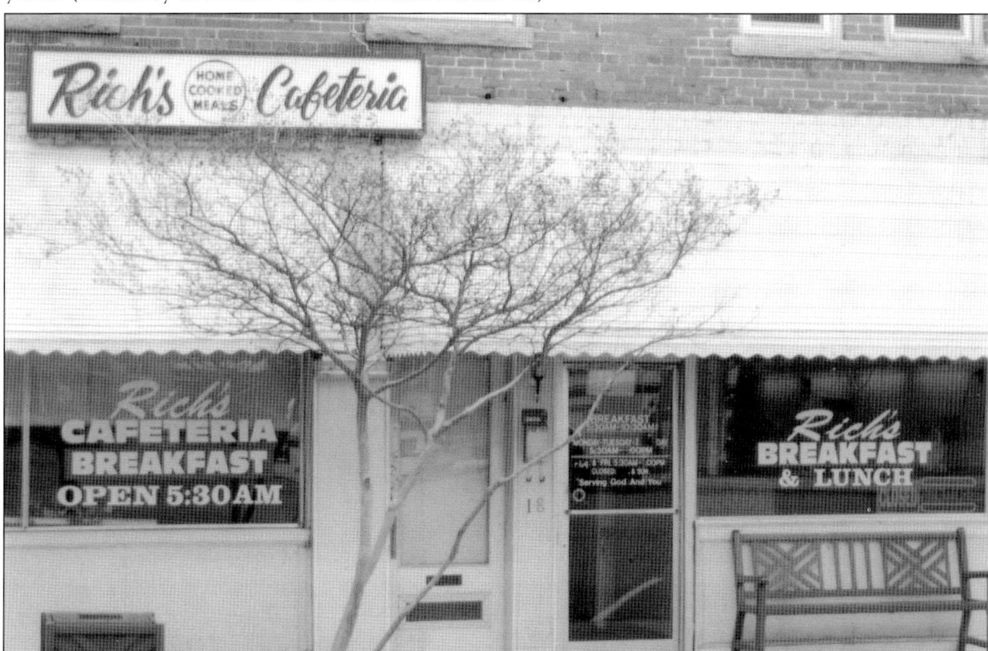

Rich's Cafeteria was a fixture on Court Square for decades. It began as Riverside Café, and was run by Bradley Rich, who renamed the restaurant Rich's. A local favorite, Rich's offered down-home country cooking just like grandma made it. (Courtesy of Graham Historical Museum.)

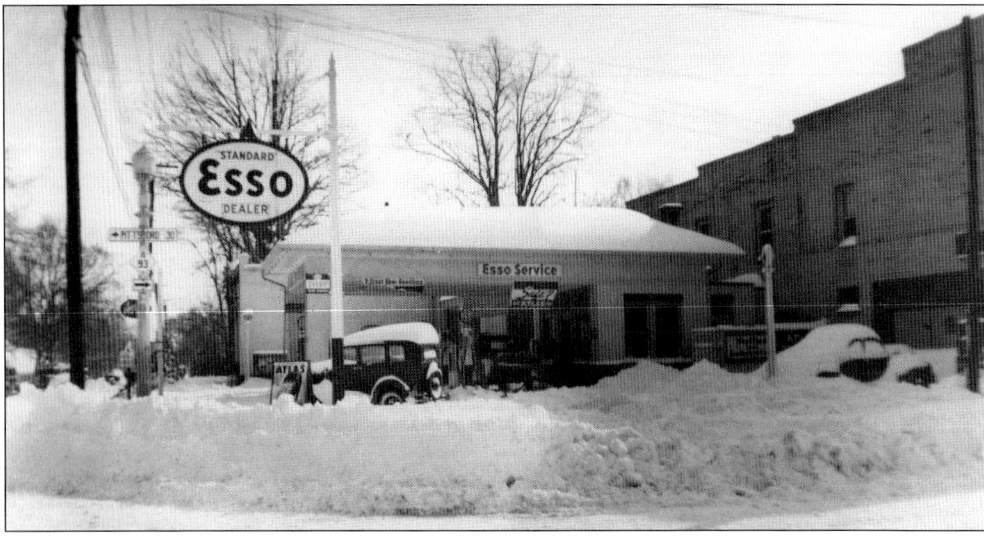

The long-running Esso station at the corner of North Main and Harden Streets changed owners many times. William Boswell's filling station is seen above during the big snow of January 24, 1940. In the 1950s photograph below, Perdue Esso advertises a sale on Atlas tires. The familiar landmark later became Lemon's Esso Station. (Above, courtesy of Don Bolden; below, courtesy of Jerry Perdue.)

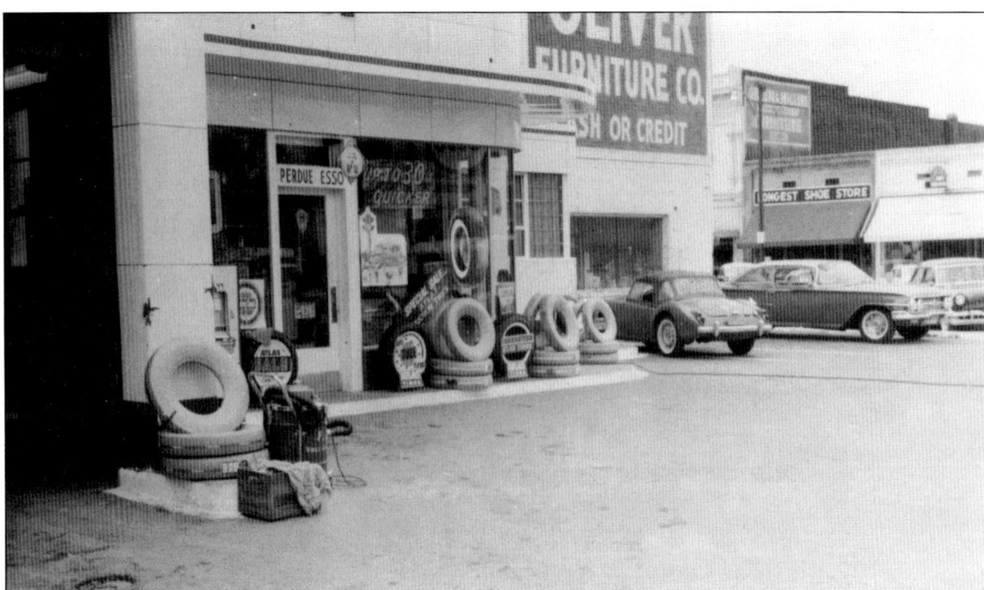

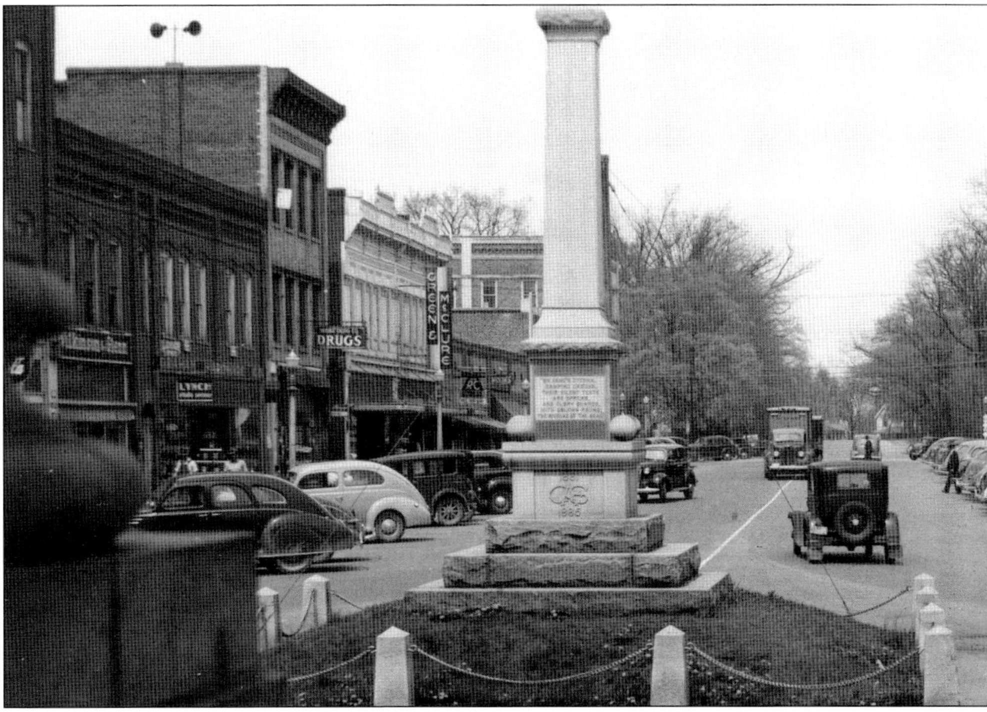

The business district bustled with activity in the years leading up to World War II. This view from the courthouse looks up North Main Street toward the Monte White Theatre. (Courtesy of Skee and Virginia Johnson.)

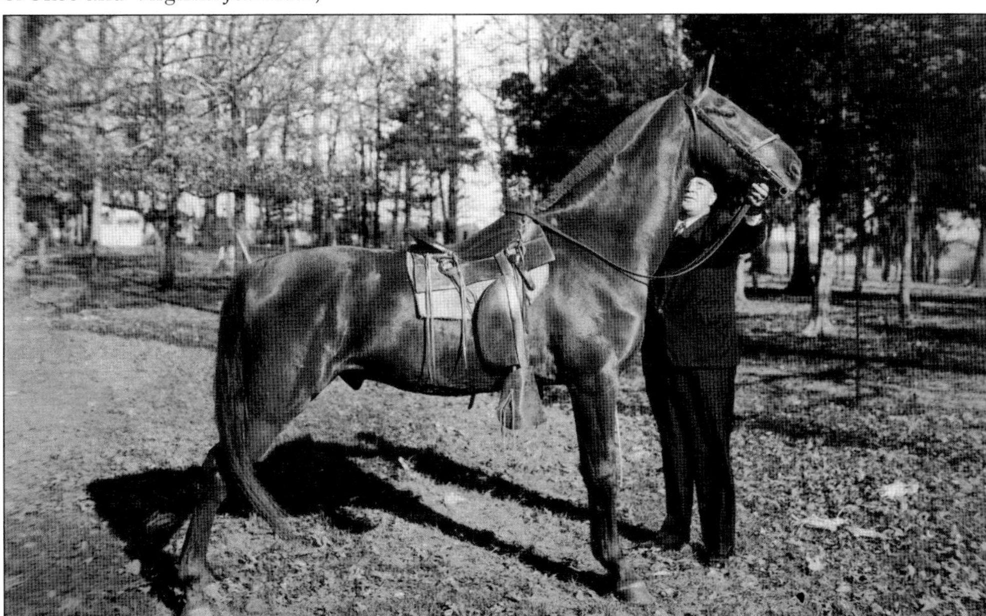

In May 1942, gasoline rationing for the war effort began. By January 1943, all pleasure driving was outlawed on the East Coast, making horses in demand again. Brothers Hallie and Bascom Moore owned a stable and rented horses on the weekends, when driving was restricted. Hallie Moore is seen here with one of his horses. (Courtesy of Bonnie Blalock.)

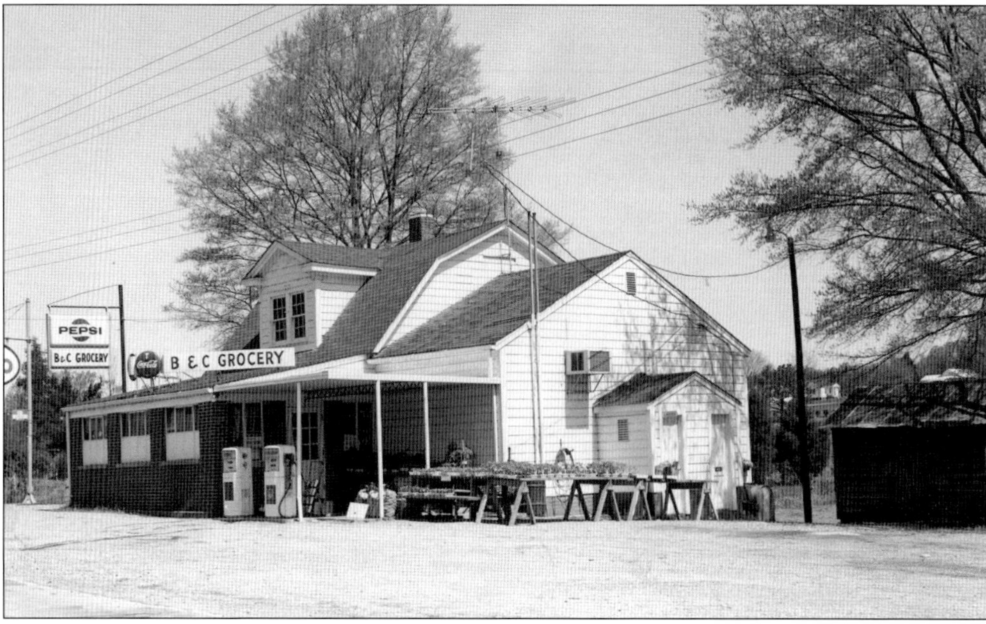

B & C Grocery on East Harden Street opened for business in 1950 and was a staple in Graham for nearly 60 years. It was run by the Whittemore brothers, Charlie, Bill, and Clyde. B & C was a popular place to buy just about everything, including gasoline, groceries, working clothes, birdseed, and plants. Folks stopped by and stayed awhile to catch up on the news of the day. (Courtesy of Charles Whittemore.)

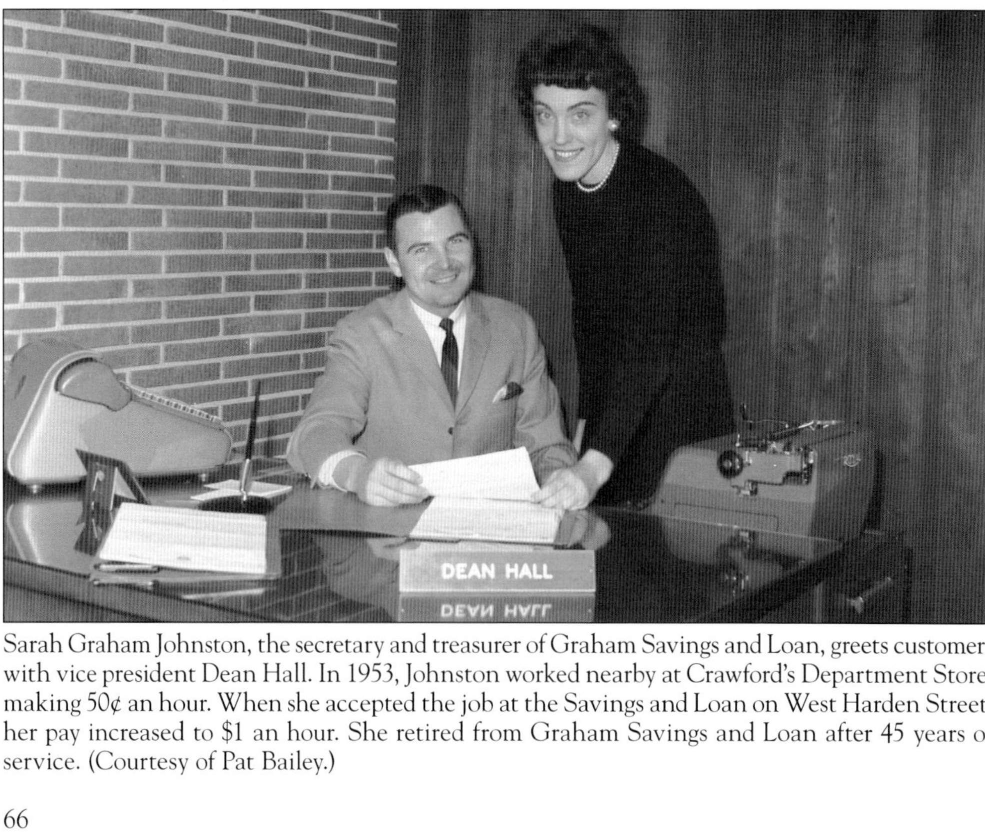

Sarah Graham Johnston, the secretary and treasurer of Graham Savings and Loan, greets customers with vice president Dean Hall. In 1953, Johnston worked nearby at Crawford's Department Store, making 50¢ an hour. When she accepted the job at the Savings and Loan on West Harden Street, her pay increased to $1 an hour. She retired from Graham Savings and Loan after 45 years of service. (Courtesy of Pat Bailey.)

Four

Serving the Community

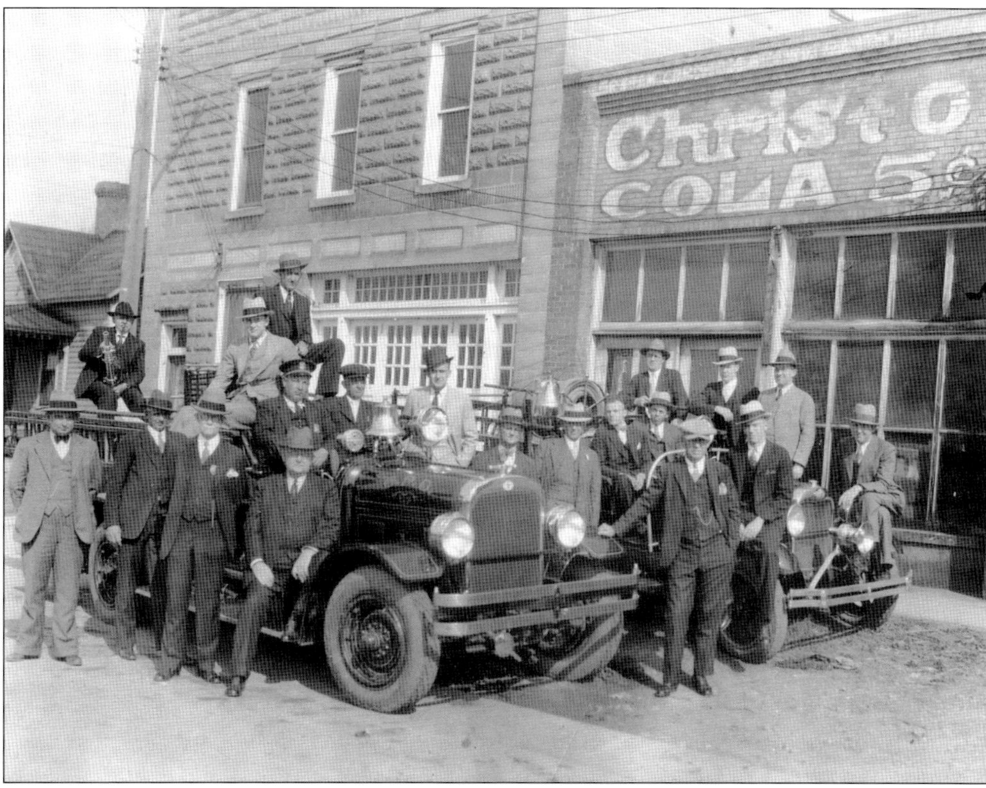

Volunteer firemen in Graham Hose Company No. 1 answered the fire bell beginning in 1903. The day the new 1930 Seagrave Suburbanite Pumper was delivered was highly anticipated, and firemen posed around it in front of the fireman's building on West Elm Street. The fire truck on the right is a 1924 Ford chemical truck. Money was tight in the 1930s, and the Seagrave was repossessed three times for nonpayment. Christo Cola Bottling Works was operated by W. Ernest Thompson. (Courtesy of Green & McClure.)

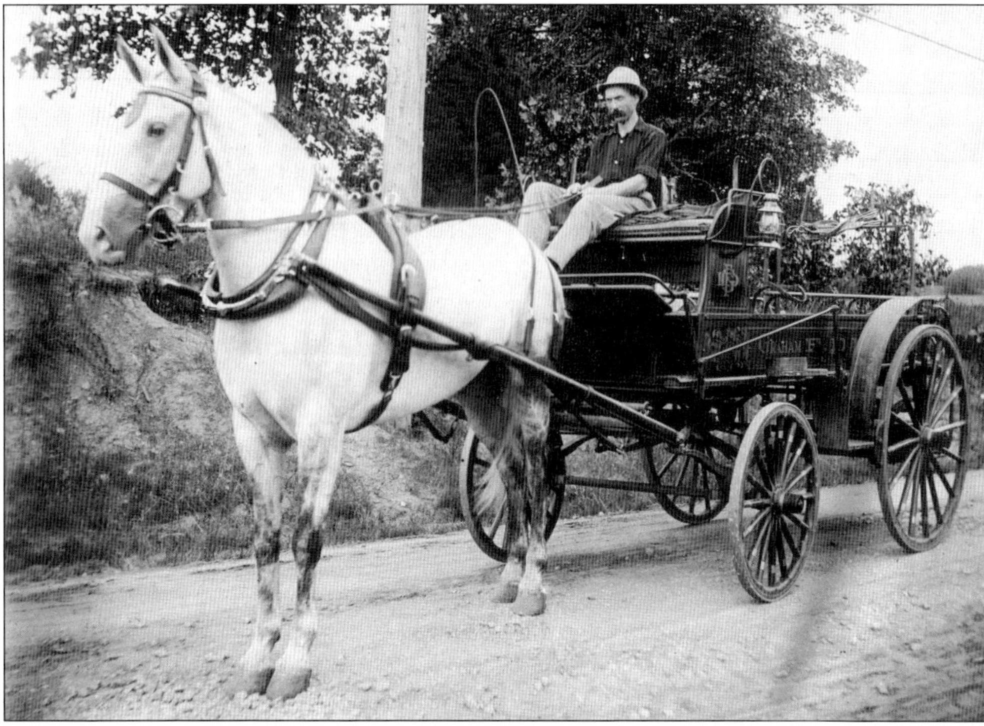

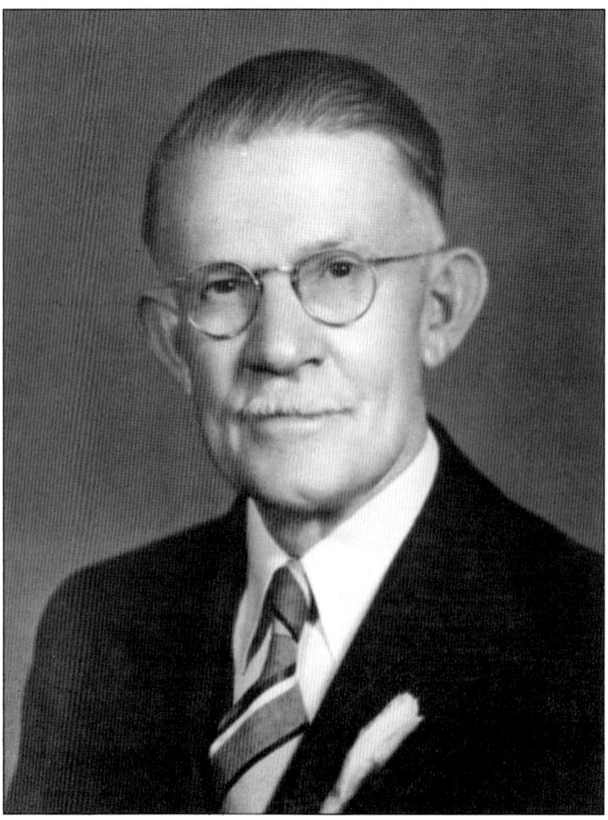

One story passed down by the fire department concerns Old Mac, seen here, the horse that pulled the fire wagon and was used to plow fields during the day. When the fire call sounded, Old Mac knew what his next job would be; he pricked up his ears and was ready to roll. (Courtesy of Green & McClure.)

Dr. William Long, a local dentist, lived in Elon in the 1890s. His home was destroyed by fire in 1895, and his wife barely escaped with their infant son. After the fire, "Dr. Will" was devoted to protecting his community. He moved his practice to Graham and was the town's fire chief from 1915 to 1954. (Courtesy of Graham Fire Department.)

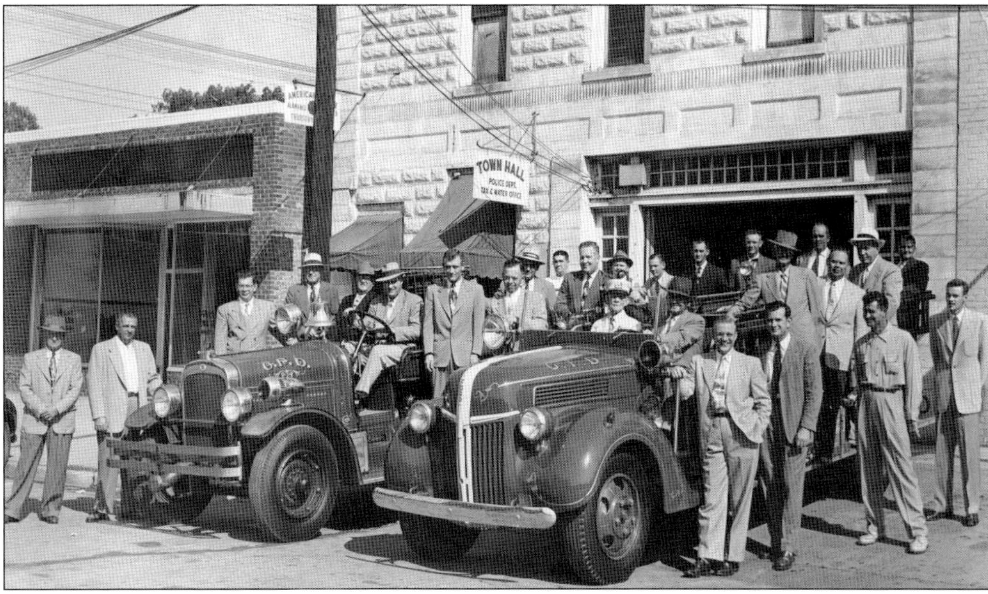

Members of the Graham Fire Department pose with the fire trucks. Dr. William Long, the fire chief, wearing white, sits in the newer fire truck. The 1930 Seagrave is on the left. The truck on the right is a 1940s Ford open-cab pumper. (Courtesy of Graham Historical Museum.)

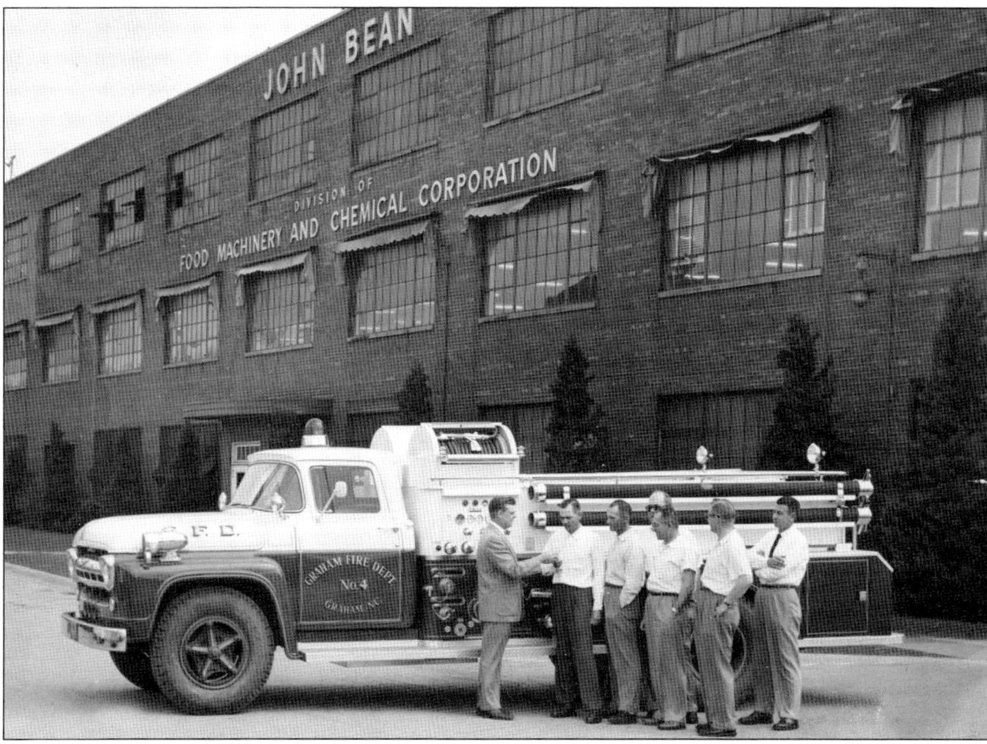

A group of firemen traveled to Detroit to pick up the new fire truck in 1957. Foster Hughes of Hughes Motor Company, a former fireman, financed the trip with $500 and accompanied the firemen on the trip. After one day on the road, Hughes called his dealership to say that they had run out of money but gave no explanation as to how they spent it so quickly. (Courtesy of Jack Henderson.)

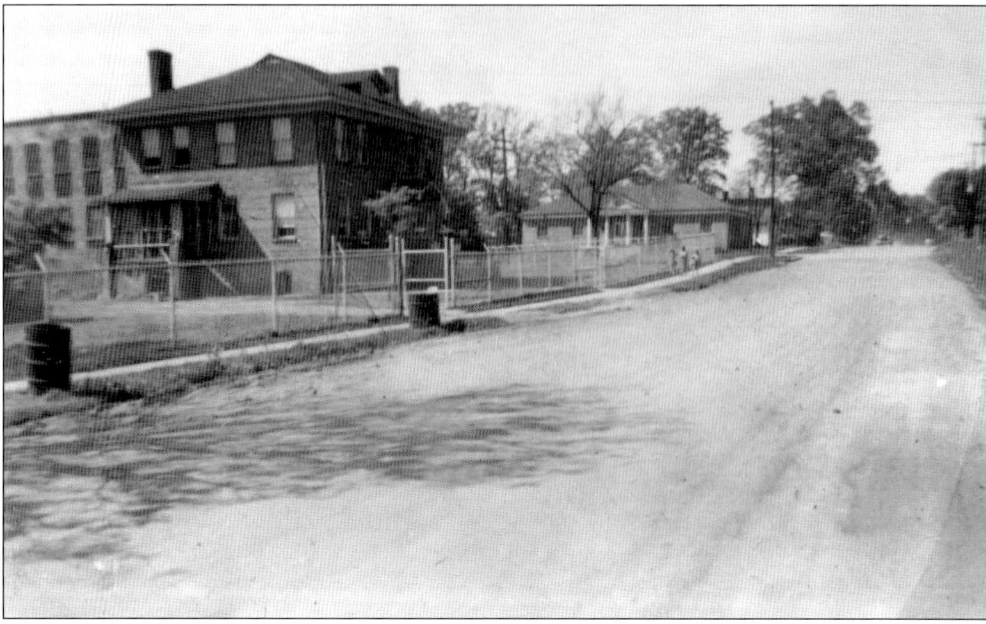

The first Alamance County Jail was built in 1853 on the corner of Maple and Elm Streets. The brick jail seen here was not as secure as modern-day facilities are. In fact, in 1913, all five prisoners escaped while the jailer and his wife were attending church. (Courtesy of Drucilla Hearn.)

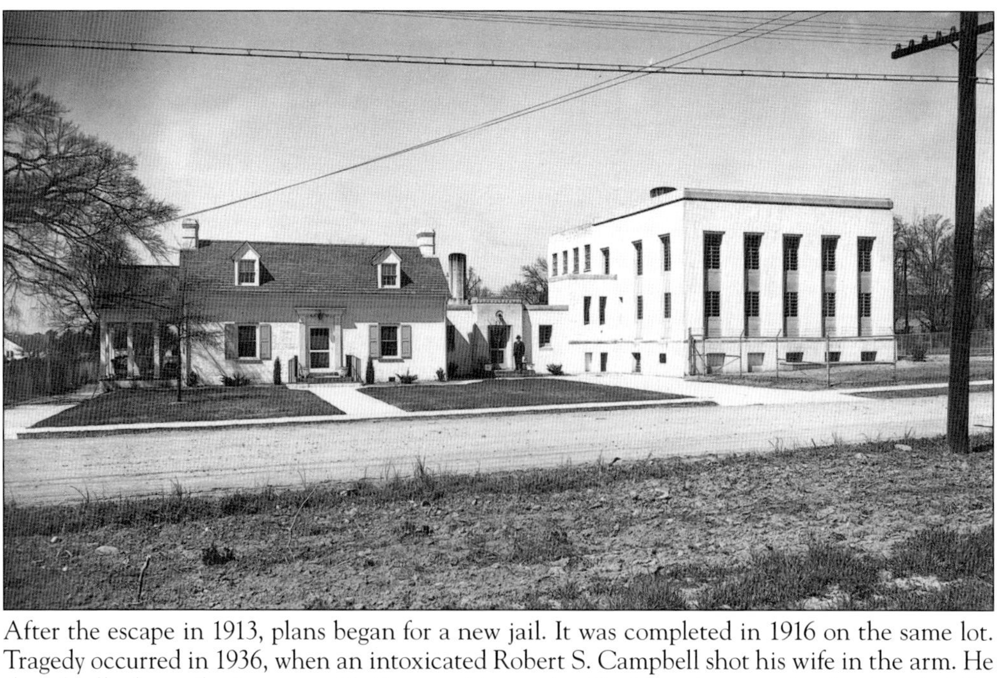

After the escape in 1913, plans began for a new jail. It was completed in 1916 on the same lot. Tragedy occurred in 1936, when an intoxicated Robert S. Campbell shot his wife in the arm. He then fatally shot jailor Lawrence G. Gowens. Gowens's wife, Alma, became the first female jailer in the county when she was appointed to serve the remainder of his term. This photograph was taken in 1943. (Courtesy of Graham Police Department.)

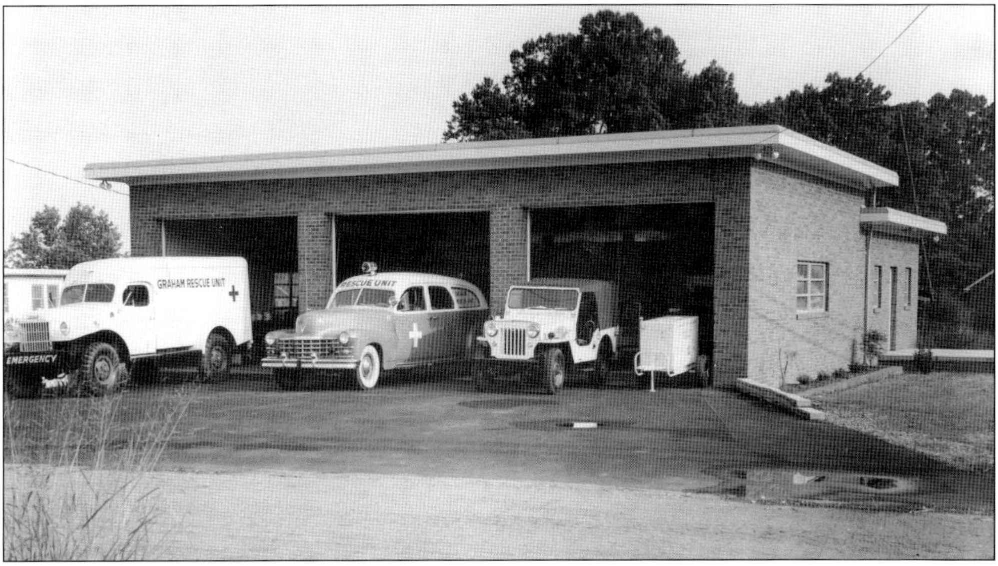

The Graham Rescue Unit was organized in 1955 by members of the Graham Fire Department. Prior to this, emergency services were provided by area funeral homes. The community provided the rescue unit's first vehicles, including an older-model hearse donated by McClure Funeral Home, a bread truck from a local business, and a jeep belonging to Bobby Simpson. (Courtesy of Carl Fitch.)

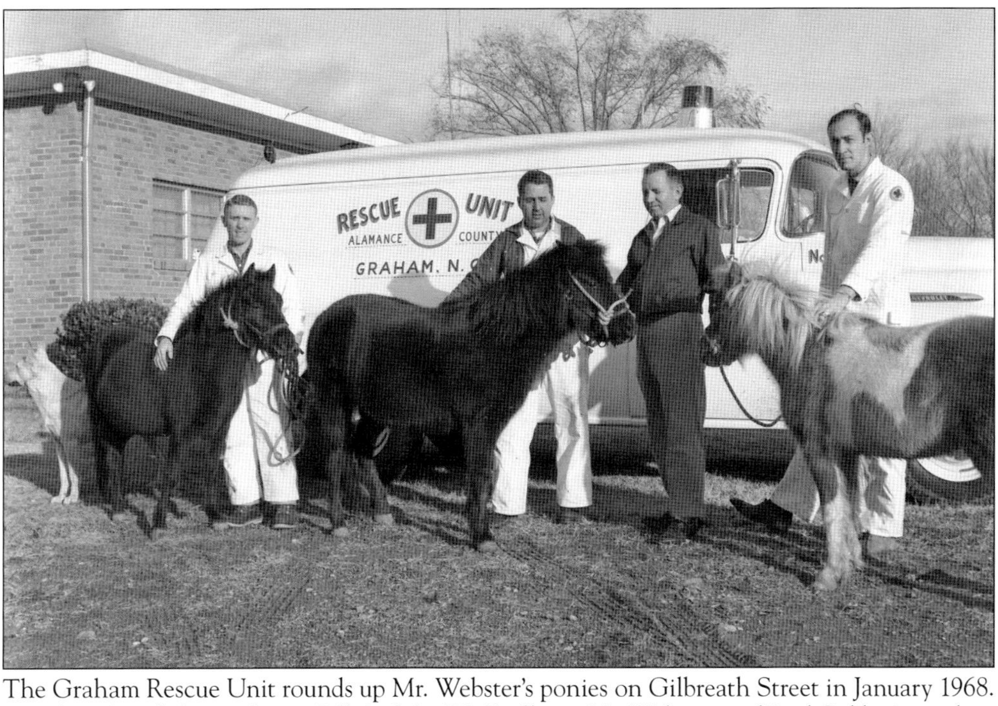

The Graham Rescue Unit rounds up Mr. Webster's ponies on Gilbreath Street in January 1968. Standing from left to right are Bill Aydt Jr., E.J. Faulkner, Mr. Webster, and Paul Cobb. According to Aydt, the truck in this photograph was hard to drive—he said it drove like a dog wagging its tail. (Courtesy of Pat Bailey.)

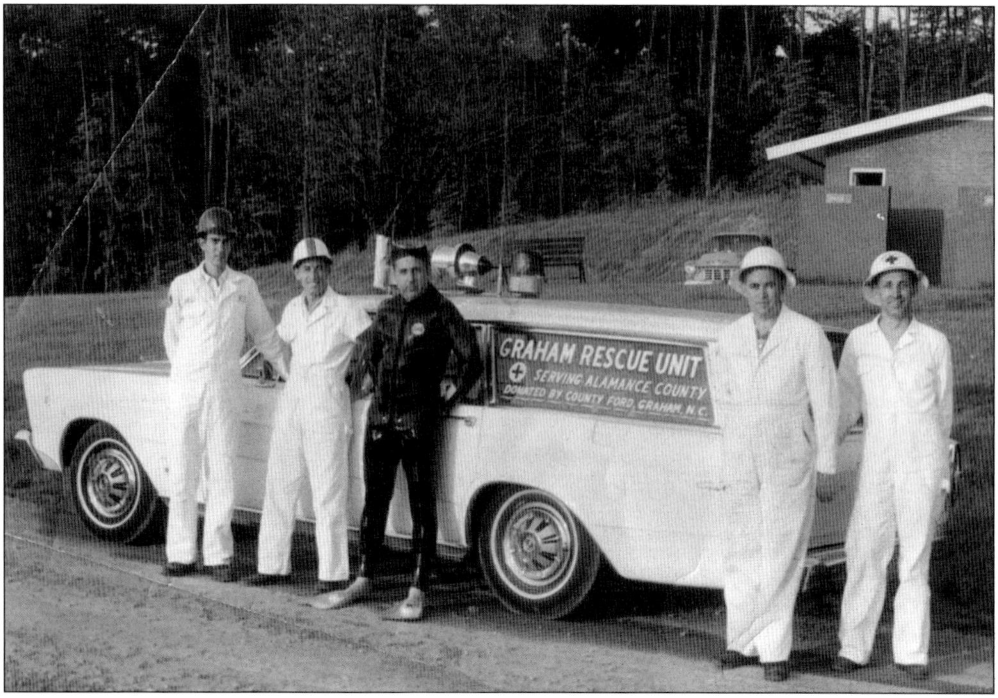

The Graham Rescue Unit responded anywhere in Alamance County. If a car drove into Burlington Lake or the Haw River, boats and divers were available. Here, leaning on the ambulance from left to right are John Brietmier, Earl Boggs, E.J. Faulkner (in diving suit), an unidentified man, and Carl Fitch. The station wagon was donated by County Ford. (Courtesy of Carl Fitch.)

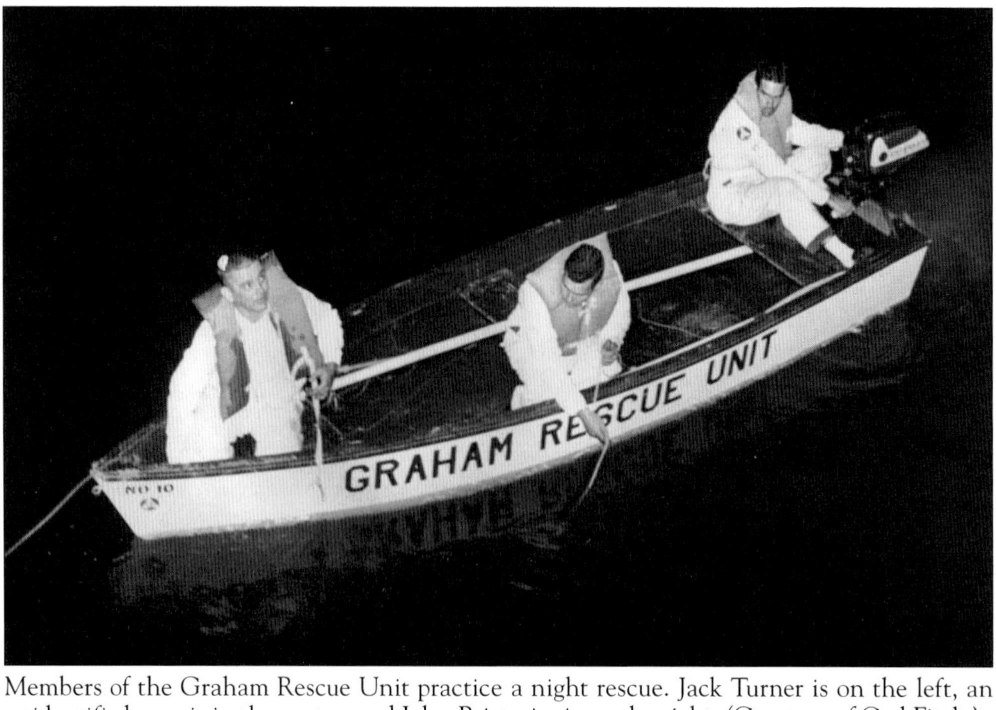

Members of the Graham Rescue Unit practice a night rescue. Jack Turner is on the left, an unidentified man is in the center, and John Brietmier is on the right. (Courtesy of Carl Fitch.)

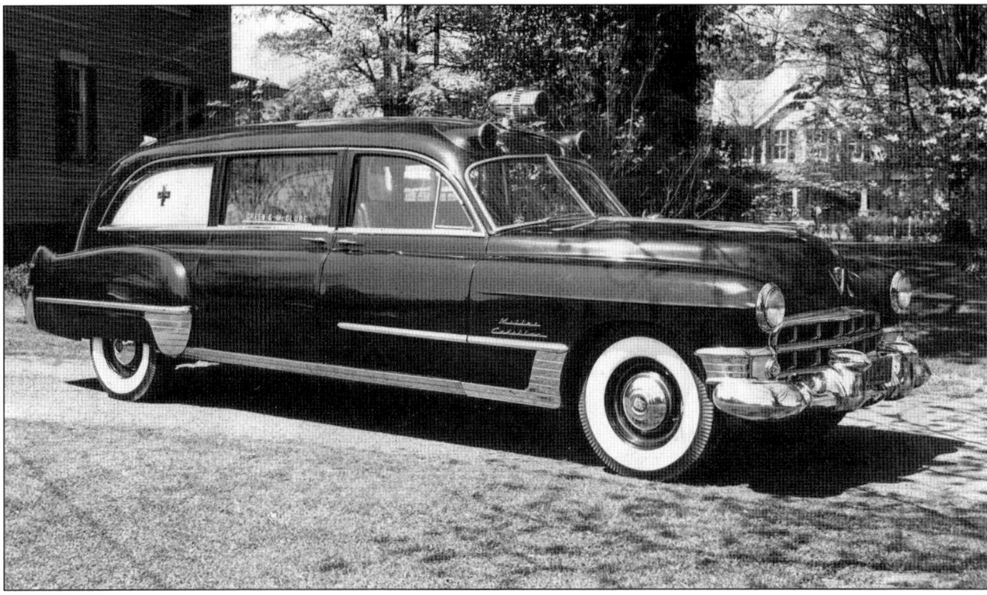

This private ambulance belonged to Green & McClure Funeral Service. Prior to 1967, ambulance services were provided by local funeral homes. At that time, the county took over ambulance calls, and the private services were discontinued. (Courtesy of Green & McClure.)

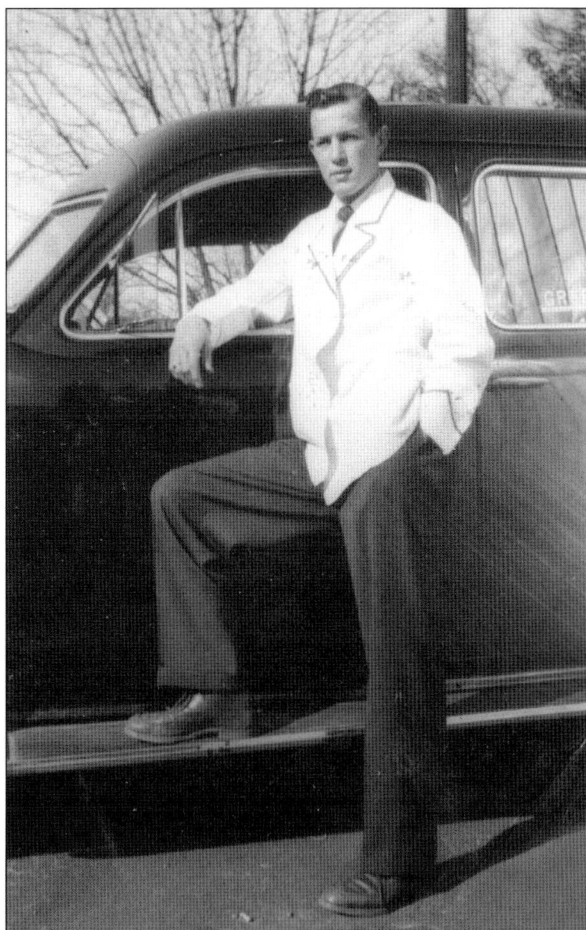

John Hardie Stockard drove an ambulance for Green & McClure. He was also a volunteer member of the Graham Fire Department. He later became the sheriff of Alamance County. The jail complex built in 1987 is named the John Hardie Stockard Law Enforcement Center in his honor. (Courtesy of Green & McClure.)

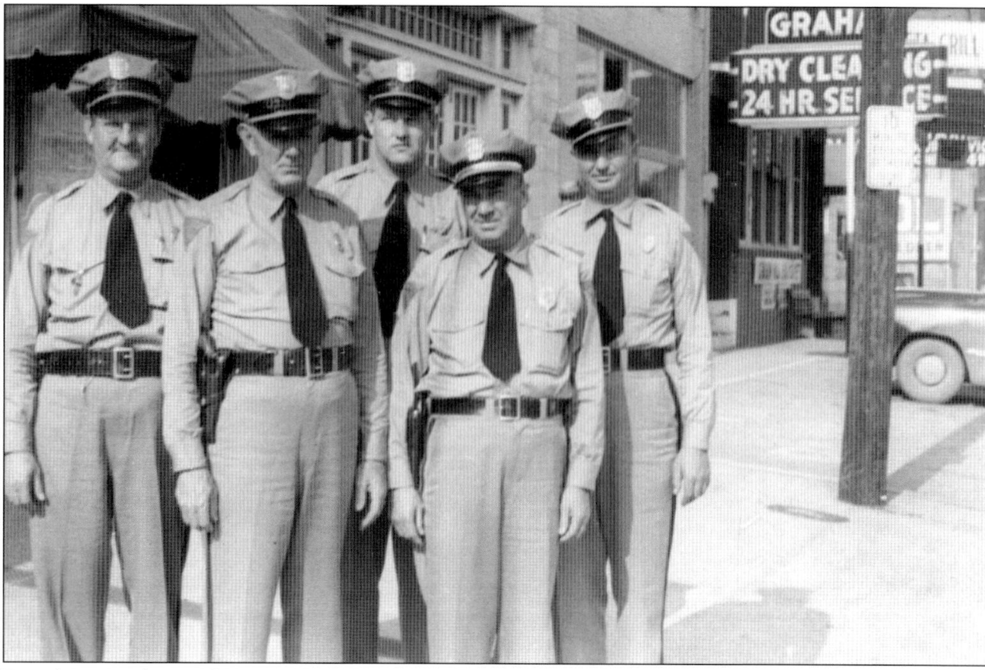

Patrolmen gather in front of city hall on West Elm Street around 1950. As late as the 1980s, officers walked a beat around Court Square, checking for open doors or anything out of the ordinary. (Courtesy of Graham Police Department.)

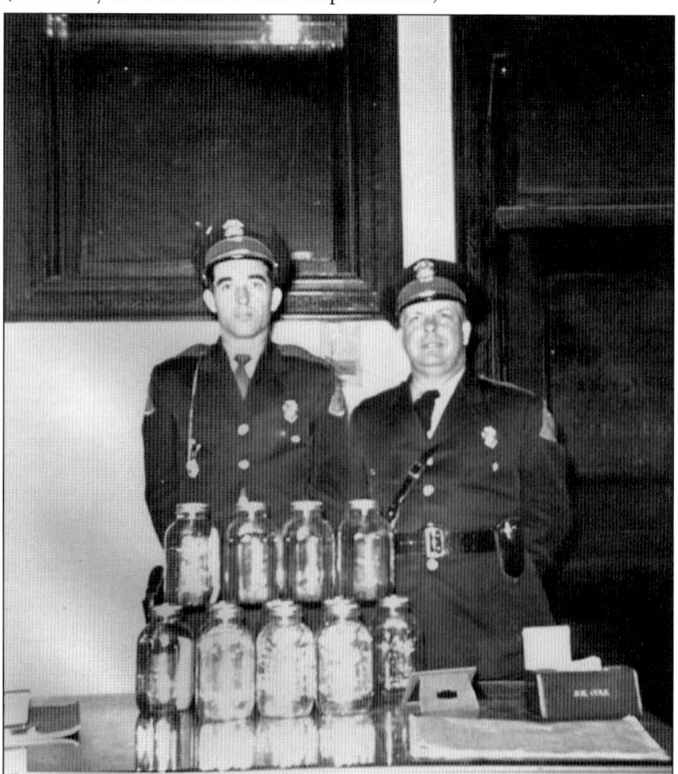

Sgt. William Miles (left) and patrolman Alvis Wilson guard jars of white whiskey confiscated in the 1950s. (Courtesy of Graham Police Department.)

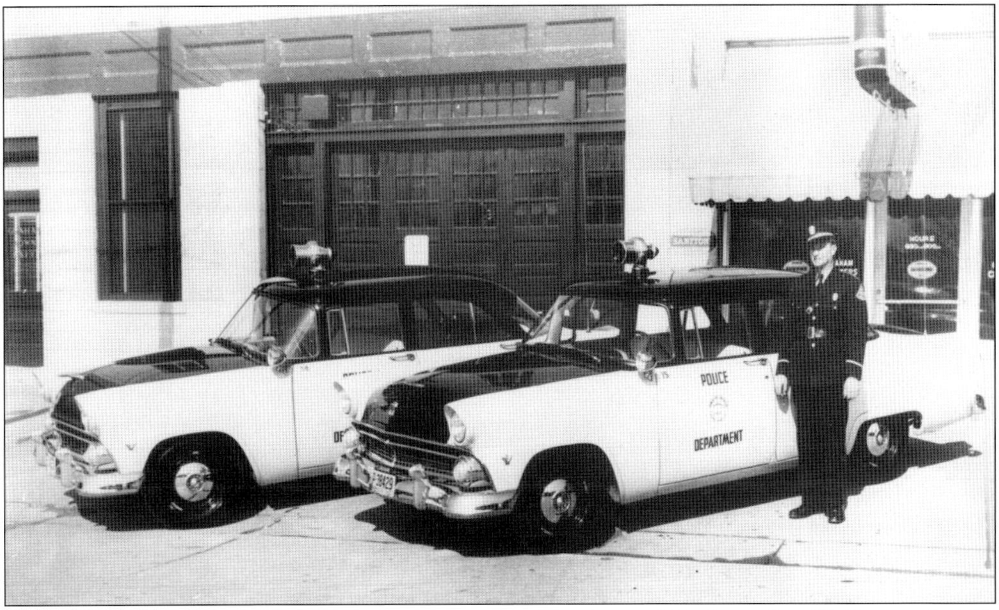

Chief Ralph E. Sykes stands with the new patrol cars in front of Graham City Hall around 1955. He joined the department in 1949, bringing the total number of police officers at that time to four. He served in the department for 25 years and was the chief of police for 14 years. (Courtesy of Graham Historical Museum.)

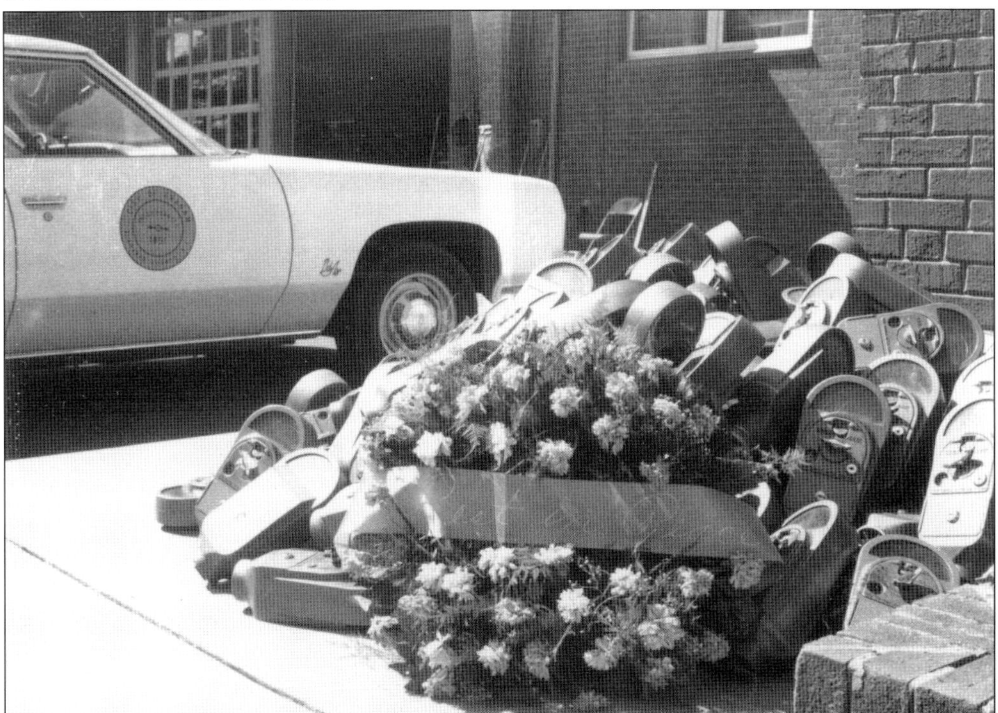

Parking meters dotted the business district until 1978. The resident who placed the wreath on these discarded parking meters must have been happy when the meters were removed. The wreath says, "Rest in Peace," with tongue-in-cheek humor. (Courtesy of Graham Historical Museum.)

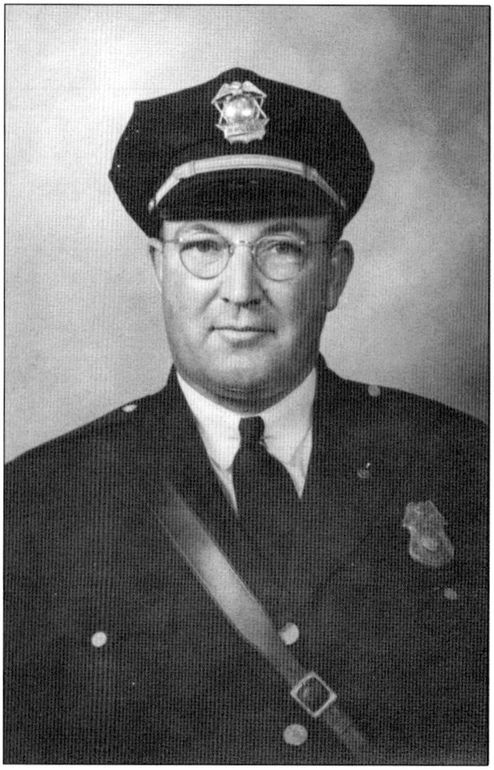

C. Harris "Hallie" Moore served as the chief of police from 1931 to 1943. He and his brother Bascom operated the White Front Market on North Main Street. Hallie was always willing to help those in need. His wife, Beulah, kept food on hand for folks who needed it. He was appointed mayor of Graham in 1945, serving two years, during which time he was elected sheriff, a position he held until 1954. (Courtesy of Bonnie Blalock.)

The police officers posing below in 1956 are, from left to right, (seated) chief of police Ralph Sykes and D.B. Paris; (standing) Jimmy Bowland, Jim Wright, Ethel Bradshaw, Johnny Adams, and Otis Massey. (Courtesy of Graham Police Department.)

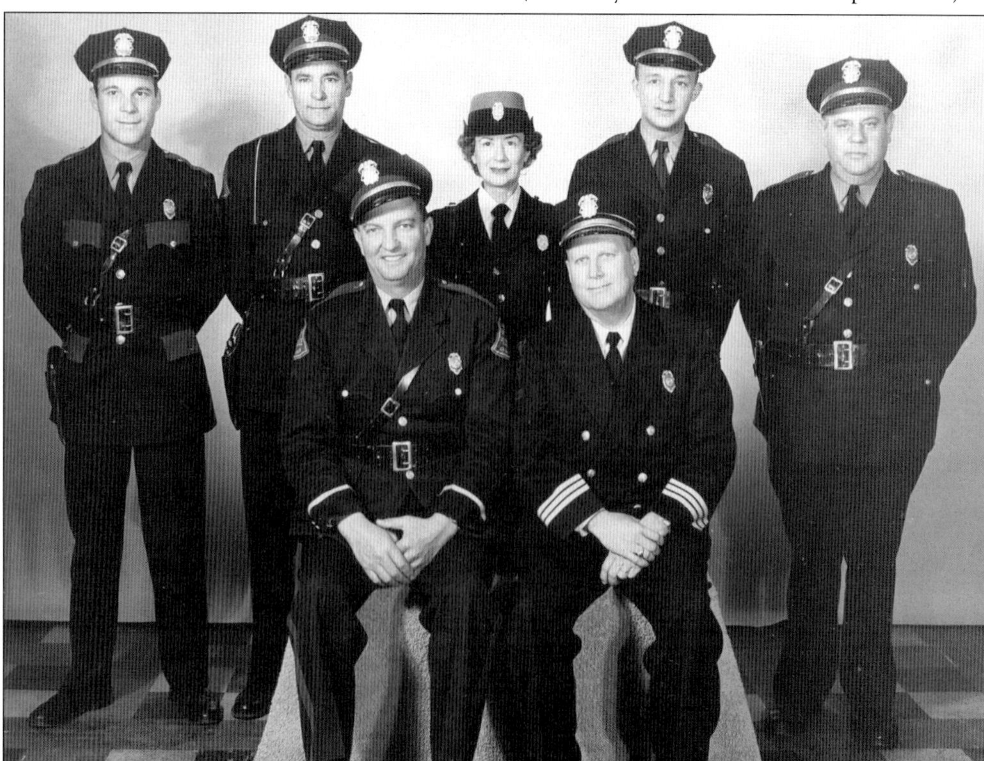

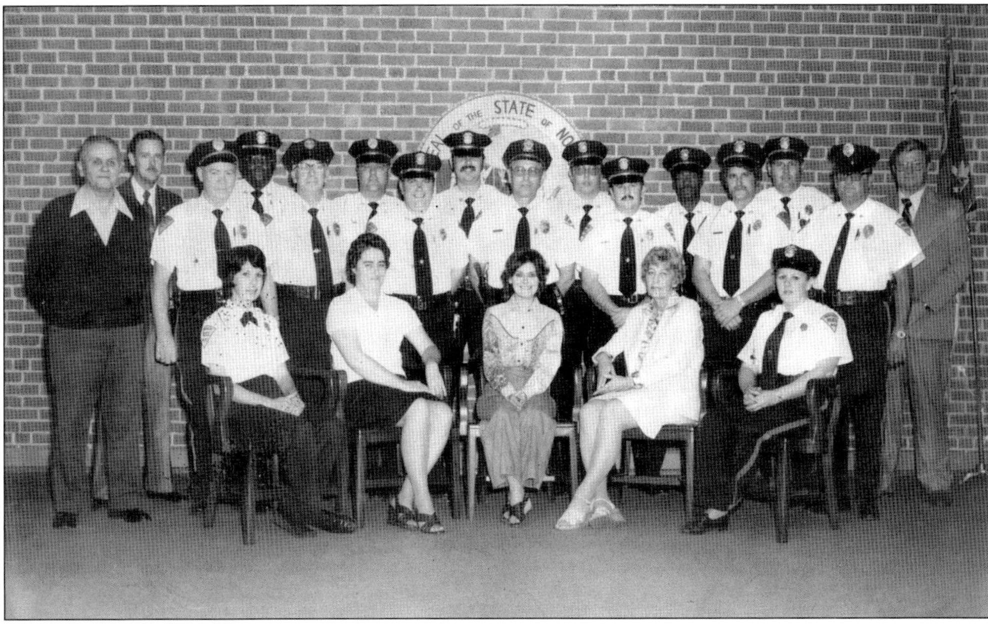

The Graham Police Department posed for this group photograph around 1978. (Courtesy of James Cooley.)

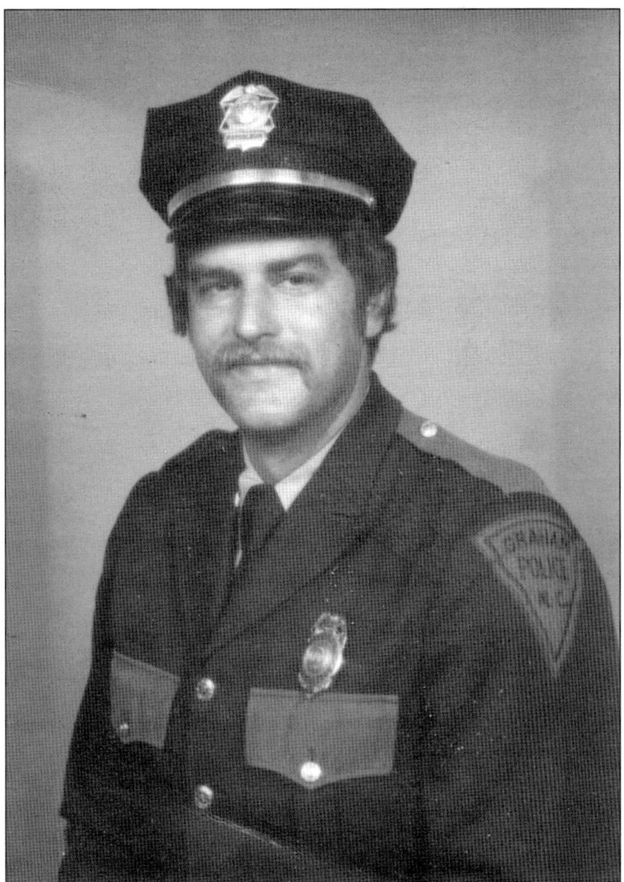

William Alton Roberson Jr. was killed on July 12, 1978, in an automobile accident during a pursuit. He was a five-year veteran on the force and is the only Graham police officer to die in the line of duty. (Courtesy of Graham Police Department.)

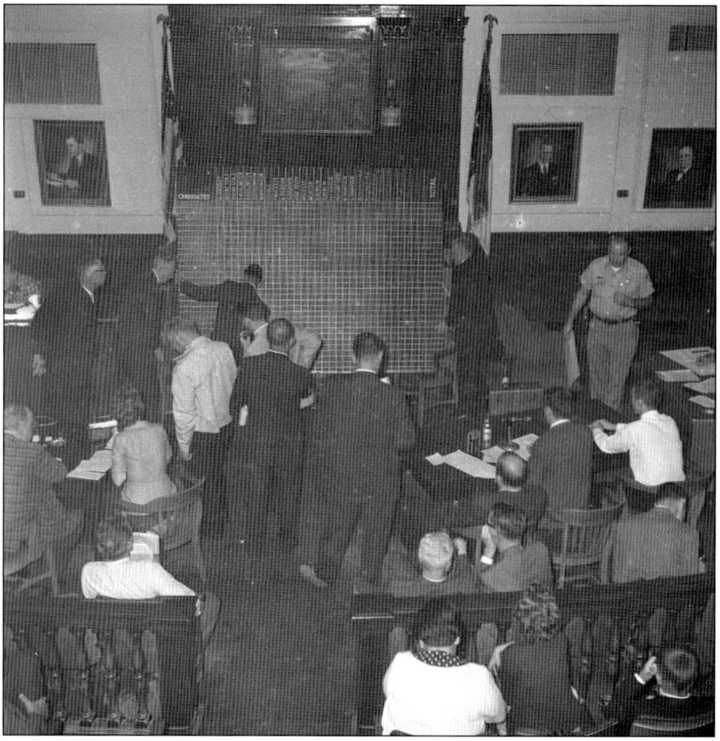

In a tradition dating from the 1800s, concerned citizens gather at the courthouse to await election returns. Ballots were counted by hand, and sometimes, voters and the press waited until the wee hours of the morning to learn the outcome. In the 1960s, results were marked on a large chalkboard as the precinct judges hand-delivered their returns. (Courtesy of Pat Bailey.)

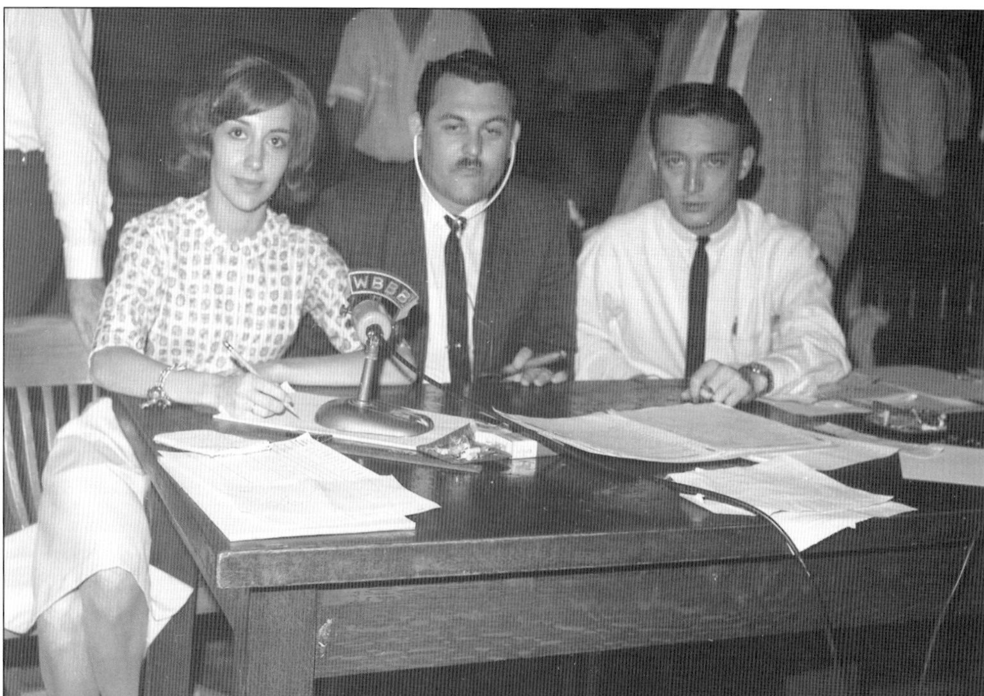

The elections were broadcast live on WBBB radio. The station sent an eight-member team to tally votes and announce the results on the air. Here, in 1962, Janet Hazelwood Butler tallies votes with Olin Campbell (center). (Courtesy of Pat Bailey.)

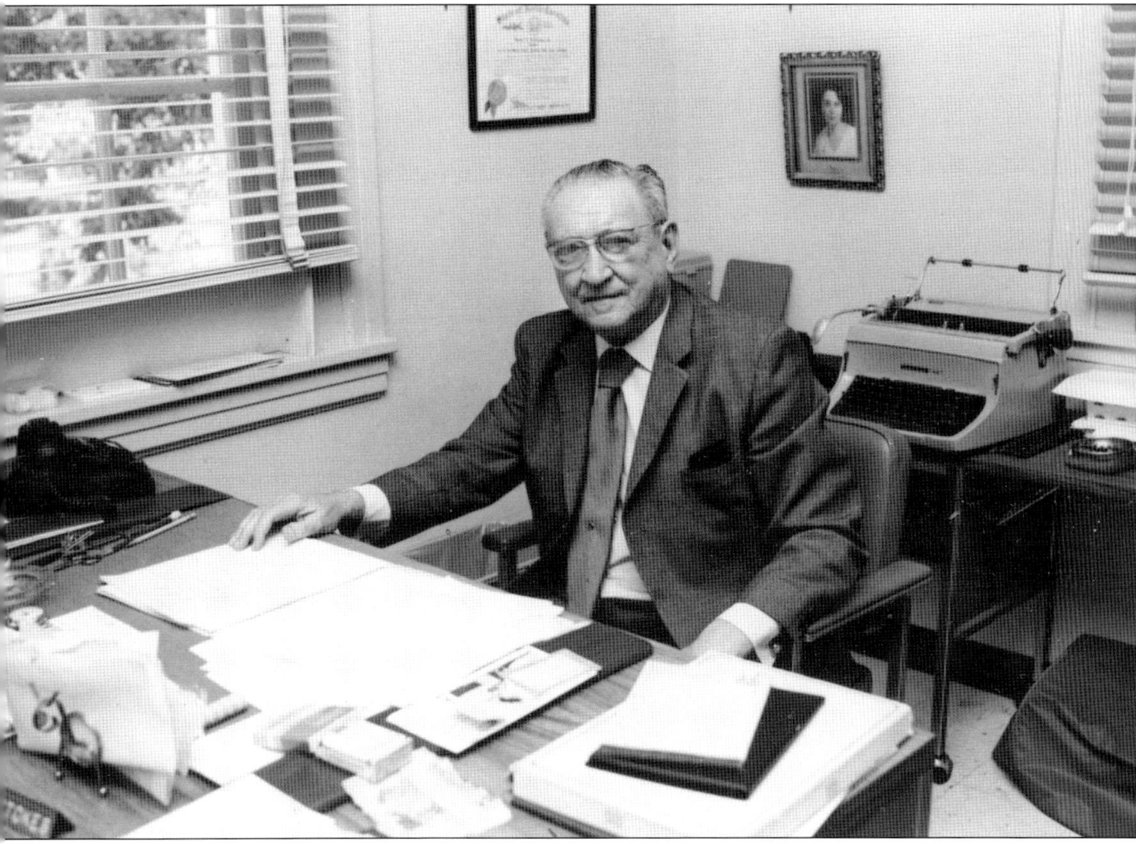

Dr. Durward T. Stokes lived in the W.J. Nicks store on Court Square for many years. He and his wife, Enita Nicks, operated his father-in-law's store from 1939 to the 1960s. While writing his book about Graham, *Auction and Action*, Stokes spent many hours at the Graham Public Library researching microfilms of the *Alamance Gleaner* for relevant facts. An elder and historian for Graham Presbyterian Church, he also authored a book of the church's history. Stokes, who taught at nearby Elon College, donated items of local interest to the Graham Historical Museum. (Courtesy of Belk Library Archives and Special Collections, Elon University.)

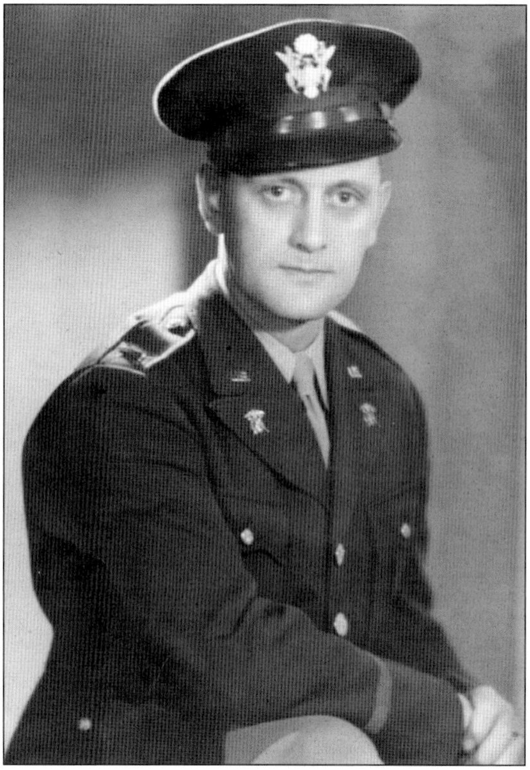

Myron A. Rhyne dedicated his life to public service. He and his wife, Sarah, moved to Graham after his tour of duty in World War II. He was the superintendent at Travora Textile Mills and the mayor of Graham for 24 years. He retired from the Army with 31 years of service, both active and reserve. Rhyne also had a large clock collection; to display them, he built a handsome addition behind his home. (Courtesy of Dennis Andrews.)

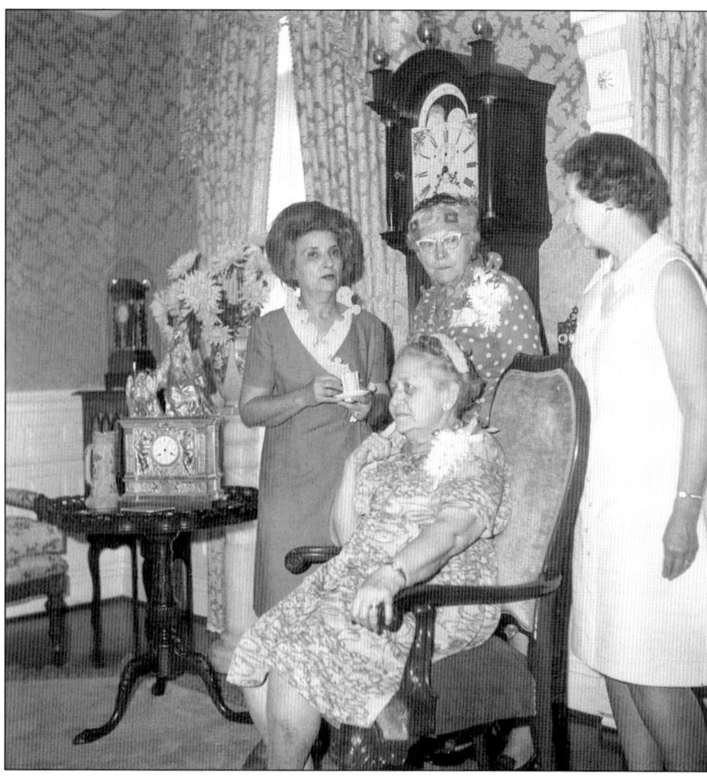

During her husband's tenure as mayor, Sarah Rhyne became known as the first lady of Graham. She devoted her time and talents to the community she loved. She stands on the left in this photograph, entertaining the ladies of the Lutheran church in the "clock house." This addition to the Rhyne home was built using portions of the original carriage house from Lynn Banks Holt's home. (Courtesy of Pat Bailey.)

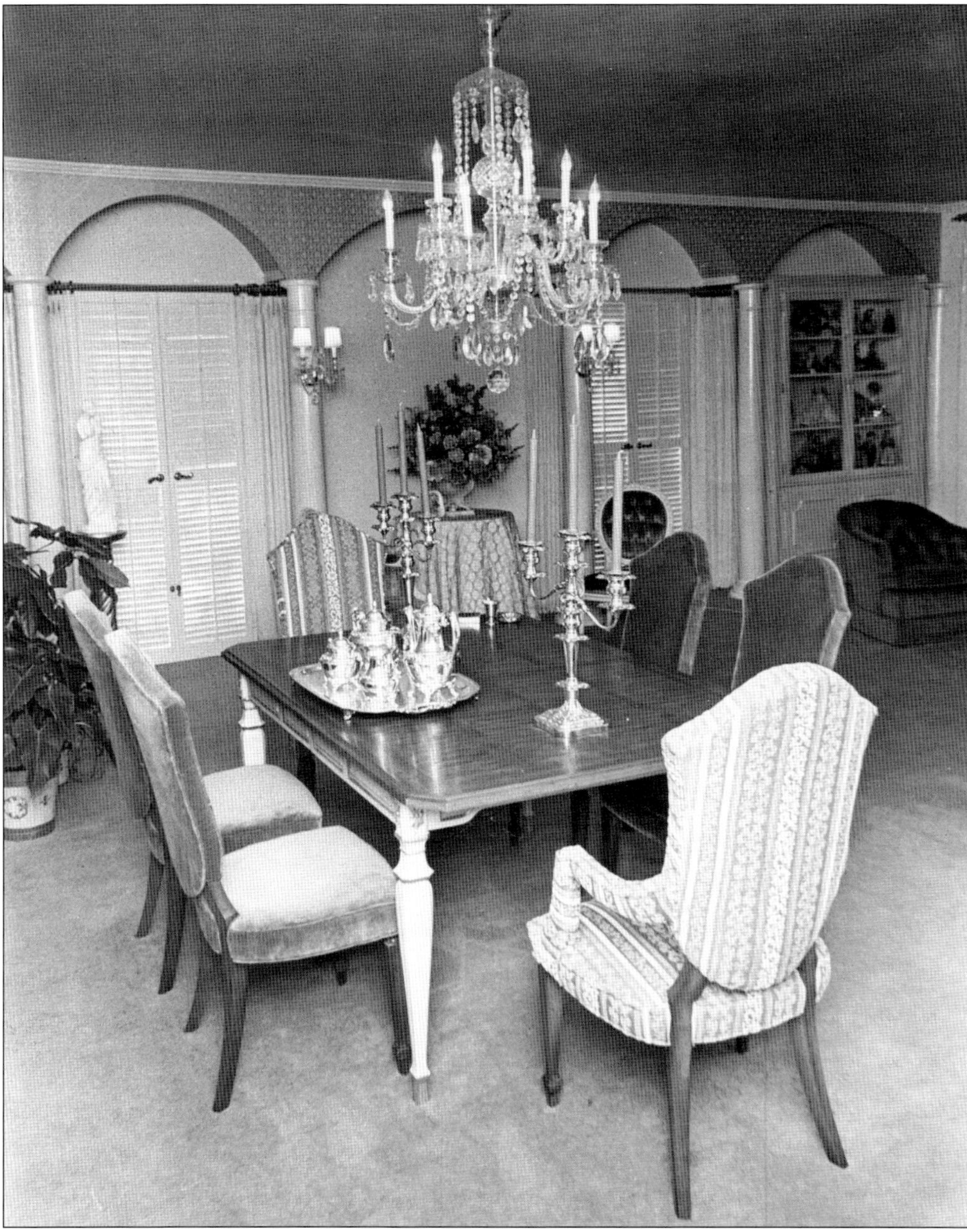

Sarah Rhyne was also thought of as the mother of the arts in Alamance County. She was instrumental in saving two of Graham's most beloved homes. She first convinced Nationsbank to restore Elmhurst on South Main Street. A few years later, she partnered with others in the community to restore the Captain White House, which is now the Alamance County Arts Center. She organized the Graham Appearance Commission and began the tradition of planting flowers throughout the downtown area, initially planting all of the flowers herself. Her achievements also extended beyond Graham. She had the vision of restoring Glencoe Mill and Glencoe Village and creating the Textile Heritage Museum at Glencoe. The grace and charm of the first lady of Graham are evident in this photograph of her lovely home on Parker Street. (Courtesy of Dennis Andrews.)

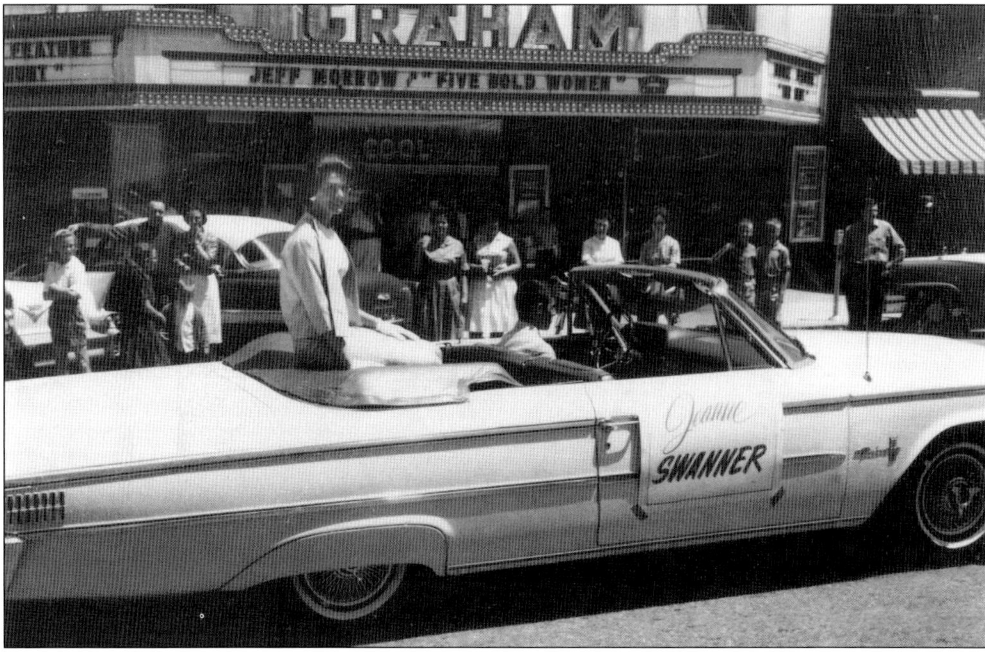

The festivities for the Miss Graham pageant began with a parade down Main Street in April 1963. Contestant Jeanne Swanner is seen here in front of the Graham Cinema. She was crowned Miss Graham later that evening. The six-foot, two-inch beauty was on her way to the Miss North Carolina pageant. (Courtesy of Graham Historical Museum.)

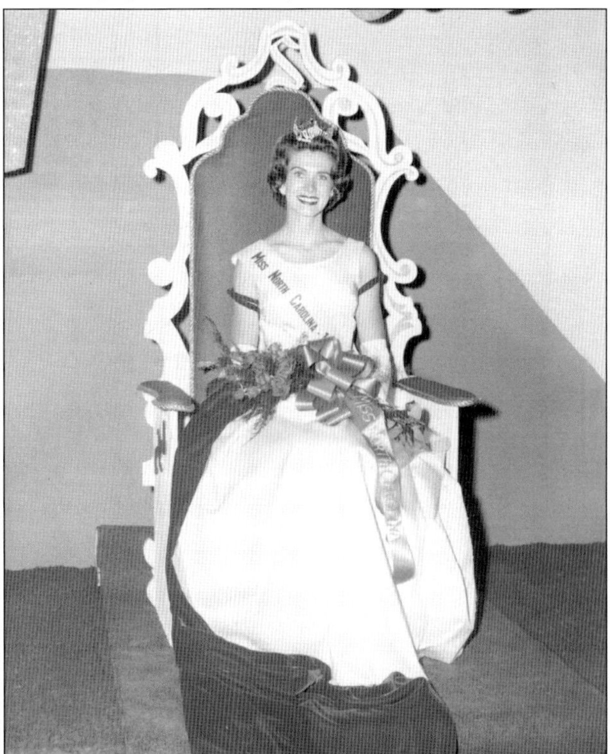

The 1963 Miss North Carolina pageant was held in July in Greensboro. Jeanne Swanner won the pageant and was crowned Miss North Carolina. When she returned home the next day, the town turned out in celebration. People lined the streets and fire apparatuses sounded a salute to alert the crowd. She was greeted by car horns and cheering. (Courtesy of Graham Historical Museum.)

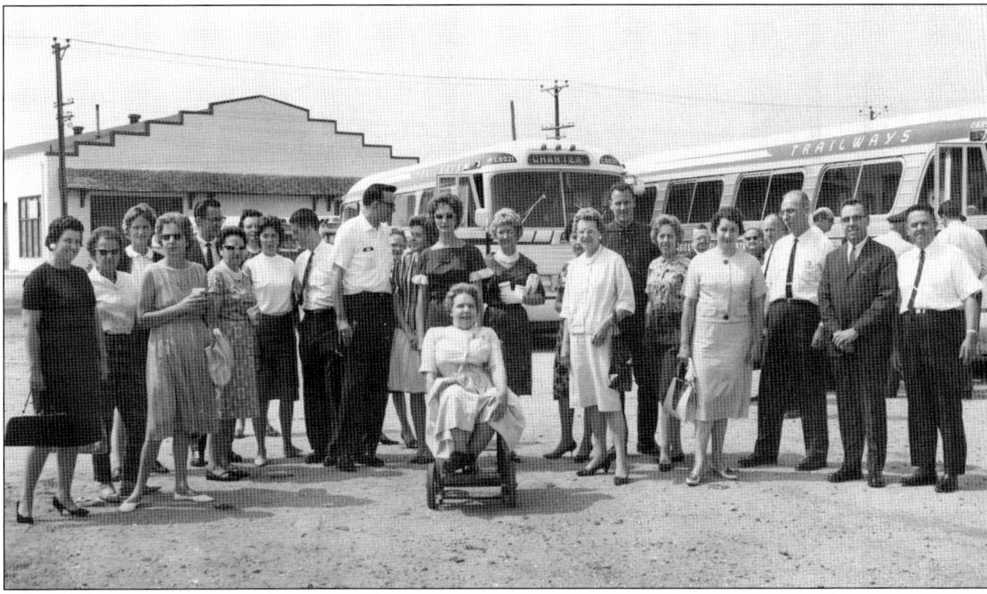

In September 1963, more than 300 people traveled to Atlantic City, New Jersey, to support Jeanne Swanner in the 1963 Miss America pageant. When asked how many people would watch the pageant on television, Sheriff John Stockard replied, "About 90 percent, the other 10 percent are in Atlantic City." Jeanne did not win the Miss America crown, but she was voted Miss Congeniality. (Courtesy of Graham Historical Museum.)

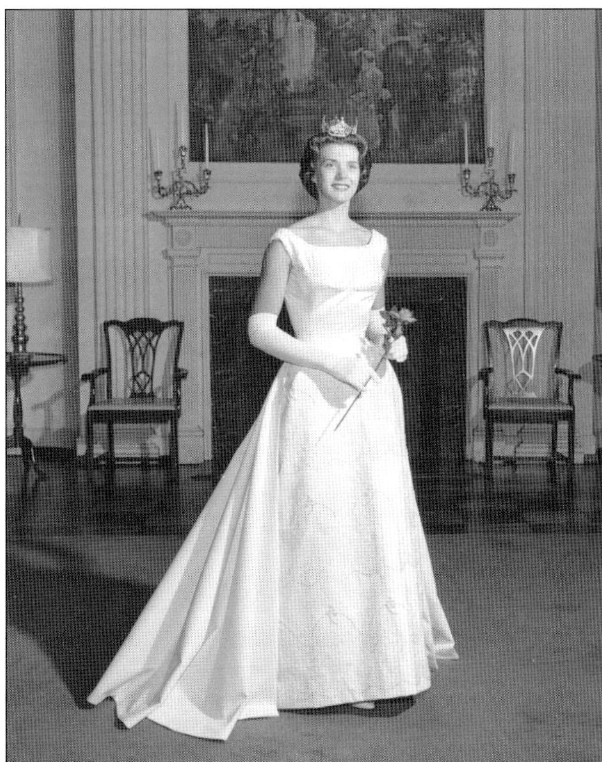

After winning Miss Congeniality in the Miss America pageant, Jeanne Swanner graduated from Auburn University. After that, she taught physical education and coached basketball for nine years before going into professional speaking on a full-time basis. Toastmasters International named Jeanne Swanner Robertson the recipient of its 1998 Golden Gavel Award. The tall girl from Graham has authored three books and continues to share her hometown's humor and charm. (Courtesy of Haw River Historical Museum.)

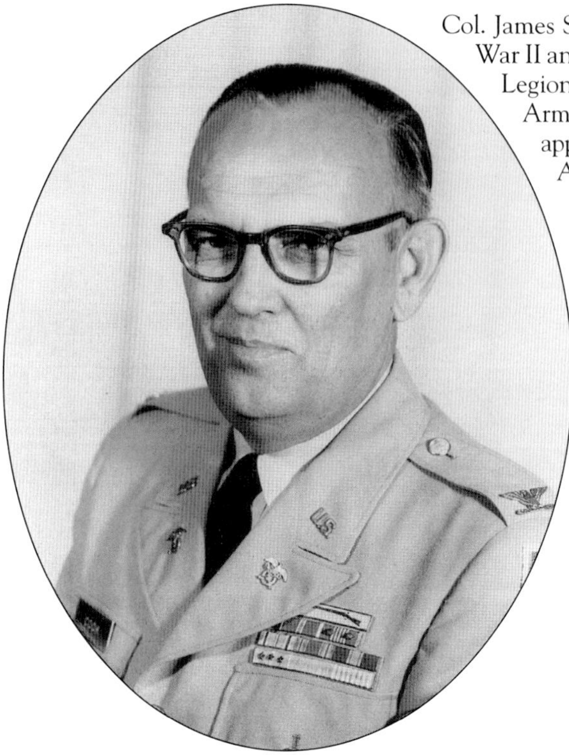

Col. James S. Cook Jr. served in the Army in World War II and in the Korean War. He was awarded the Legion of Merit, the Bronze Star Medal, and the Army Commendation Medal. He was eventually appointed chief of the Heraldic Branch of the Army. (Courtesy of Jack Henderson.)

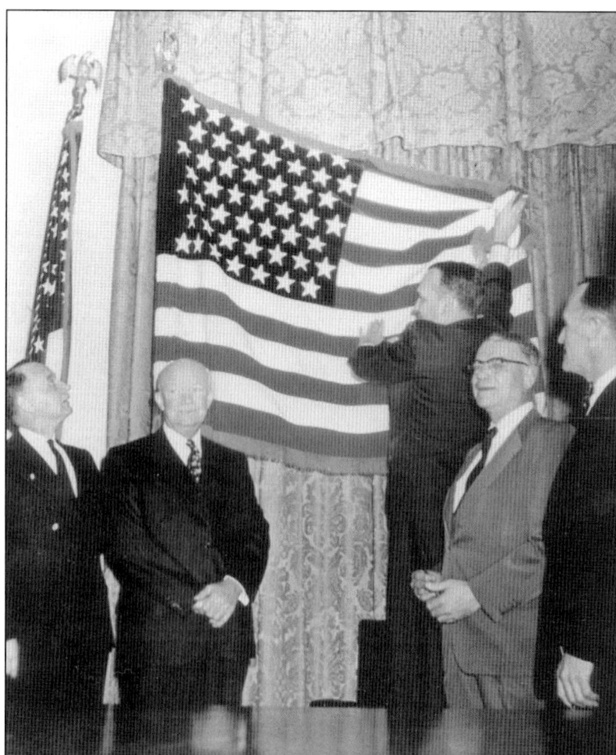

Col. James S. Cook Jr. worked on a committee to design both the 49-star and the 50-star American flags. He personally carried both new flags to the White House and assisted the president in their original unfurling. Standing here in the president's chair in the Oval Office in 1960, he holds the flag for Pres. Dwight D. Eisenhower. Cook Drive, located at Fort Bragg, is named in his honor. (Courtesy of Jack Henderson.)

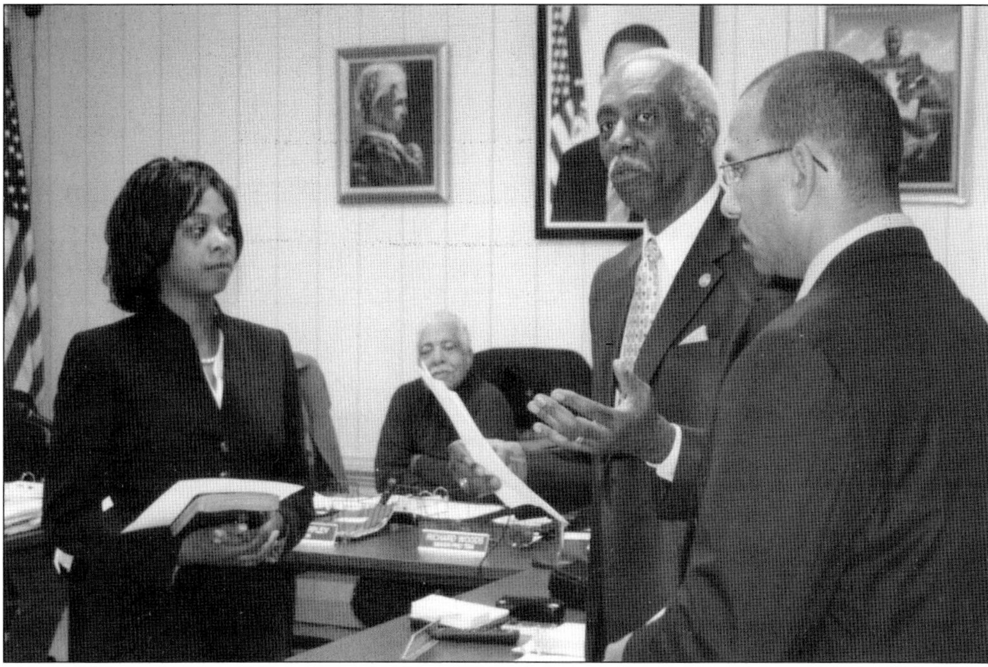

Tony Foriest was elected to the North Carolina state senate in 2006, serving two terms. An army veteran, he graduated from Elon University and worked for the Xerox Corporation in Greensboro for 24 years. He served on many boards, including those of the United Way and the Friendship Center. He was also a two-term chairman of the Alamance County Democratic Party. In this photograph, Foriest (standing, center) speaks with councilwoman Carissa Graves of nearby Green Level. (Courtesy of Tony and Clara Foriest.)

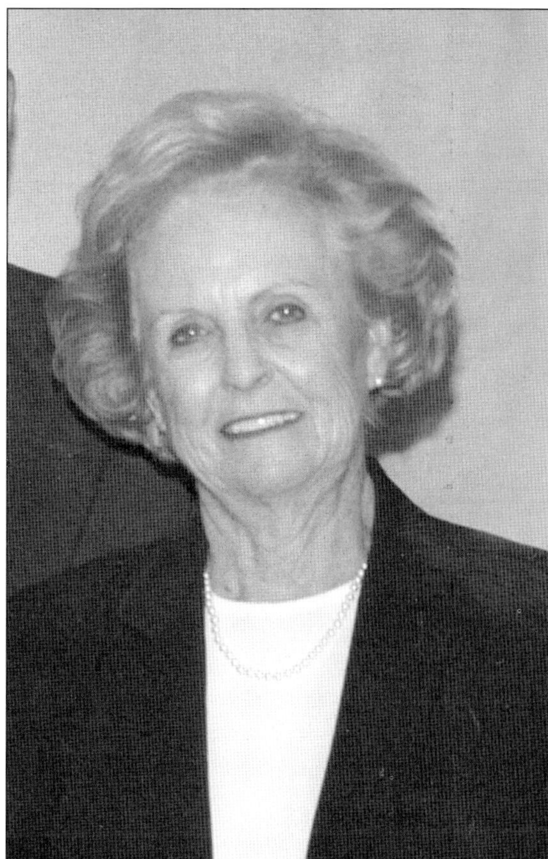

Carrie Stanford Thompson made history in 1989 by becoming the first woman elected to the Graham City Council. She attended Elon College and has served on the Graham Appearance Commission, the Graham Historical Committee, and as a member of the boards for Family Abuse Services and Alamance County Public Libraries. (Courtesy of City of Graham.)

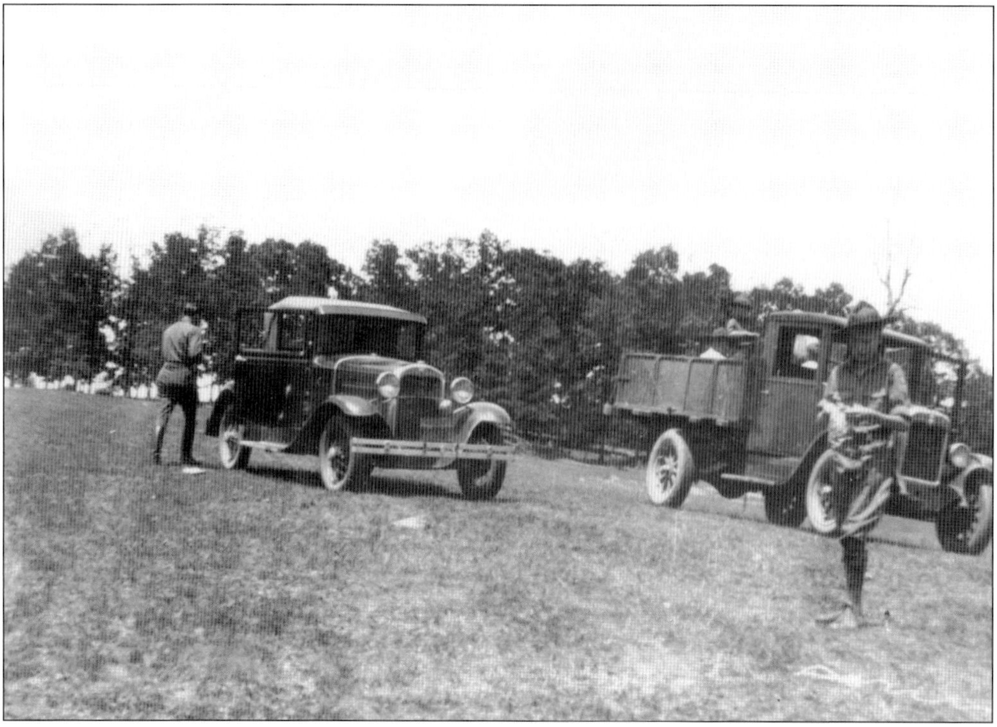

Boy Scouts of America was organized in 1912. Troop 1 in Graham was the seventh unit in North Carolina. Lon G. Turner was the first scoutmaster. During World War I, Troop 1 raised $80,400 in Liberty Bond sales, with 21 scouts receiving medals for their work. In this photograph from the 1930s, Graham Boy Scouts have fun on an outing. (Courtesy of Bartialette Thompson.)

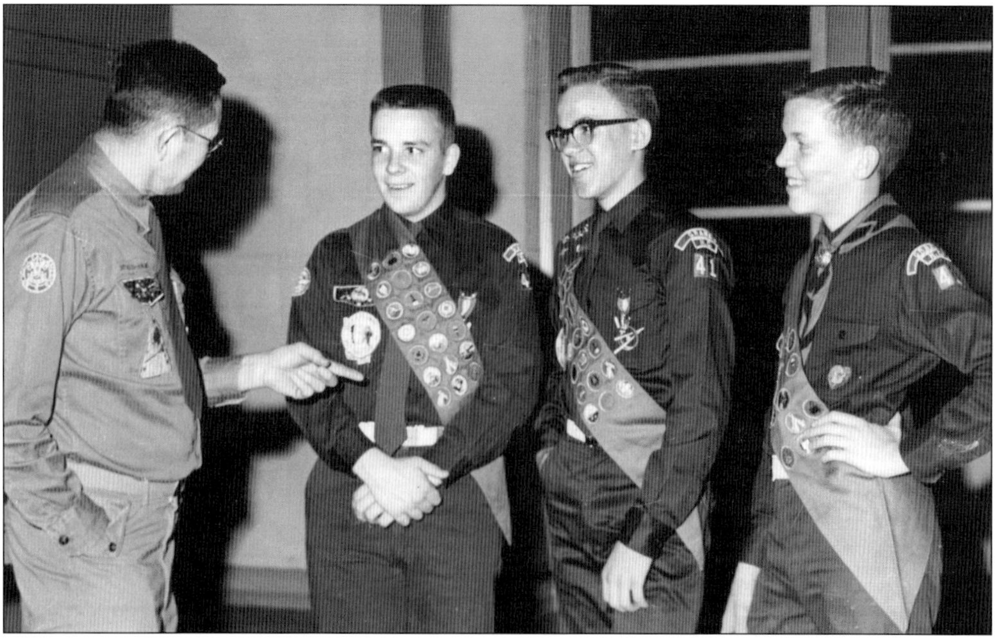

Boy Scouts in Troop 41 receive instructions from scoutmaster Charles A. Cates. (Courtesy of Graham First United Methodist Church.)

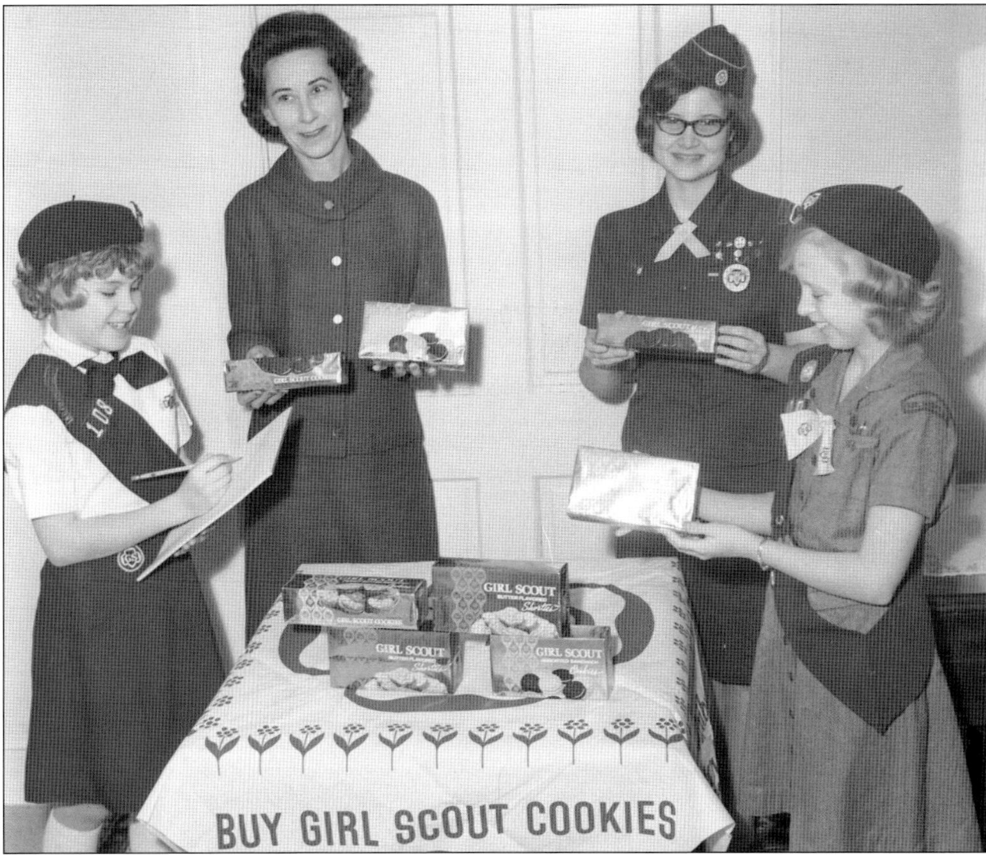

Girl Scouts first sold cookies nationwide in 1937. These Graham Girl Scouts prepare for a cookie sale in February 1965. (Courtesy of Pat Bailey.)

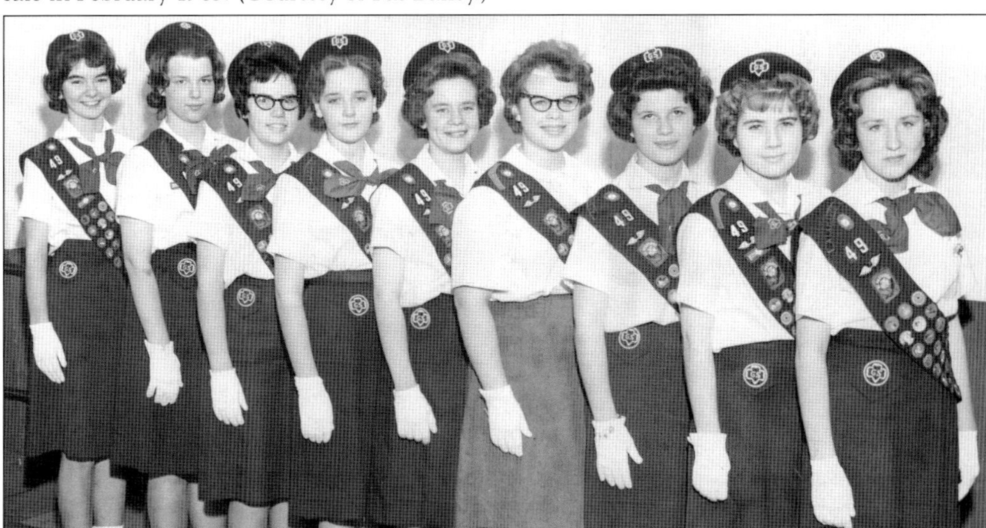

Graham Girl Scouts received Curved Bar Awards at Graham Methodist Church in 1963. Seen here from left to right are Becky Loy, Pam Foust, Sue Wiggins, Faye Shoffner, Marilyn Owens, Pat Harden, Hazel Wheeler, Mary Lou Graham, and Starr McMullan. (Courtesy of Starr Henderson.)

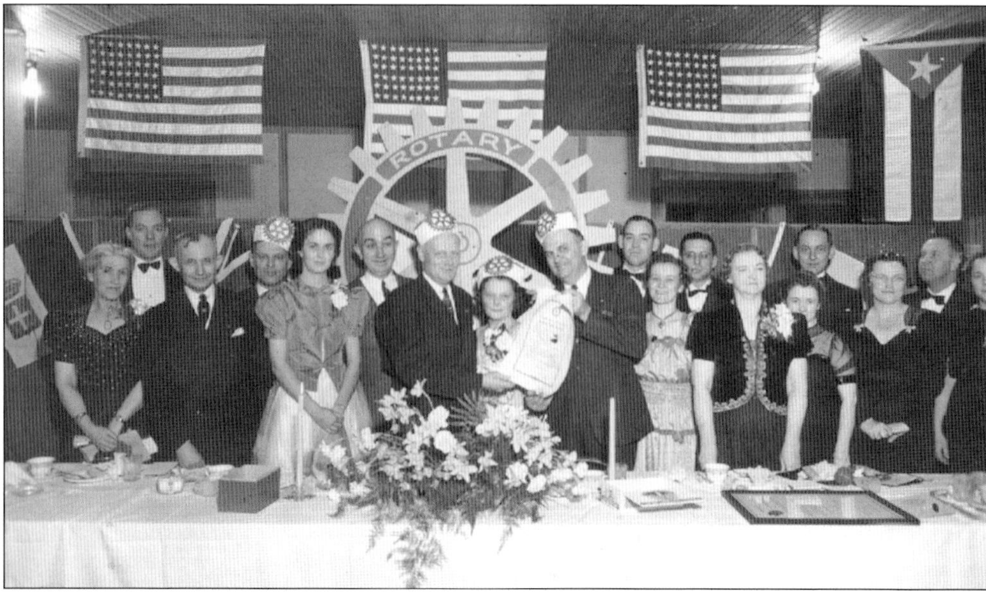

Graham Rotary Club received its charter on March 14, 1940, and began its long history of service to the community. The club's first president was H.D. "Tarvia" Jones. (Courtesy of City of Graham.)

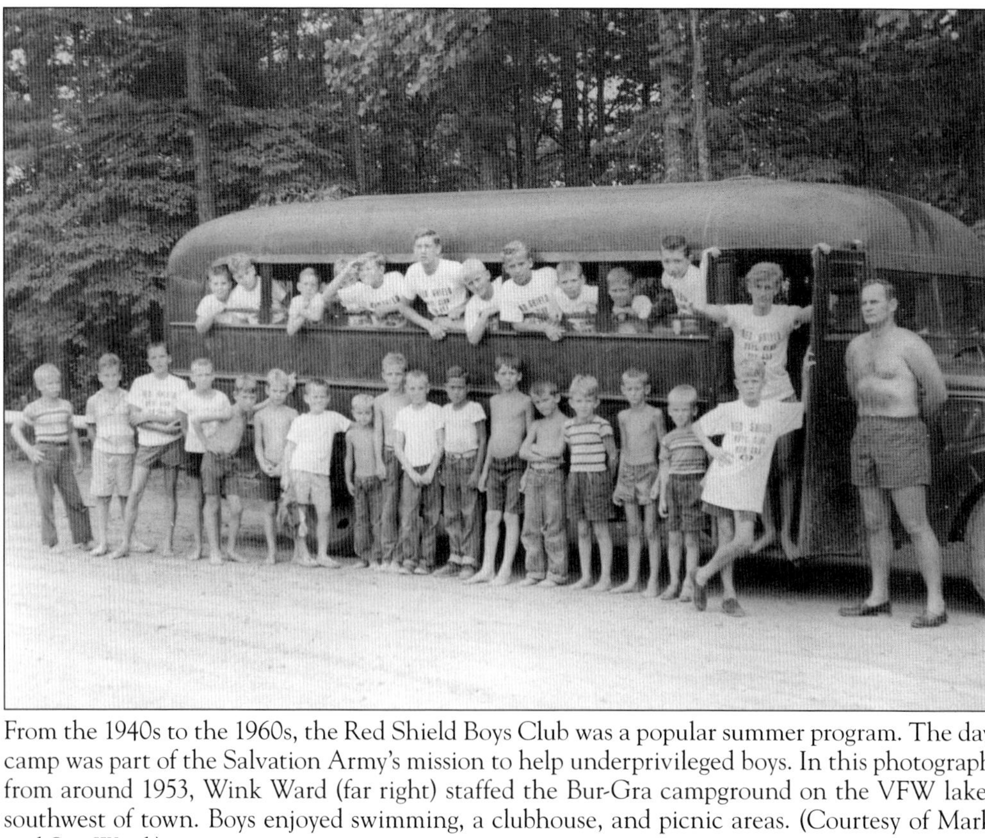

From the 1940s to the 1960s, the Red Shield Boys Club was a popular summer program. The day camp was part of the Salvation Army's mission to help underprivileged boys. In this photograph from around 1953, Wink Ward (far right) staffed the Bur-Gra campground on the VFW lake, southwest of town. Boys enjoyed swimming, a clubhouse, and picnic areas. (Courtesy of Mark and Sue Ward.)

Five

Faith

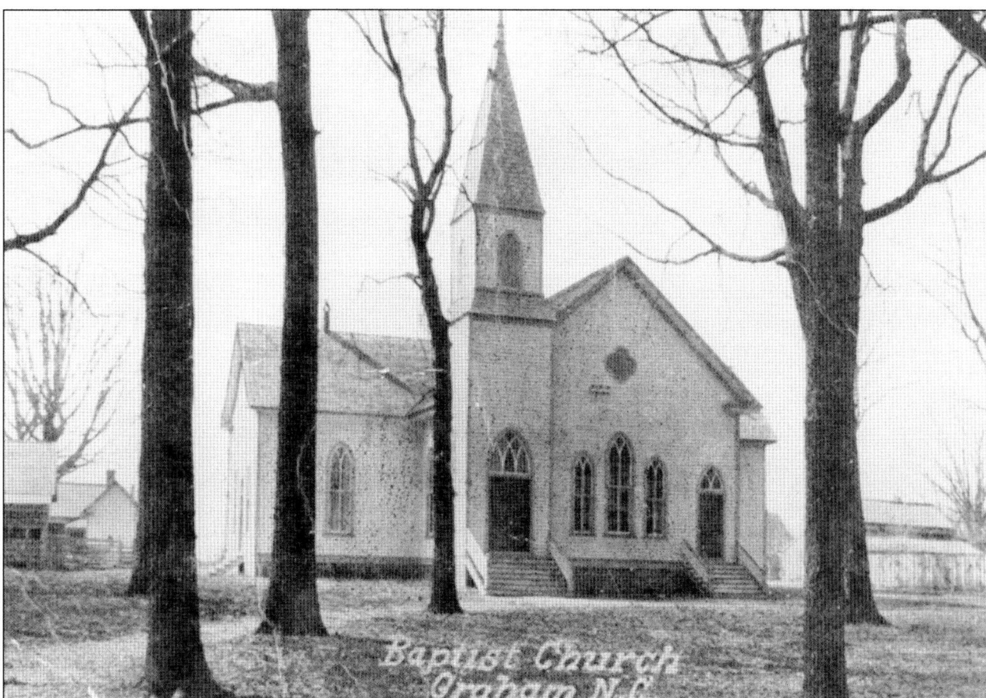

Seven men and women met at the courthouse in June 1874 to organize the Graham Baptist Church. The first pastor, Rev. W.T. Farrow, was called to preach twice a month. In 1877, the original frame church seen here was built on North Main Street. It has been modified several times through the years and was replaced by a colonial brick sanctuary in 1959. (Courtesy of First Baptist Church of Graham.)

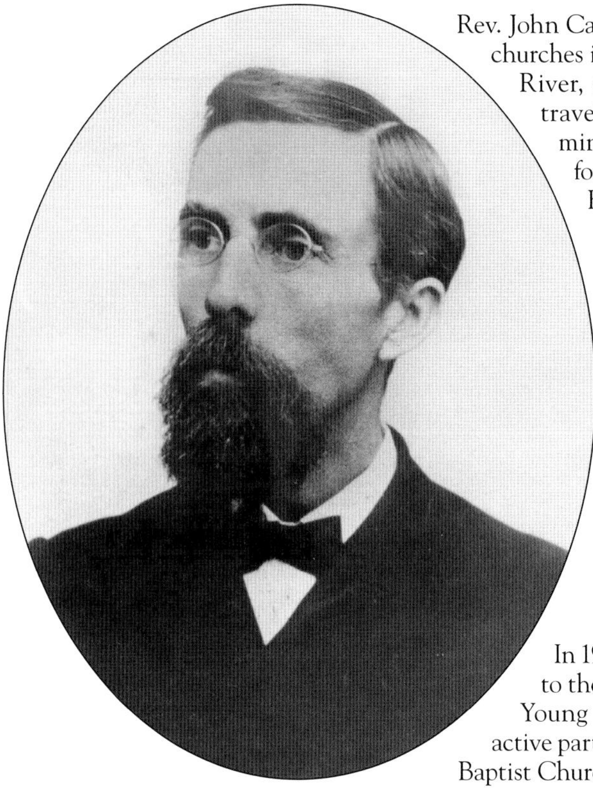

Rev. John Caswell Hocutt was the pastor at Baptist churches in Burlington, Glencoe, Graham, Haw River, and Carrboro. In the 1800s, pastors traveled throughout their districts, often ministering in a church as a supply pastor for only a year or two. Hocutt led the First Baptist Church of Graham from 1893 to 1900 and again from 1911 to 1912. He is buried in Linwood Cemetery. (Courtesy of First Baptist Church of Graham.)

In 1942, the name of the church was changed to the First Baptist Church of Graham. The Young People's Department (below) was an active part of the congregation. (Courtesy of First Baptist Church of Graham.)

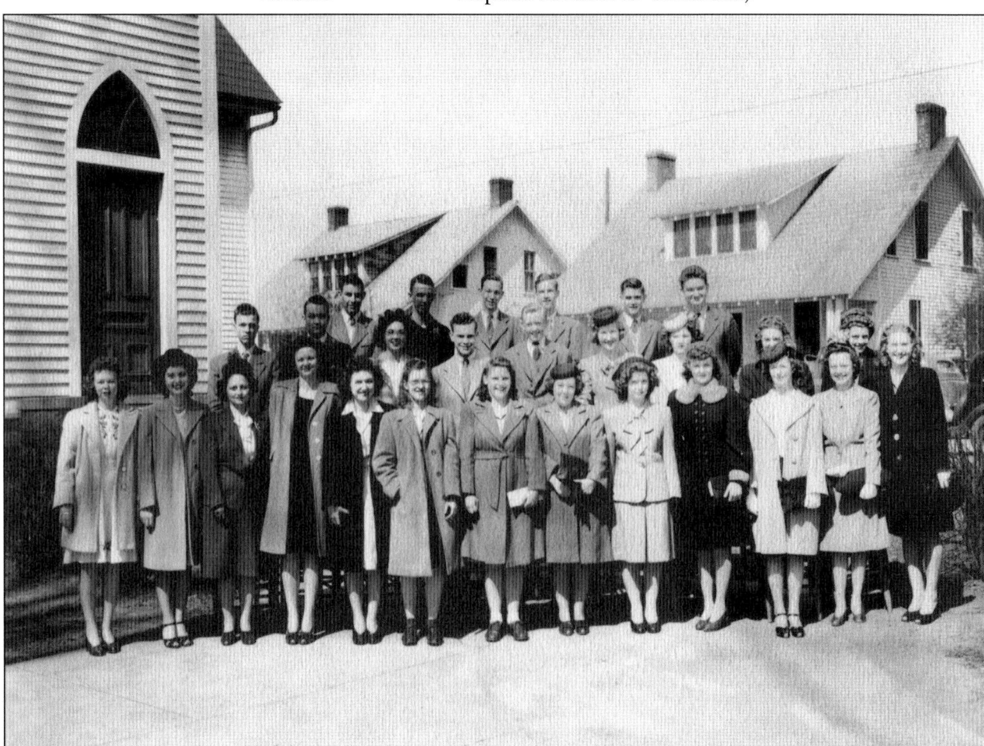

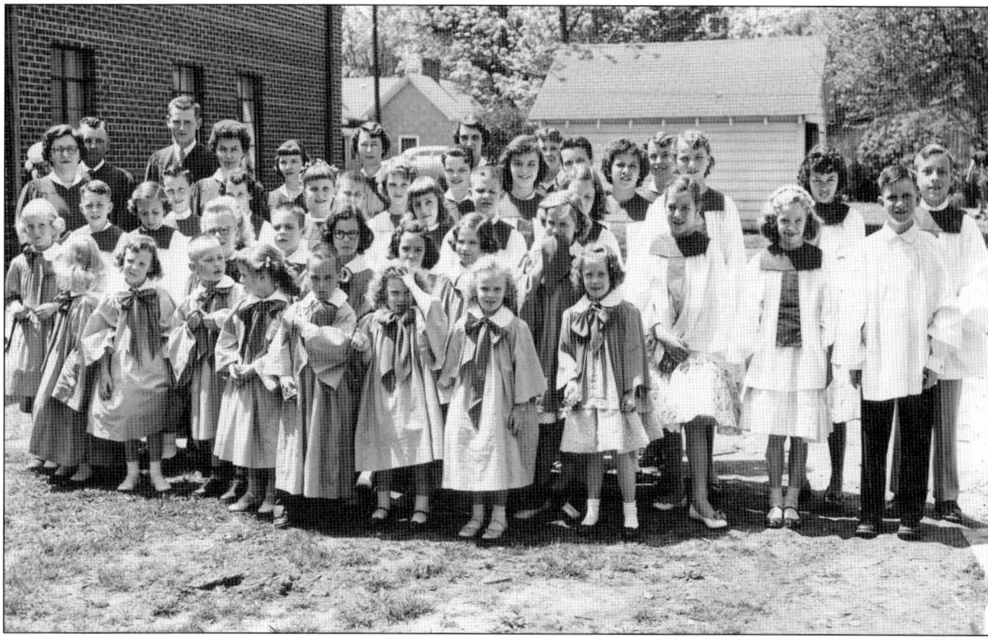

Construction of the brick sanctuary began in 1949. The children's choir (above) sang at the ground breaking for the educational building and chapel, which was completed in 1959. (Courtesy of First Baptist Church of Graham.)

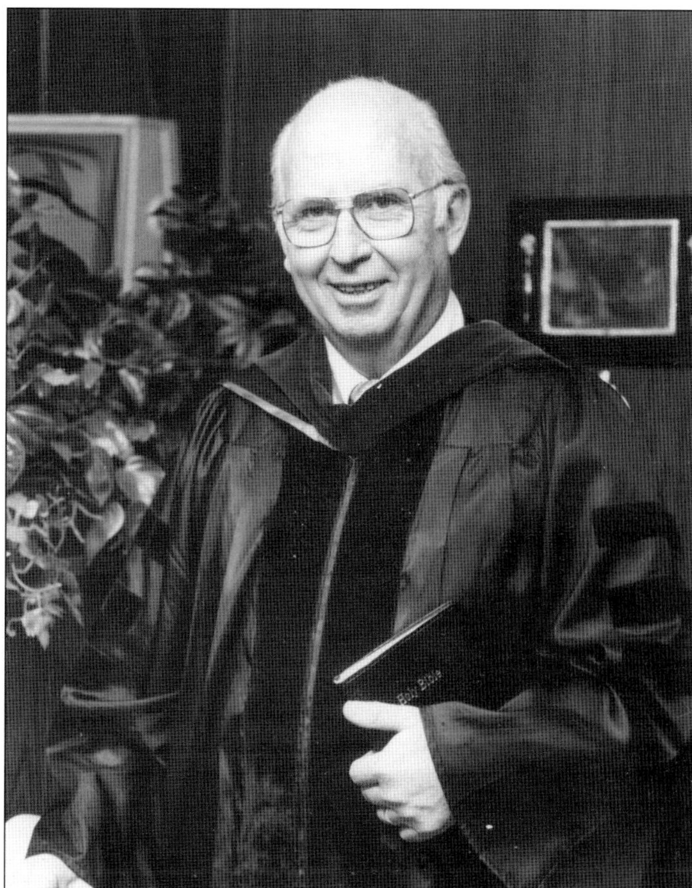

Rev. Ralph E. Jones Jr. served as the pastor of the First Baptist Church of Graham from 1960 to 1989. (Courtesy of the First Baptist Church of Graham.)

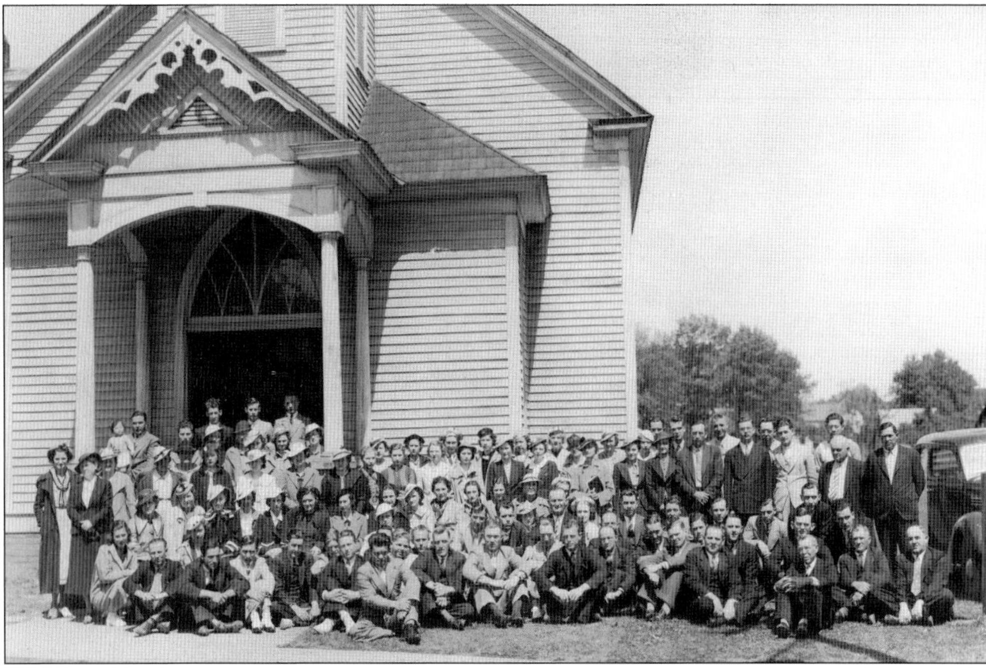

Graham Friends Meeting was established in 1907 by David E. Sampson and his wife, Sallie Marshburn Sampson. Services were held in a house on Oneida Street until this church was completed on Parker Street in 1909. The men's and ladies' Sunday school classes joined for this photograph in 1938. John Permar and Josie Crisco were the teachers. (Courtesy of Graham Friends Meeting.)

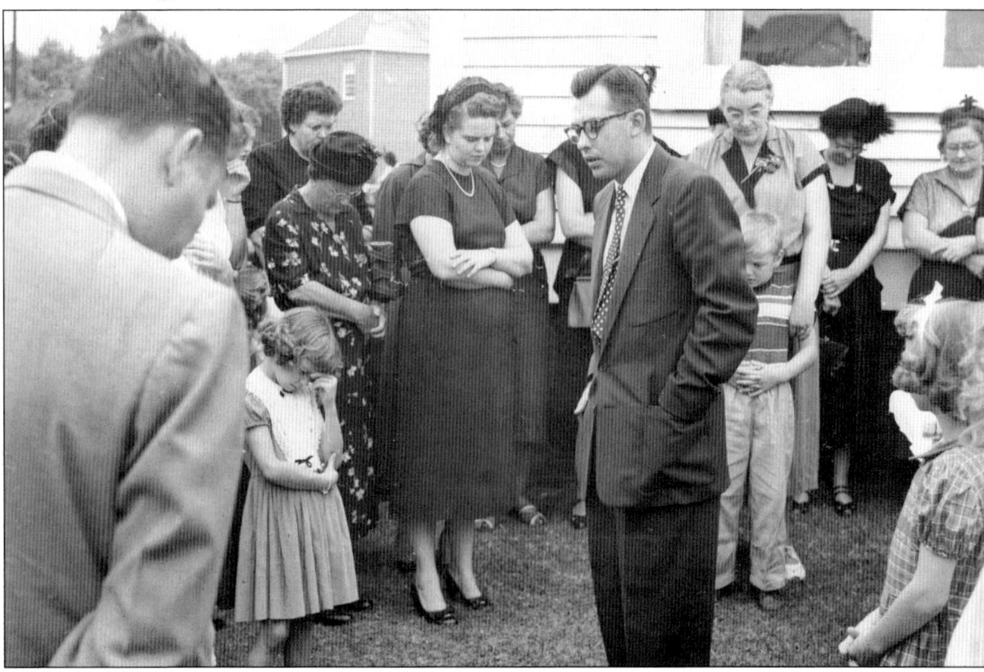

Homer Barker, the pastor of Graham Friends Meeting from 1949 to 1953, prays before the homecoming dinner on the grounds. (Courtesy of Graham Friends Meeting.)

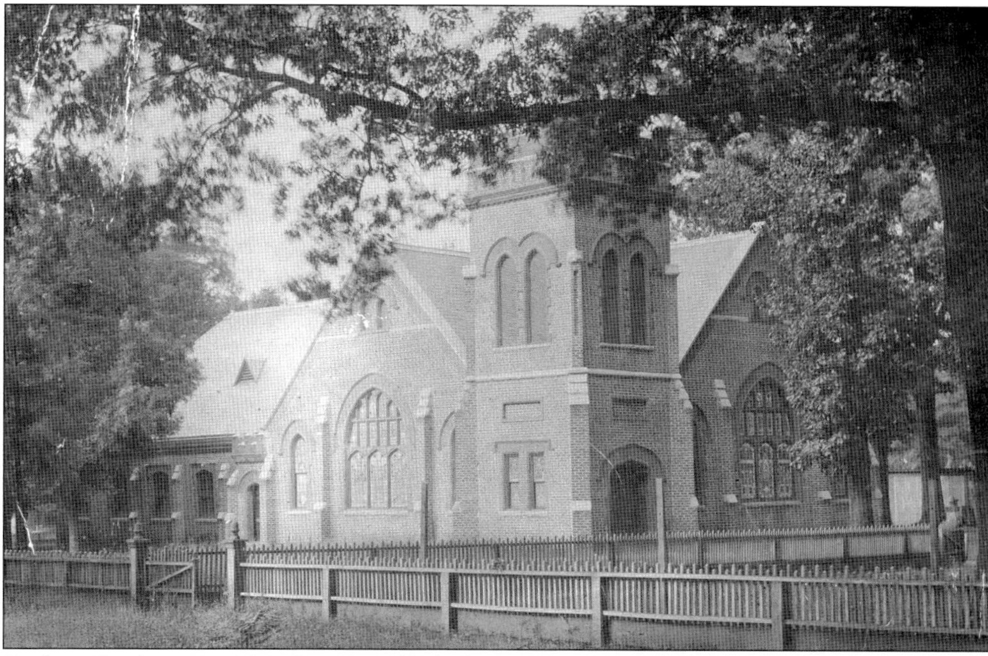

Graham Presbyterian Church was established in 1850 at the corner of Harden and Maple Streets. The first pastor was Rev. Archibald Currie. A small cemetery was just across Harden Street, but in 1896, the congregation decided to move the 32 graves a few blocks away to the town cemetery. (Courtesy of Graham Presbyterian Church.)

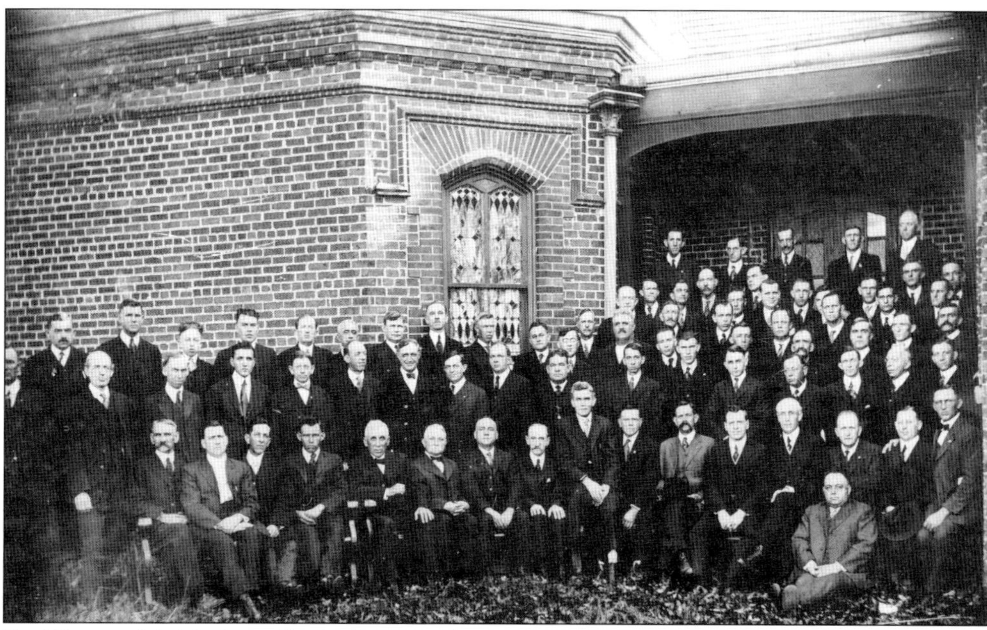

Dr. Thomas M. McConnell, Graham Presbyterian Church's new pastor in 1914, noticed men loitering around Court Square on Sunday mornings instead of attending church. He asked E.S. Parker Jr. to start a Sunday school class for them. The nondenominational Brotherhood Class, seen here around 1929, began under the trees beside the courthouse and served the community for decades. (Courtesy of Graham Historical Museum.)

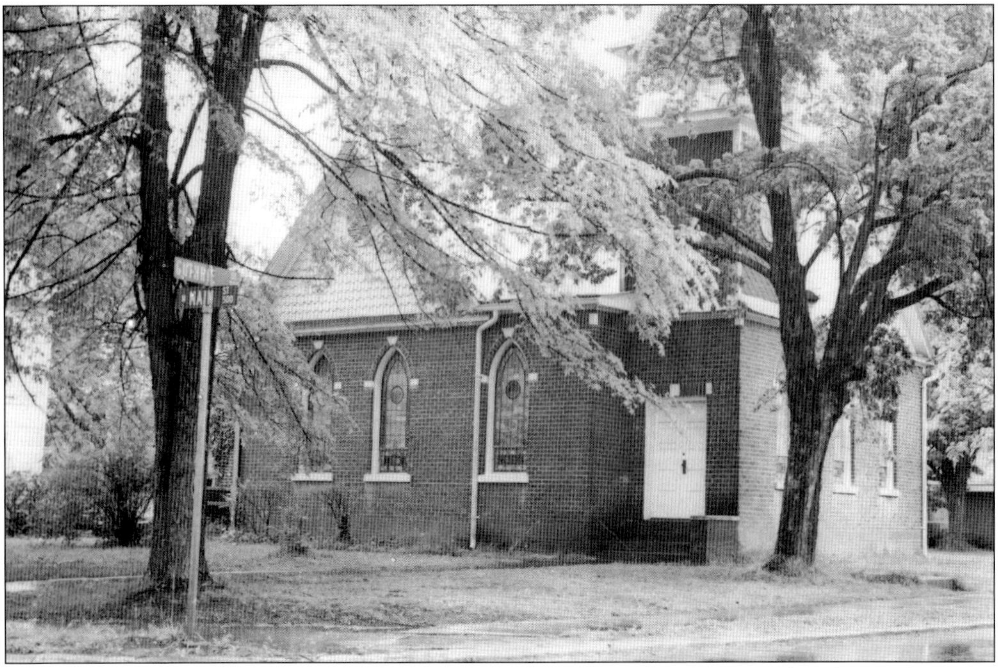

Organized in 1864, First Baptist Church is the oldest African American church in Alamance County. Sister Sarah Ruffin Bland remembers the old log church with plank windows and lighted oil lamps where Spencer Thomas served as pastor for the first two years. This sanctuary was built in 1930 on North Maple Street and served the congregation until 1975, when a larger church was constructed. (Courtesy of Sallye L. Morrow.)

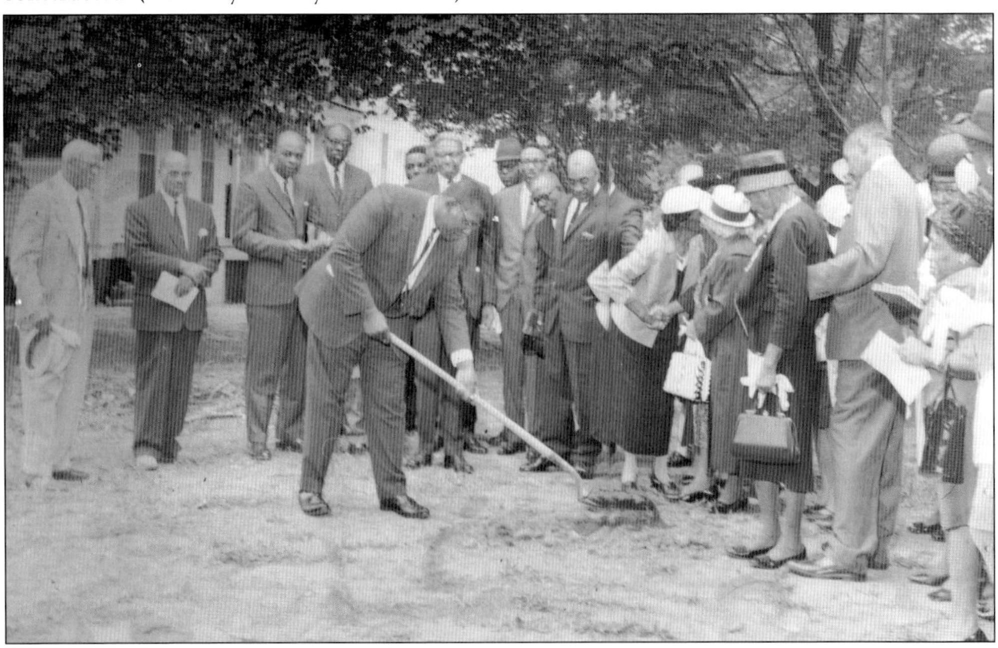

Members of the First Baptist Church attended the ground-breaking service for the educational building in May 1968. Rev. C.R. Trotter scoops up a shovel of earth at the ceremony. (Courtesy of Sallye L. Morrow.)

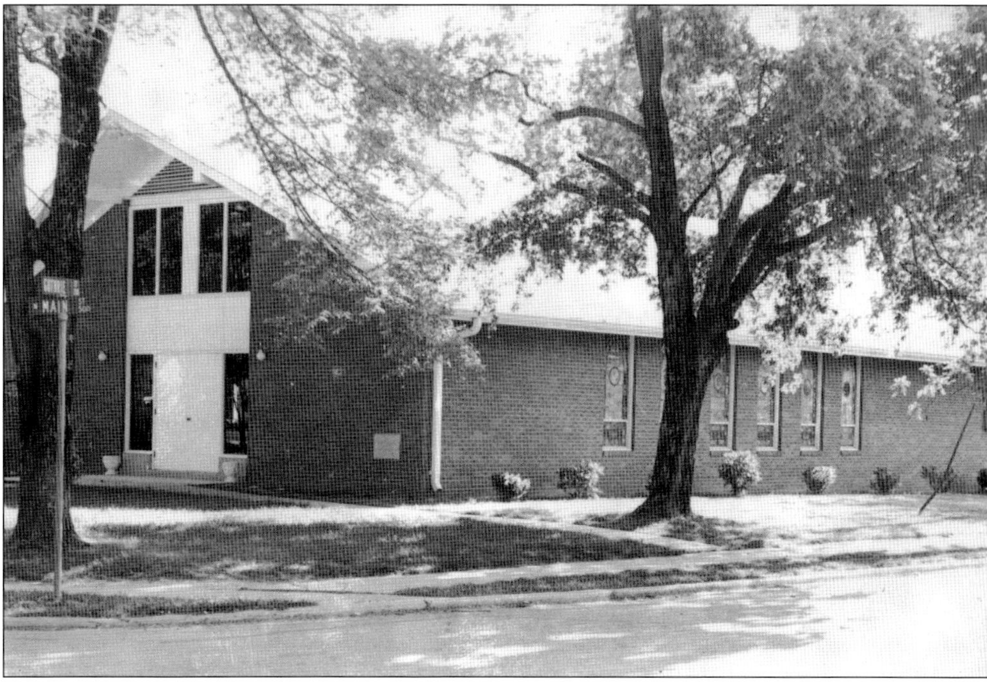

In 1975, Rev. C.R. Trotter was pastor when First Baptist Church held its first service in the new church, seen here. (Courtesy of Sallye L. Morrow.)

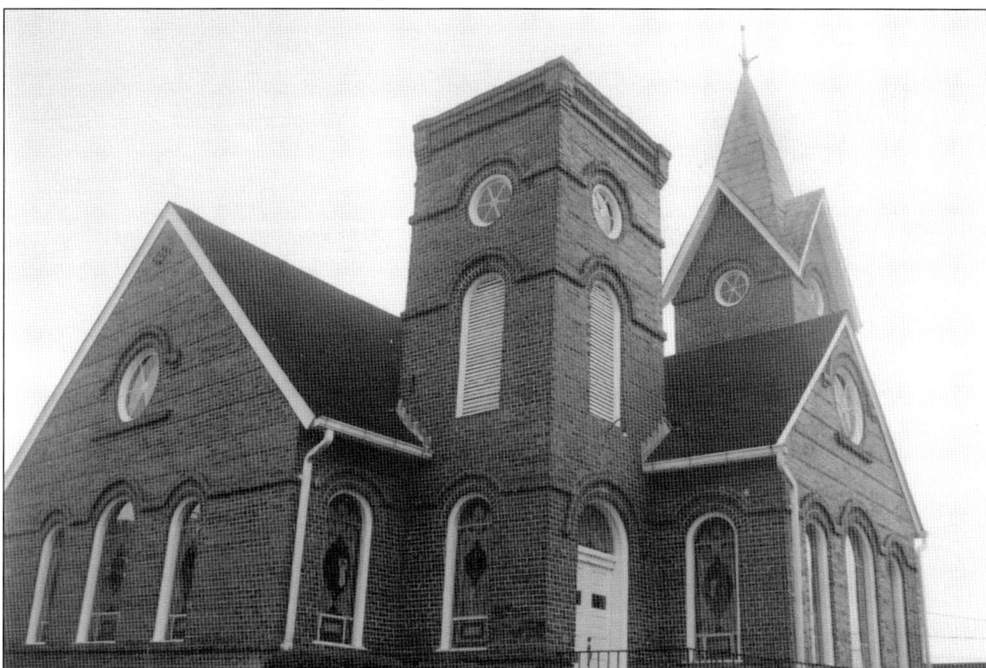

Children's Chapel United Church of Christ was organized in 1875. African American worshippers who attended Providence Church were led by Rev. J.W. Wellons. The congregation built their first frame church in 1876 on East Harden Street. They began a church cemetery, and in 1911, this brick sanctuary was completed. (Courtesy of Children's Chapel.)

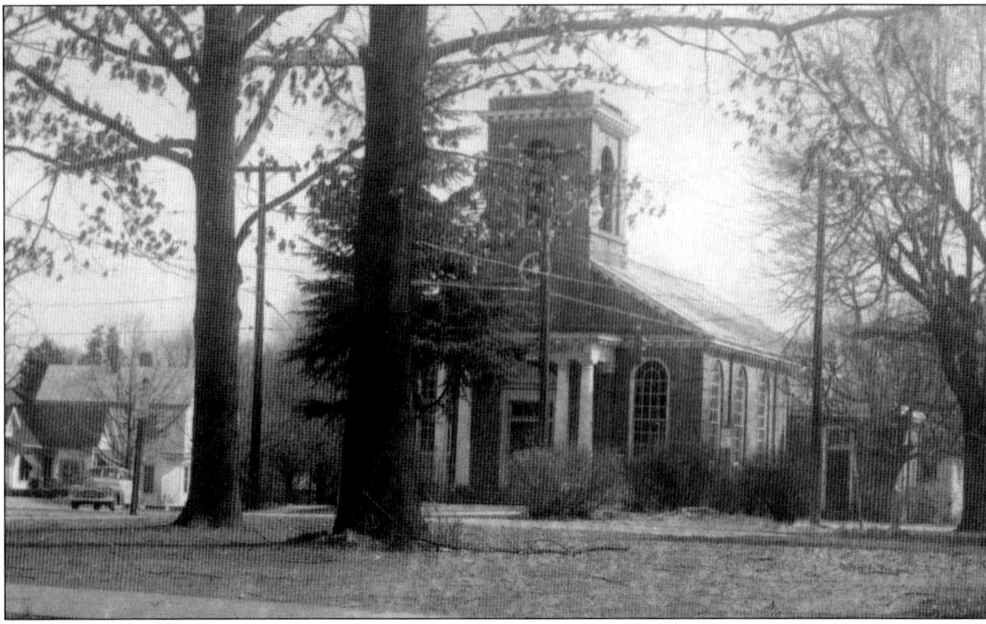

Graham Methodist Episcopal Church, South, was established in 1897 at the fork of North Maple and North Main Streets. After a fire in 1913, this church was built. In 1939, the church merged with the Methodist Protestant Church to form the Graham Methodist Church. The new, larger congregation moved to its present location on North Main Street in 1956. (Courtesy of Graham First United Methodist Church.)

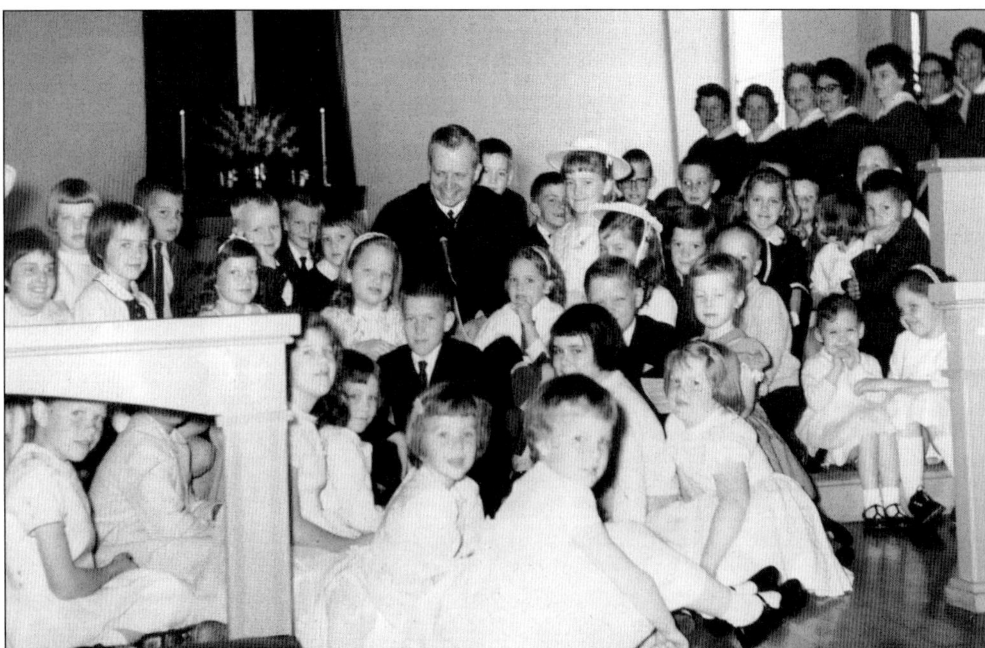

Children gather at the front of Graham Methodist Church with Rev. Langill H. Watson (center) for a children's sermon. Services were held in the fellowship hall until the sanctuary was completed. (Courtesy of Graham First United Methodist Church.)

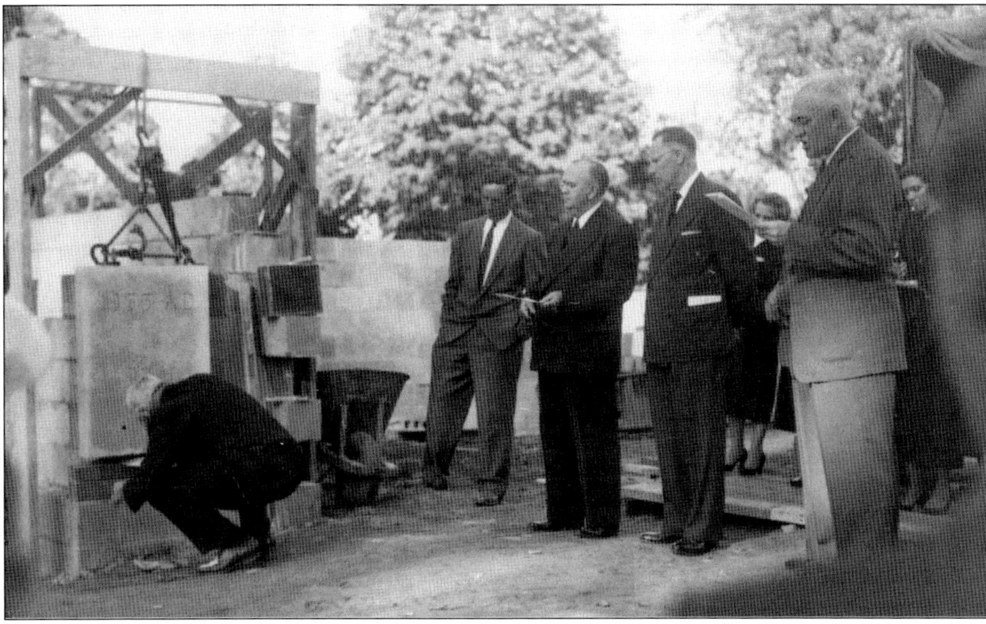

After the merger of the two Methodist Churches, preparations began for a new building. Bishop Garber is seen here cementing the cornerstone for the Graham Methodist Church in 1955. (Courtesy of Graham First United Methodist Church.)

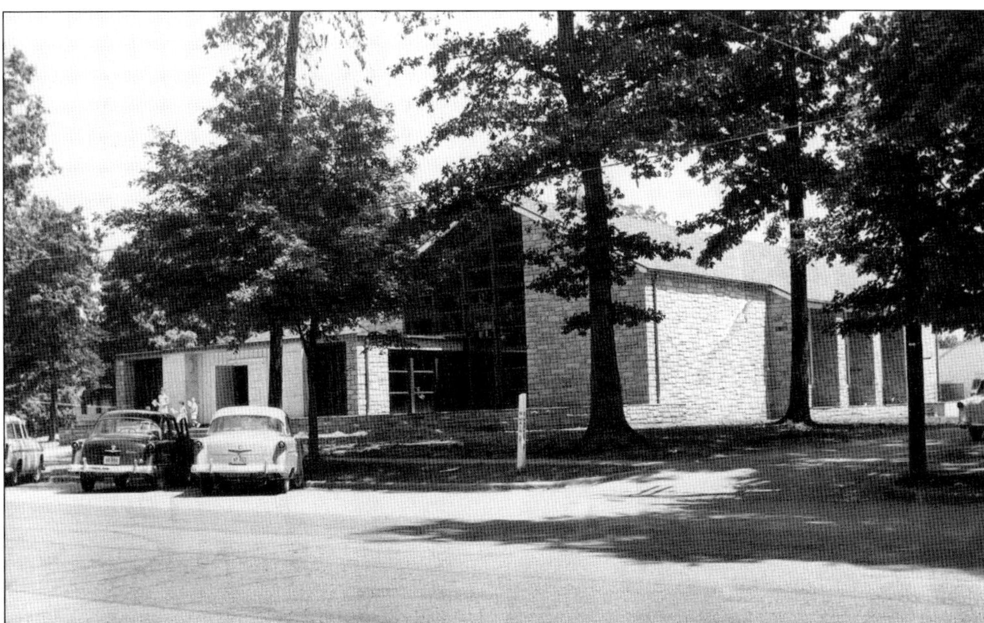

The first service in the Graham Methodist Church was held on August 5, 1956. After Sunday school was held at the old church, worshippers walked to the new church for the regular service, conducted by Rev. T.J. Whitehead. (Courtesy of Graham First United Methodist Church.)

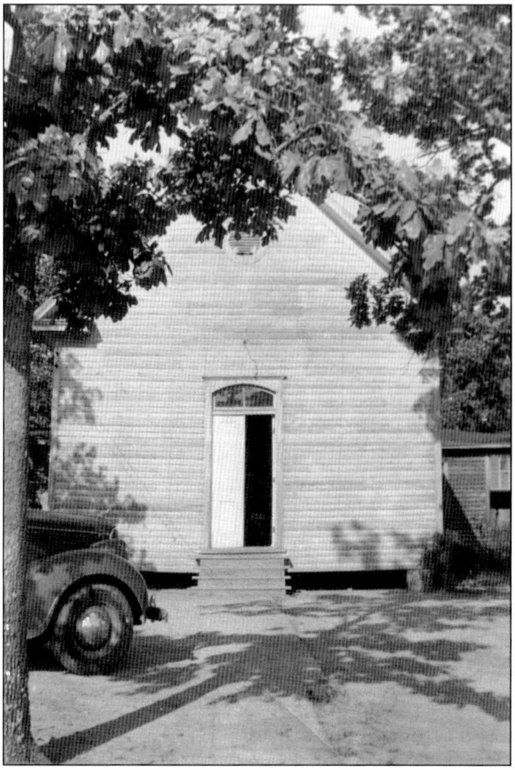

Bethany Presbyterian Church began in 1882 as a Sunday school outpost that met in a schoolhouse south of Graham. This frame church was constructed two years later on land donated by the George Curtis family. The church was officially organized in May 1892. (Courtesy of Bethany Presbyterian Church.)

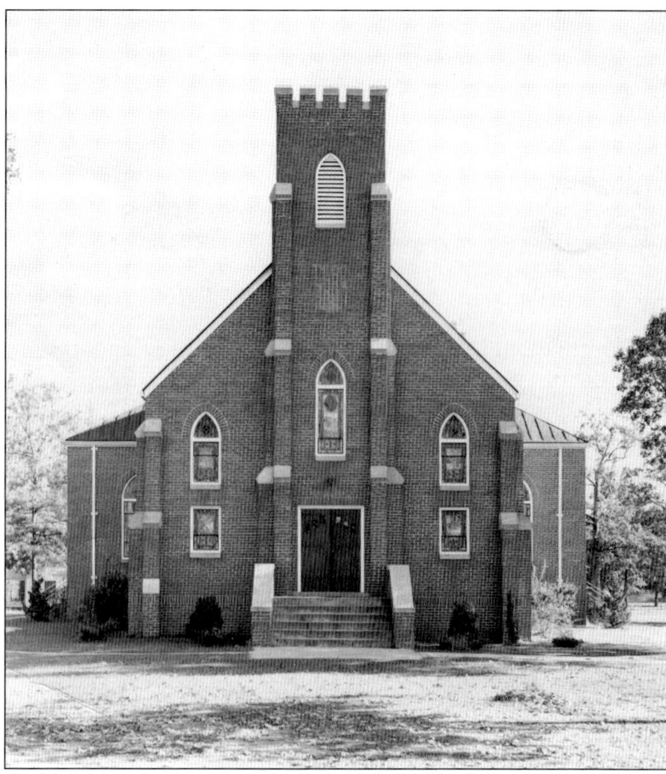

It took two years to complete the new brick sanctuary and classroom complex at Bethany Presbyterian Church, which was dedicated in 1943. A fellowship hall and educational wing were added later. (Courtesy of Bethany Presbyterian Church.)

In 1868, William Clendenin deeded land to Wyatt Outlaw on North Main Street for a church. The church was shared by two African American congregations: the Baptists and the Methodists. Wayman Chapel, seen here, was organized in 1883 as part of the African Methodist Episcopal Zion Church. The congregation built their first church simultaneously with the African Methodist Episcopal Church in Company Shops. Cornerstone ceremonies were even held on the same day. (Courtesy of Wayman Chapel.)

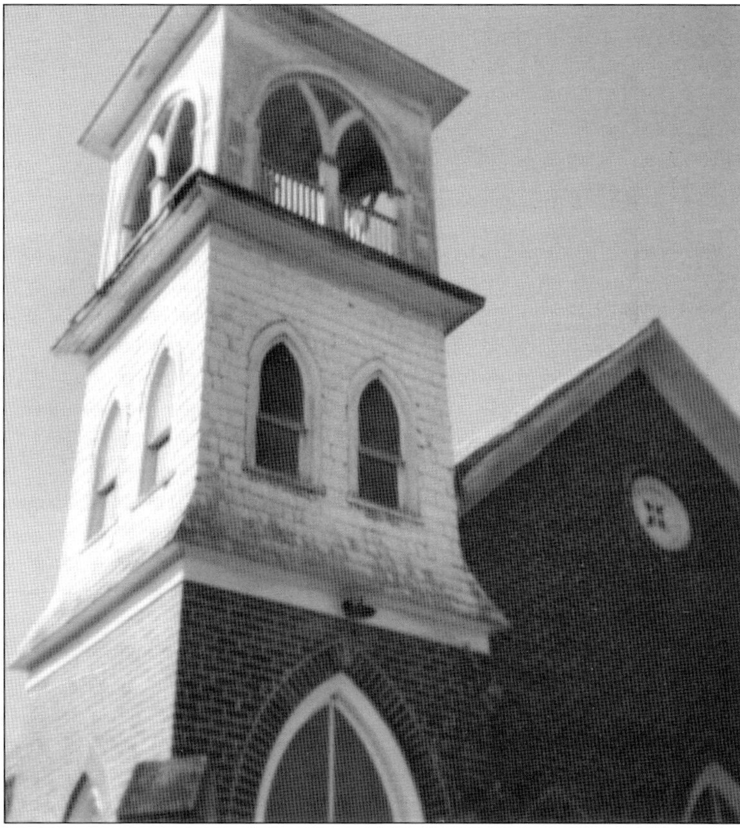

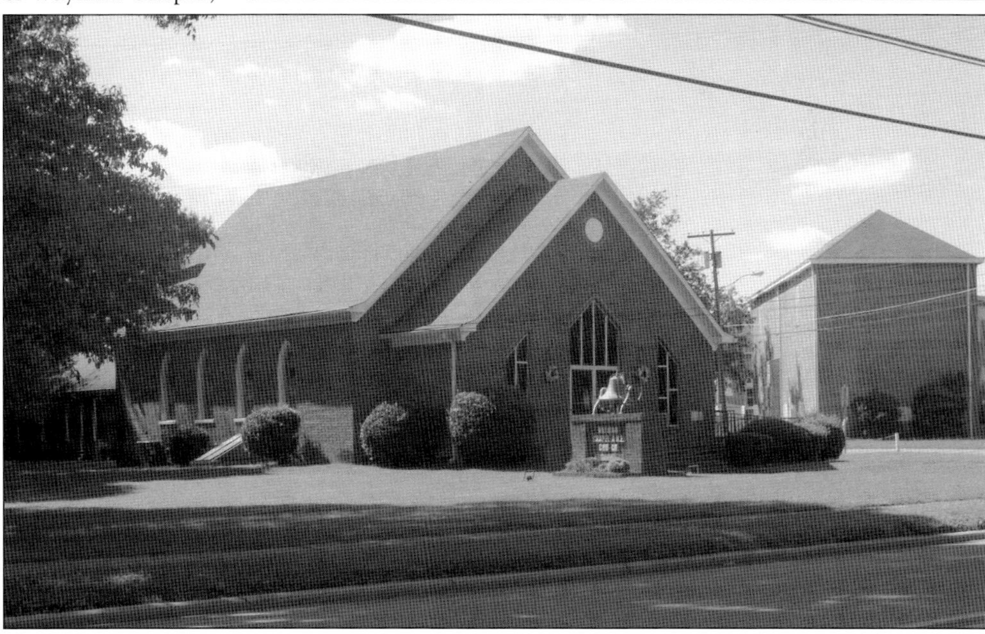

The cornerstone on Wayman Chapel states that the sanctuary was built in 1925, while Rev. R.E. Ligon was the pastor. The church was remodeled in 1979 under the leadership of pastor W.E. Diggs. (Courtesy of Wayman Chapel.)

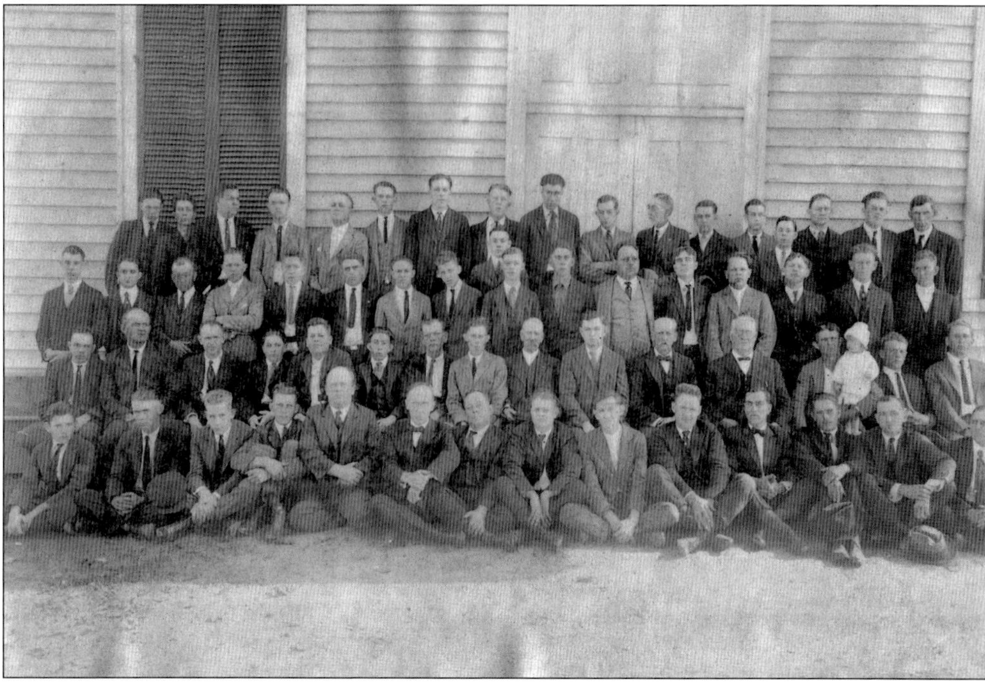

Providence Christian Church was the backdrop for the assembled men in this early photograph, taken before 1927. (Courtesy of Providence Christian Church.)

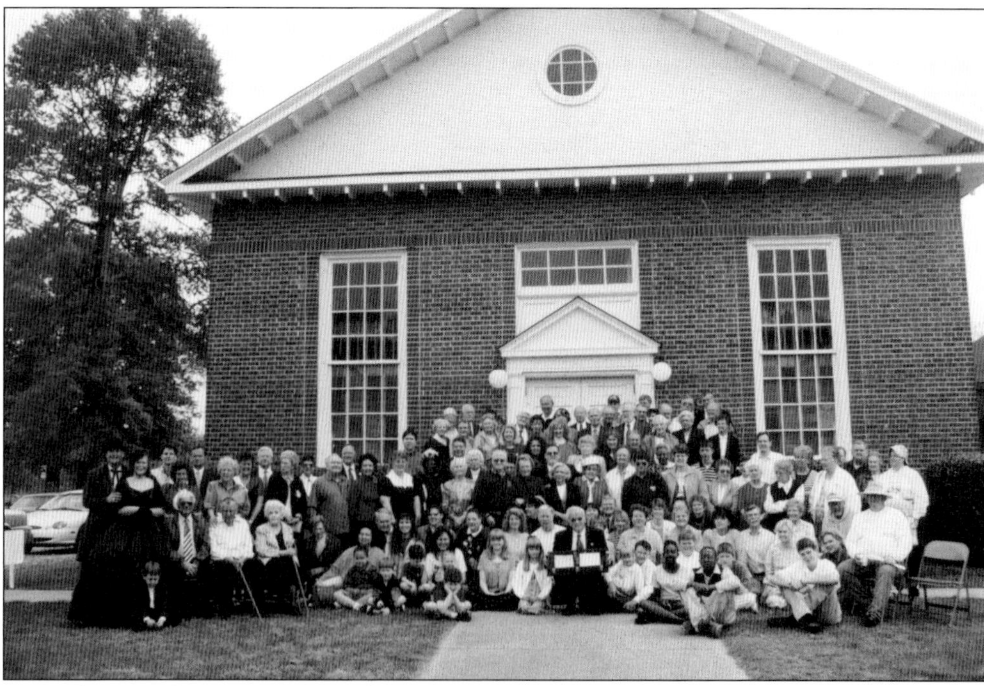

In April 1999, Alamance County observed its 150th birthday. The sesquicentennial celebration began with a full day of activities at Providence Christian Church. (Courtesy of Providence Christian Church.)

Six

Schools

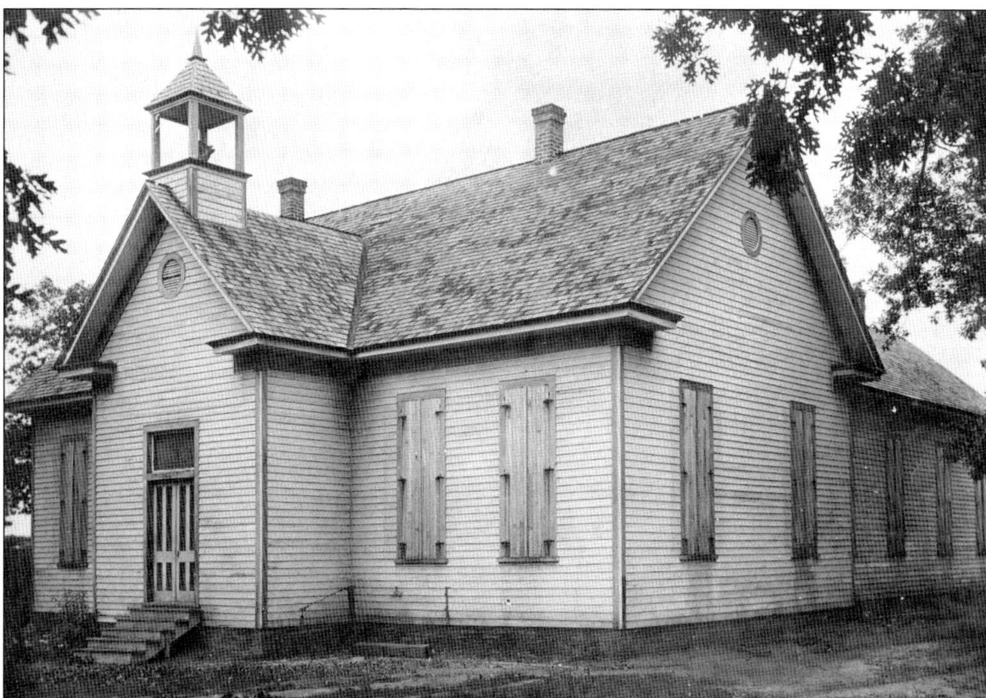

Few records remain of Graham's early one-room schools. The first school operated out of Providence Church before 1830. Children walked to small schools near their farms and neighborhoods. One early school was on Lynn Banks Holt's farm in the 1880s. The Graham Public School building seen here was originally located on Melville Street. It was moved to North Main Street around 1900. When the larger Graham Graded School opened in 1903, this school was no longer needed, and it was dismantled in 1906. (Courtesy of Graham Historical Museum.)

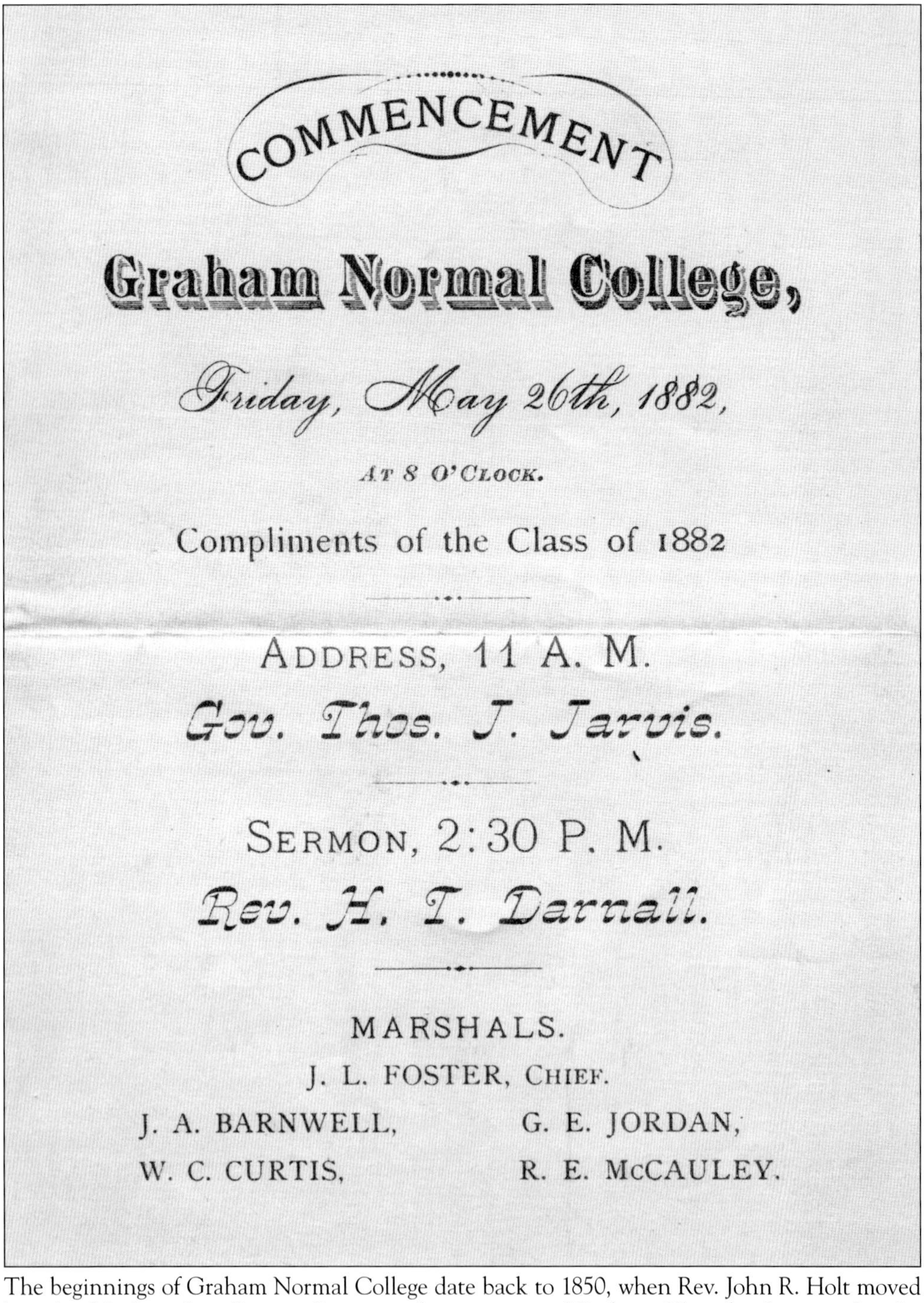

COMMENCEMENT

Graham Normal College,

Friday, May 26th, 1882,

AT 8 O'CLOCK.

Compliments of the Class of 1882

ADDRESS, 11 A. M.

Gov. Thos. J. Jarvis.

SERMON, 2:30 P. M.

Rev. H. T. Darnall.

MARSHALS.

J. L. FOSTER, CHIEF.

J. A. BARNWELL, G. E. JORDAN,

W. C. CURTIS, R. E. McCAULEY.

The beginnings of Graham Normal College date back to 1850, when Rev. John R. Holt moved his school for boys from Orange County to the new town of Graham. The school operated under several names in its early years, including Graham College, Graham Institute, and Graham Normal College. The school closed in 1863 because of the Civil War and was reopened a few years later by William S. Long. The school burned to the ground in 1892. (Courtesy of Belk Library Archives and Special Collections, Elon University.)

William S. Long believed in the importance of education. He borrowed money from his father to attend Graham College before 1863 and went on to establish his own school after the war. In addition to repaying his father, he also provided college educations for his siblings. (Courtesy of Belk Library Archives and Special Collections, Elon University.)

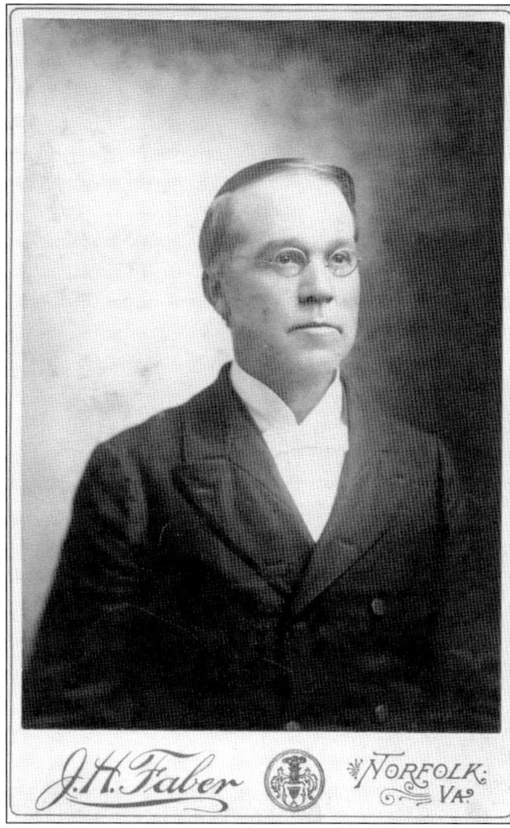

In 1892, Long moved his school to Mill Point, the railroad stop that would later become Elon University. In the group photograph below of Elon College's founders, he is standing in the second row on the far left. His brother Daniel, who taught with him in Graham, sits in the center of the first row with his arms crossed. (Courtesy of Belk Library Archives and Special Collections, Elon University.)

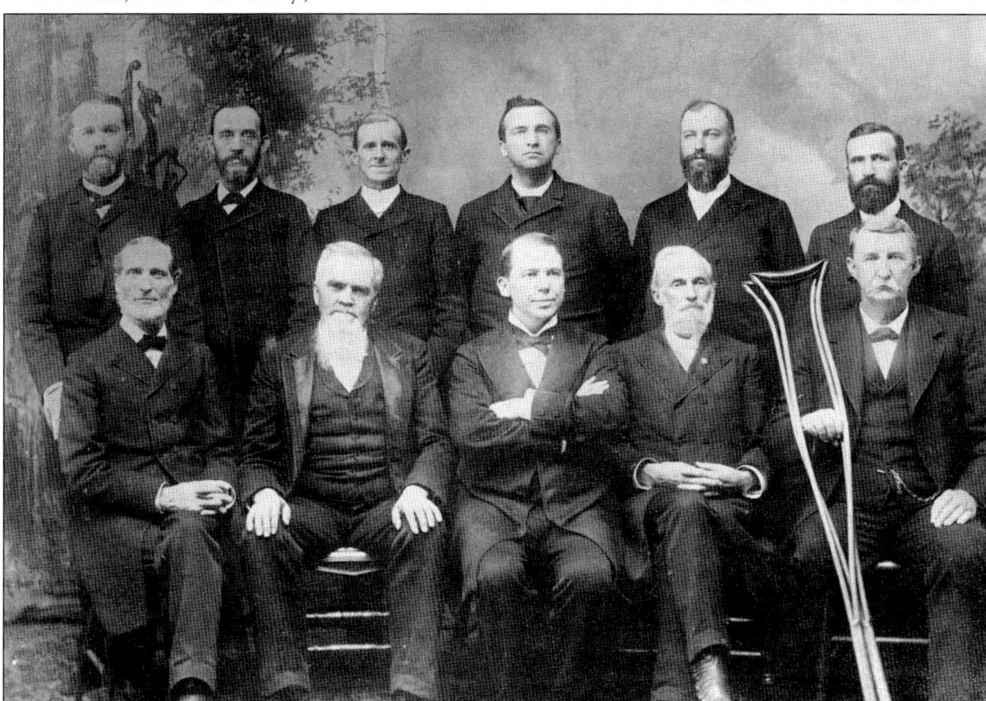

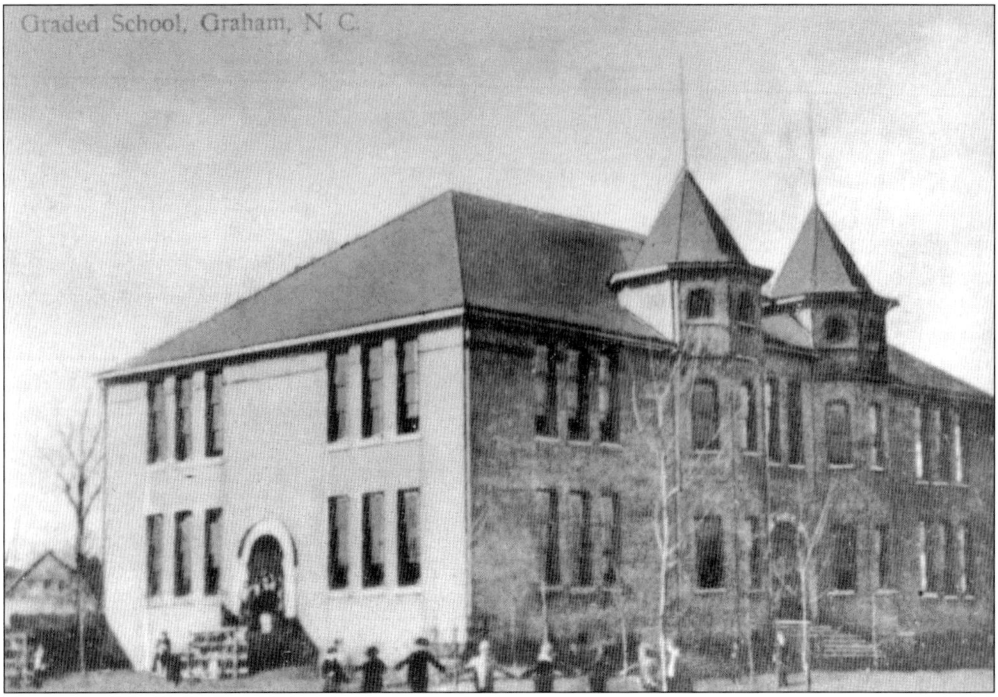

By 1896, large graded schools, which students attended from elementary school through high school graduation, were becoming common across the state. Citizens called for a central school for all students to attend, and Graham Graded School opened in 1903. The new school had eight teachers, who served 350 students in nine grades. This postcard is dated 1910. (Courtesy of North Carolina State Archives.)

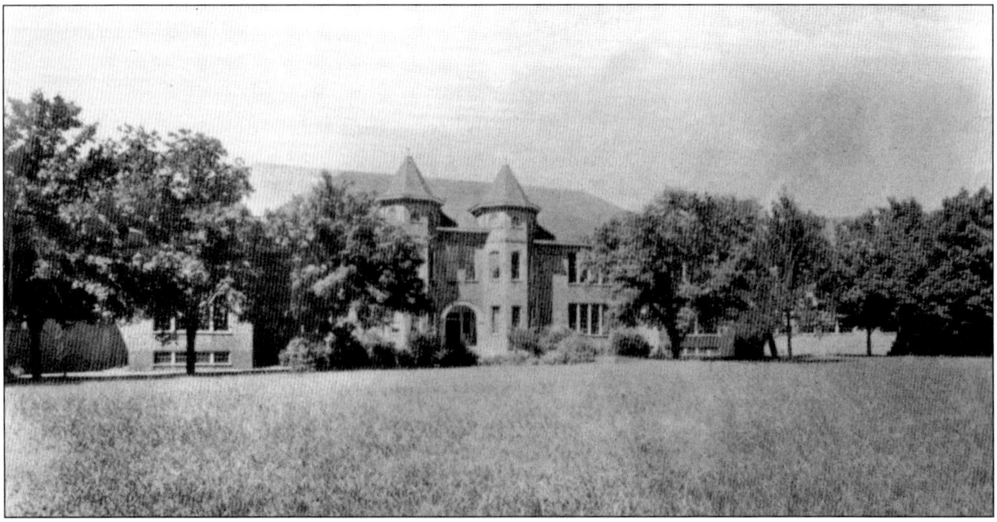

The school, located on North Main Street, served students from 1903 until 1971. Many Graham residents can remember one or more generations of their family who attended. This photograph was taken after wings were added to the main section. (Courtesy of Graham Historical Museum.)

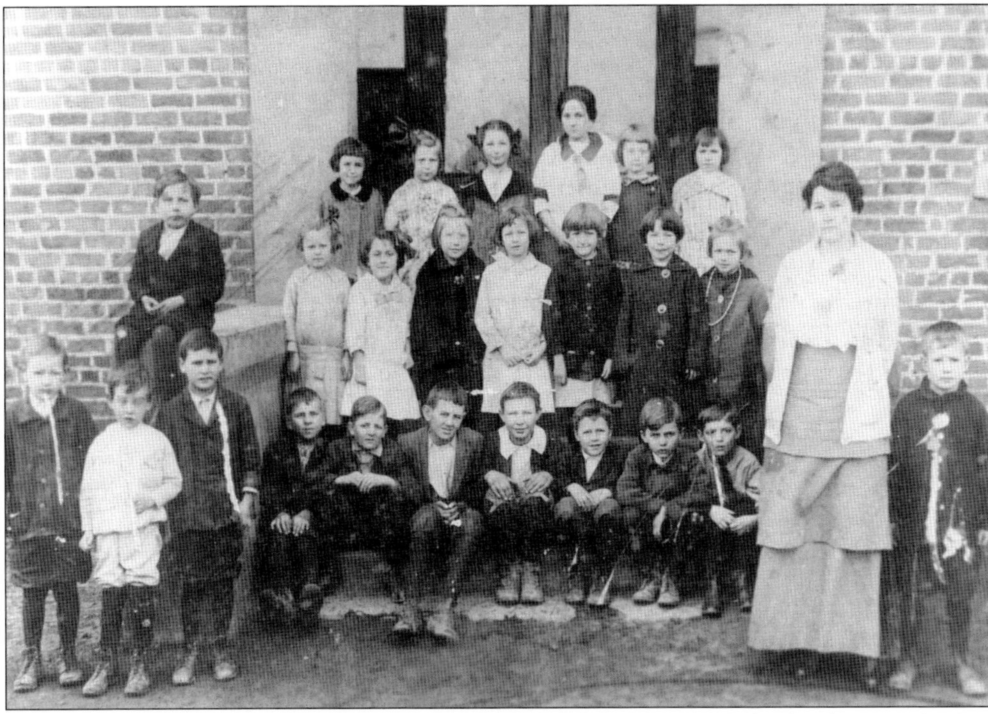

These two class photographs were taken around 1911 at Graham Graded School on North Main Street. (Both, courtesy of Graham Historical Museum.)

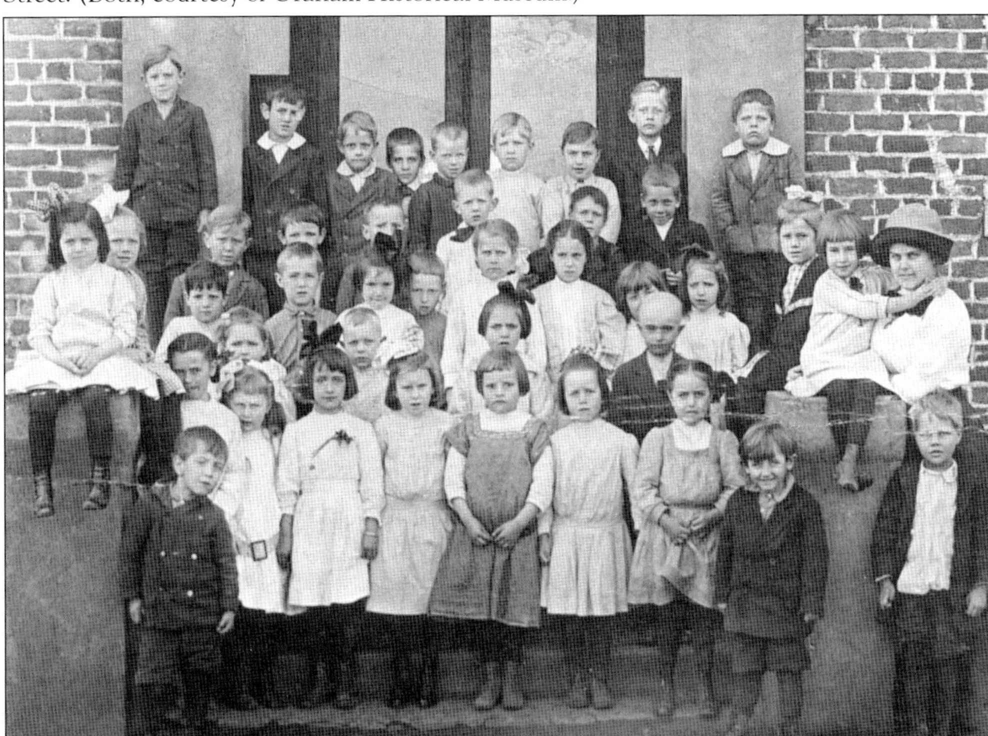

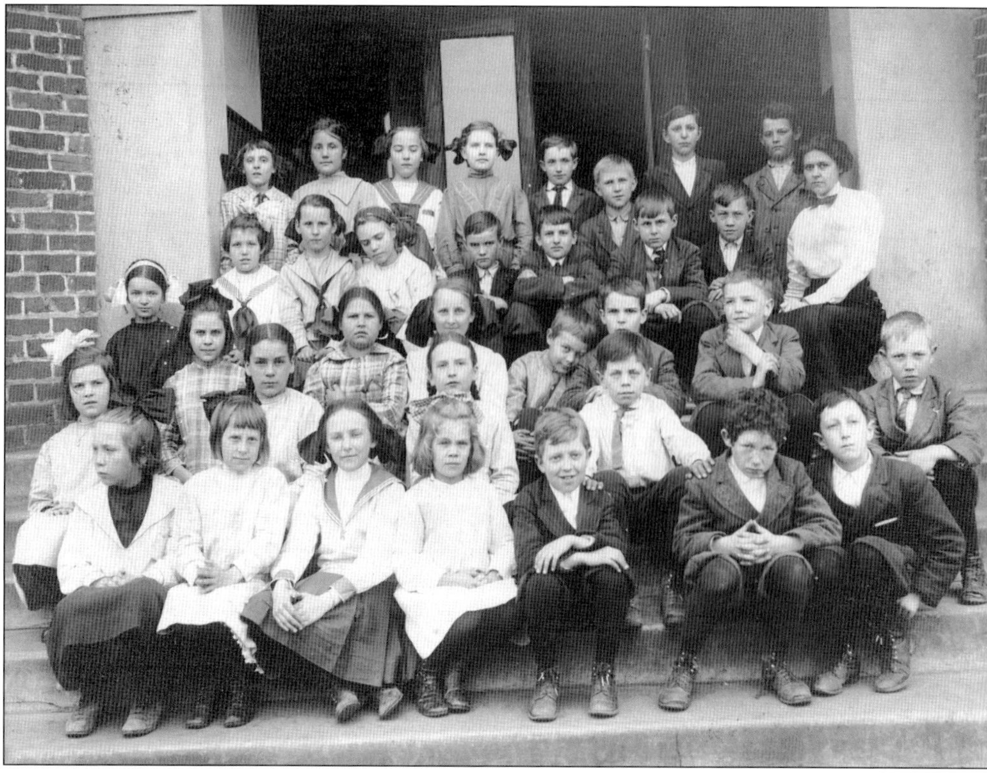

Mrs. Pickard's second-grade class at Graham Graded School gathers on the steps of the school for a photograph in 1923. (Courtesy of Graham Historical Museum.)

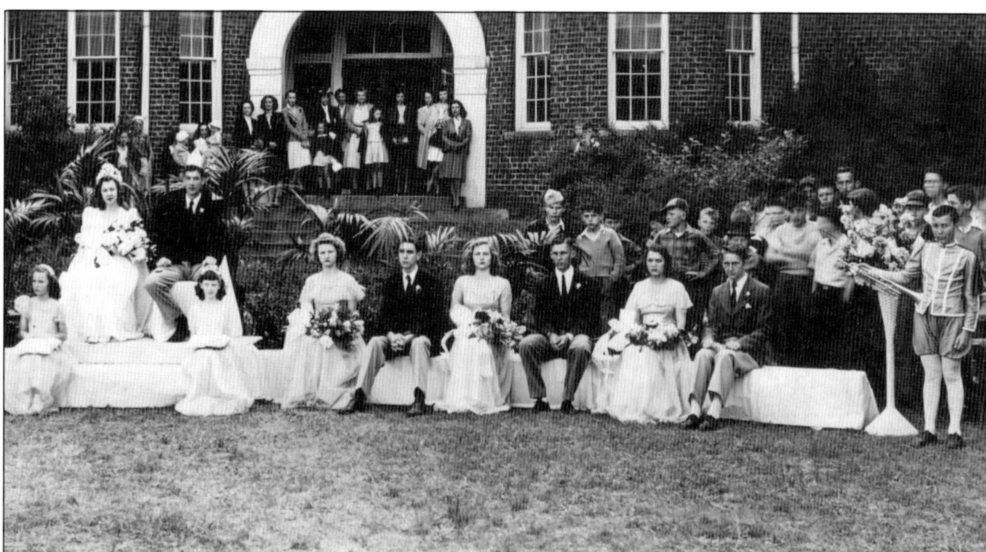

The May Day court sits on the lawn of Graham High School on North Main Street around 1947. Activities included a procession and the plaiting of the maypole. (Courtesy of the family of Foust Thompson.)

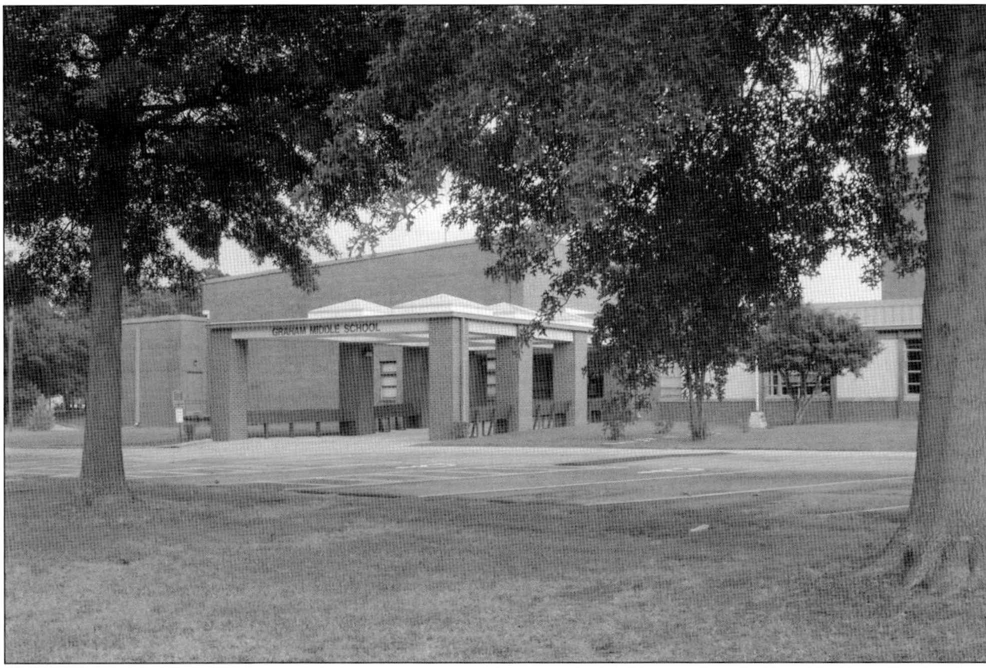

This school on Pine Street began in 1951 as Graham High School. In 1968, it became Graham Middle School when the schools were consolidated and the high school students were relocated to Central High School on Trollinger Road. (Courtesy of Alamance County Public Libraries.)

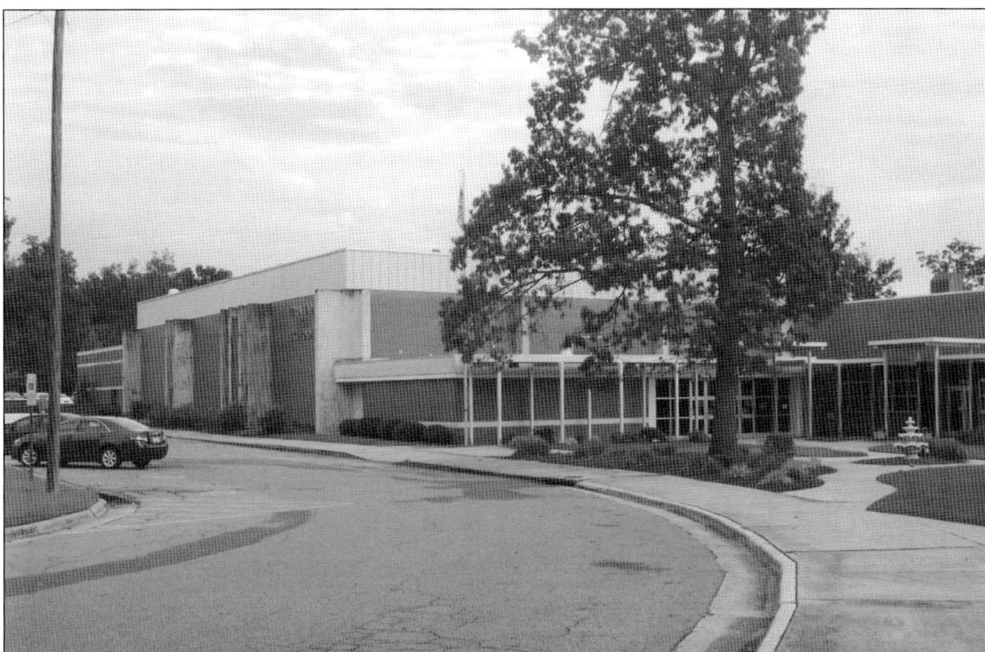

Central High School opened in 1961 as the African American high school. Before it opened, African American students attended the school on Gilbreath Street, which had operated since 1882. When the schools were consolidated in 1968, the school's name was changed to Graham High School, and students of all races attended. (Courtesy of Alamance County Public Libraries.)

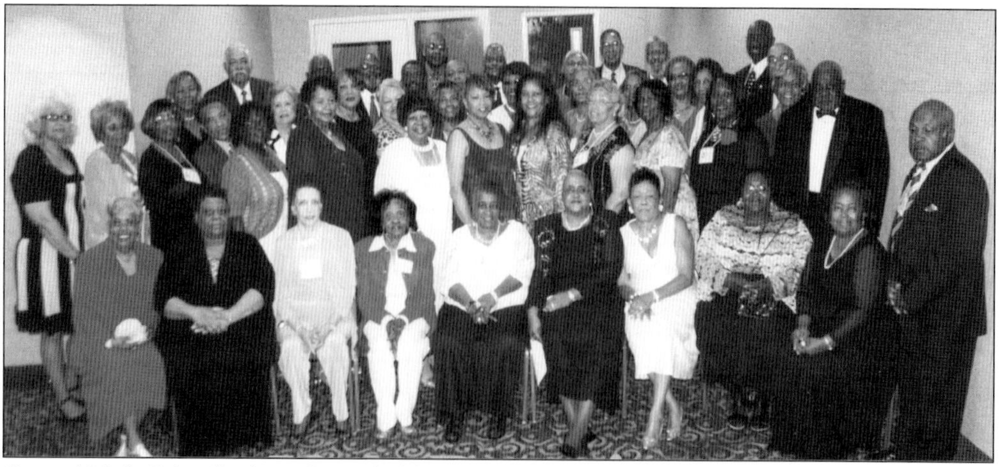

Central High School's class of 1962 held its 50th reunion in 2012. These classmates were in the first graduating class at Central High School. (Courtesy of Dorothy Spence.)

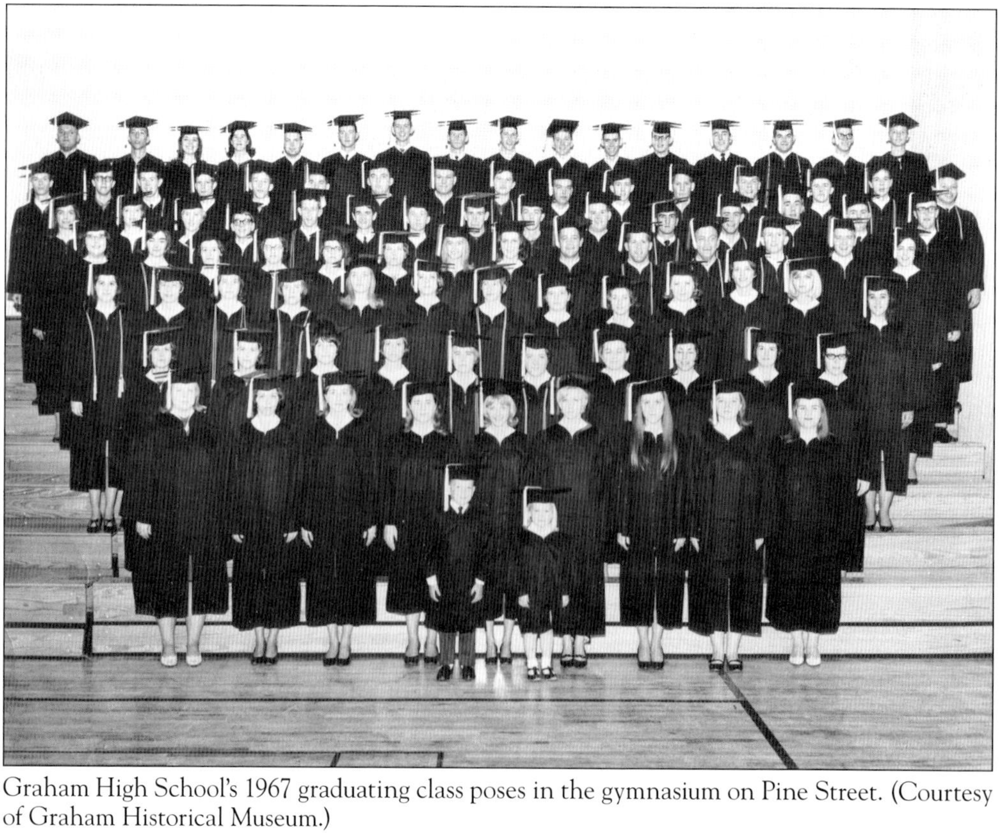

Graham High School's 1967 graduating class poses in the gymnasium on Pine Street. (Courtesy of Graham Historical Museum.)

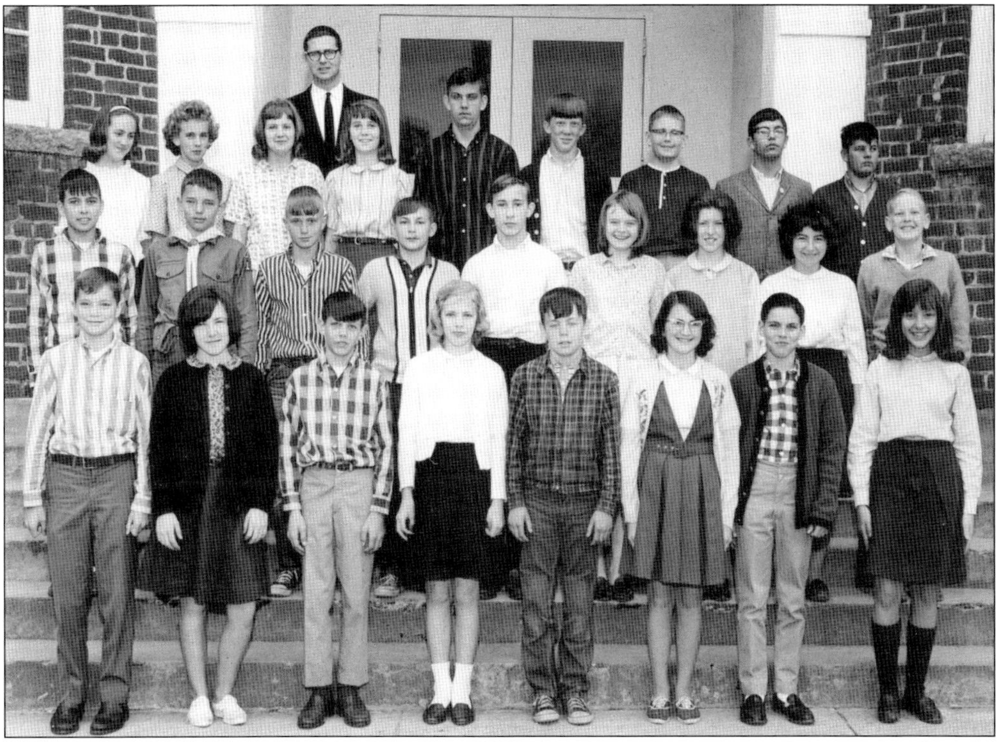

These two classes gather on the front steps at North Graham Elementary School on North Main Street. Mr. Abercrombie's class is seen above around 1963. Below, Lizzie Lewis's sixth-grade class poses for a class photograph in 1964. (Both, courtesy of Graham Historical Museum.)

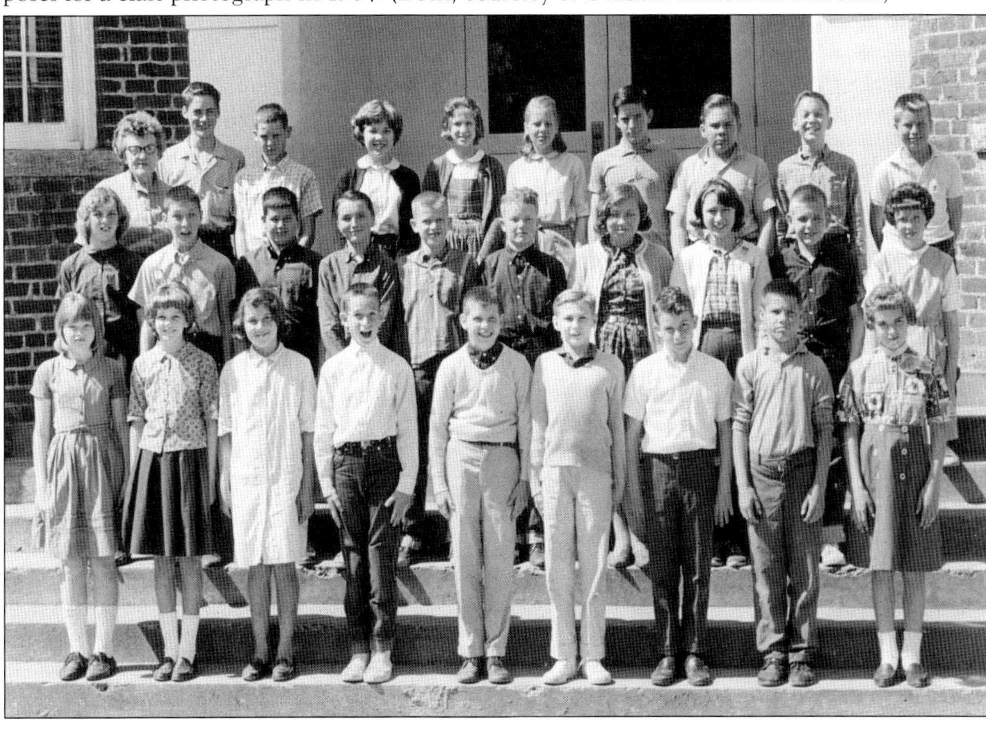

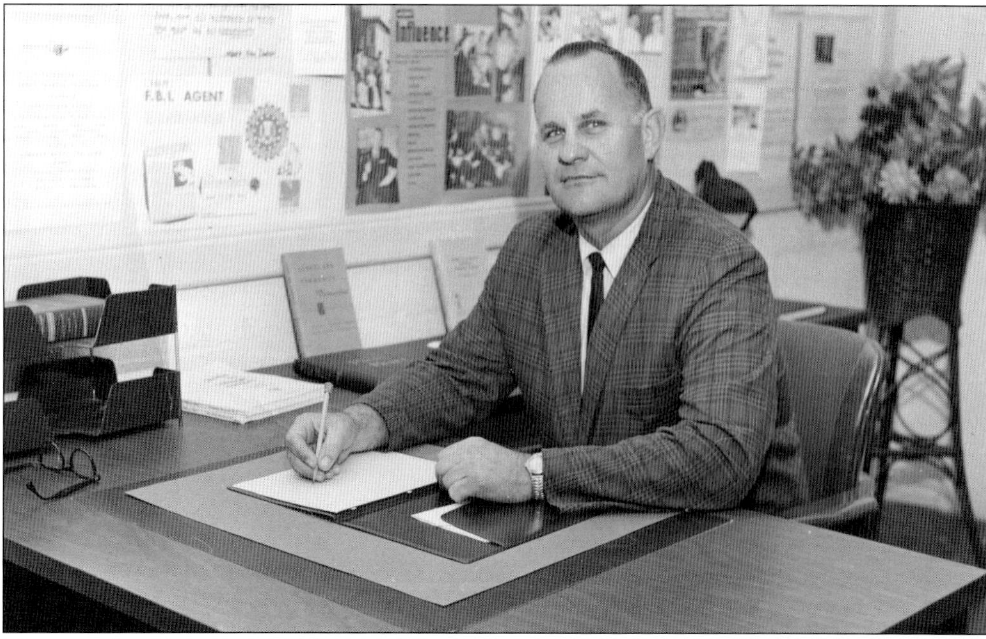

Many students knew Winfred H. "Wink" Ward as their principal. Before he served with the school system, he was director of the Red Shield Boys Club, and his work in education included positions as the principal of both North Graham Elementary School on North Main Street, and Graham Middle School on Pine Street. (Courtesy of Mark and Sue Ward.)

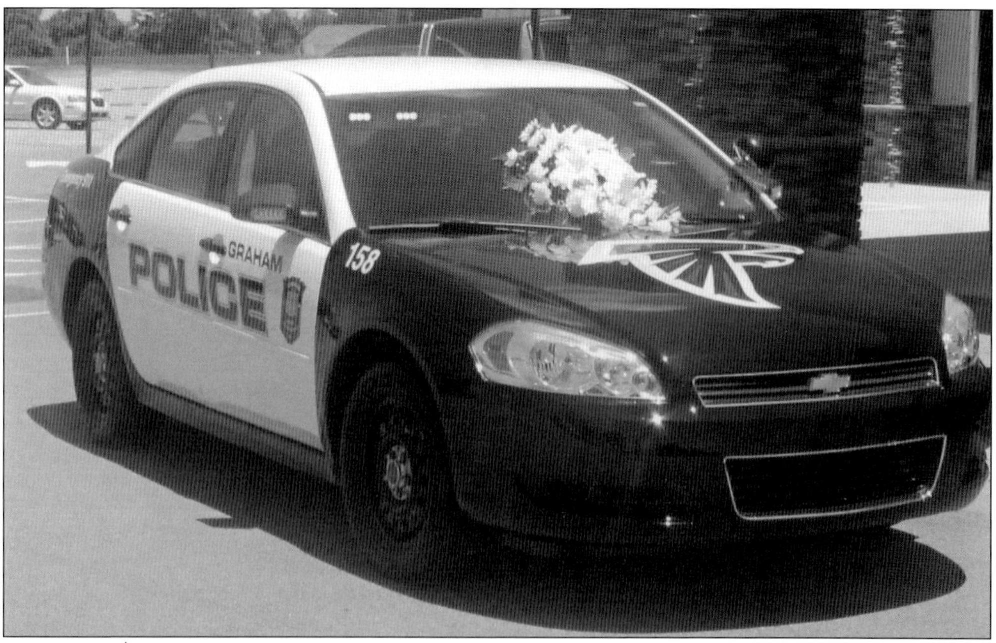

Graham police officer David G. Lewis worked closely with students and faculty as the school resource officer at Graham Middle School. He passed away in June 2012 after a short illness. He touched many lives and is missed by the community. His patrol car, with its falcon emblem on the hood, stands as a memorial in front of the Graham Police Department. (Courtesy of Graham Police Department.)

Seven

Sports and Entertainment

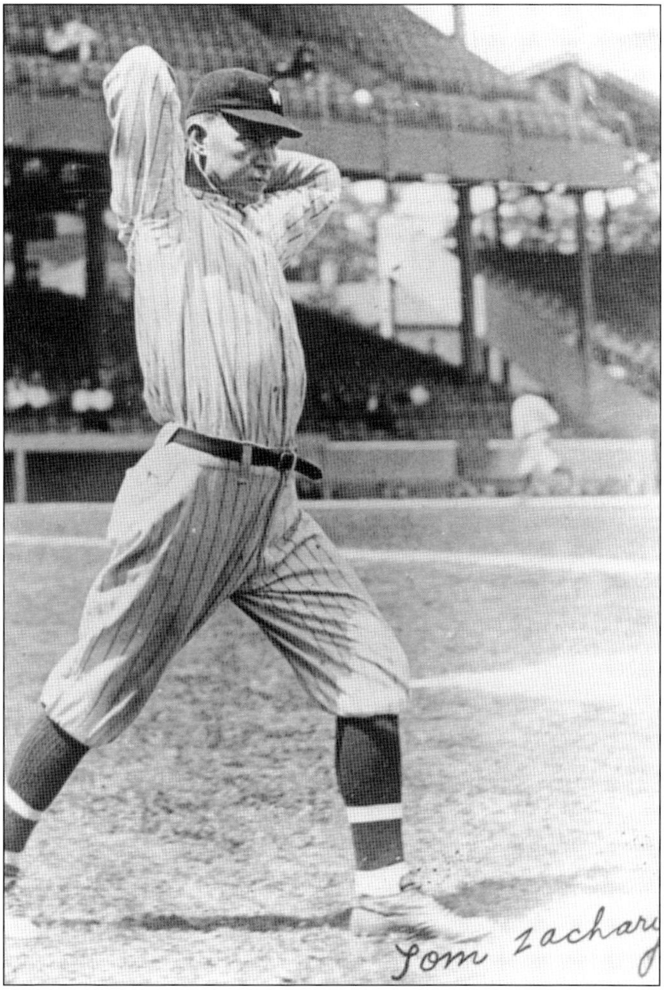

Tom Zachary began his 19-year career as a Major League Baseball pitcher in 1918. He pitched the game that launched the Washington Senators into the 1924 World Series. It was described as the most historic game in the Senators' history. Unfortunately, Zachary is remembered for a single, ill-fated pitch that would eclipse his many accomplishments. When the Senators faced the Yankees in the last game of the 1927 baseball season, Zachary faced Yankees slugger Babe Ruth. He threw the pitch that Ruth hit over the right-field wall for his 60th home run of the season, a record that stood for 34 years. In 1929, when Zachary was Ruth's teammate on the Yankees, he pitched a perfect season with 12 wins and no losses. Zachary Baseball Field at Graham Middle School is named in his honor. (Courtesy of Graham Sports Hall of Fame.)

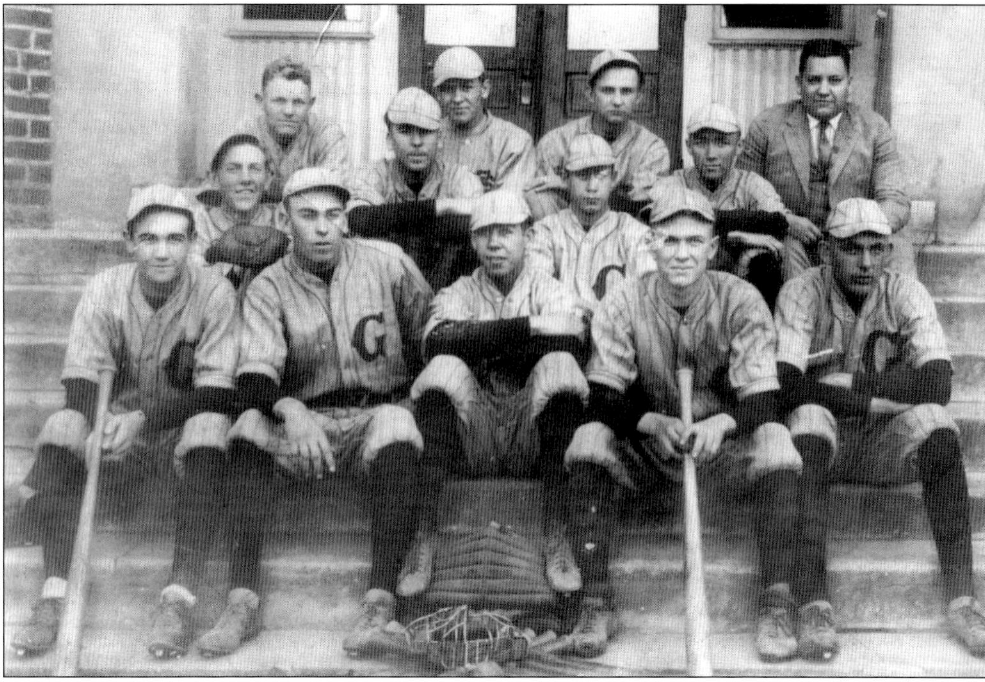

The Graham High School baseball team is seen here around 1918. Tom Zachary is on the far right in the first row. Talmadge Nelson (second row, second from left) often joked, "Zachary was the second best baseball player I ever saw. Talmadge Nelson was the best." (Courtesy of Graham Historical Museum.)

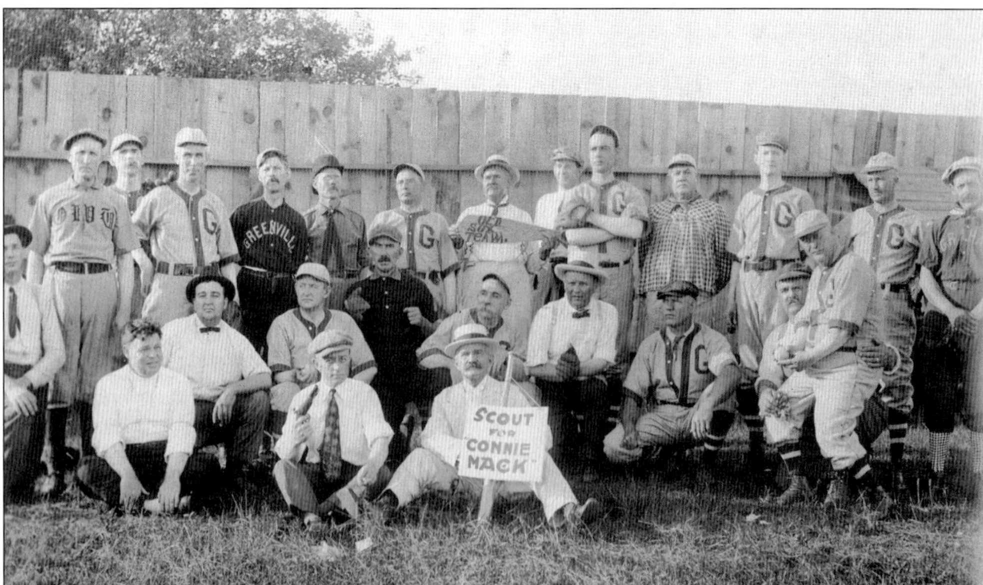

Prominent men in the community chose teams and played an exhibition game on July 3, 1915. The Old Sox Team and Scouts for Connie Mack came together for this group photograph. Familiar faces in the game included, in no particular order, E.P. McClure, J.D. Kernodle Sr., Ned Parker Jr., W.J. Nicks, and Bob Cook, the sheriff. (Courtesy of Graham Historical Museum.)

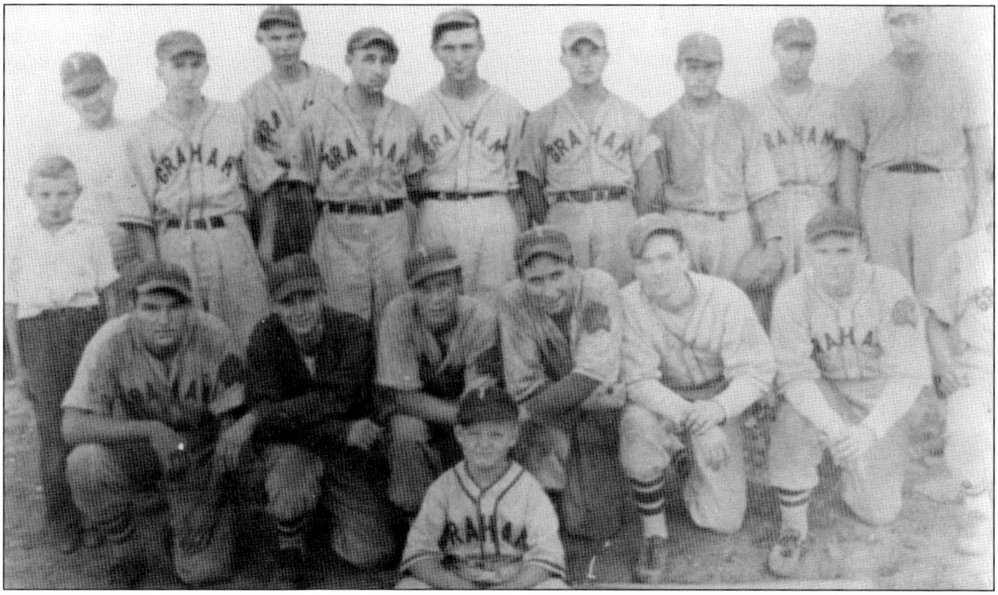

The Graham Tigers won three county championships in the 1930s. The team disbanded when World War II began. Bill Frick is the batboy in this team photograph from 1938. Doodle Lee, the mascot, is the child in the white shirt standing on the left. (Courtesy of Jack Henderson.)

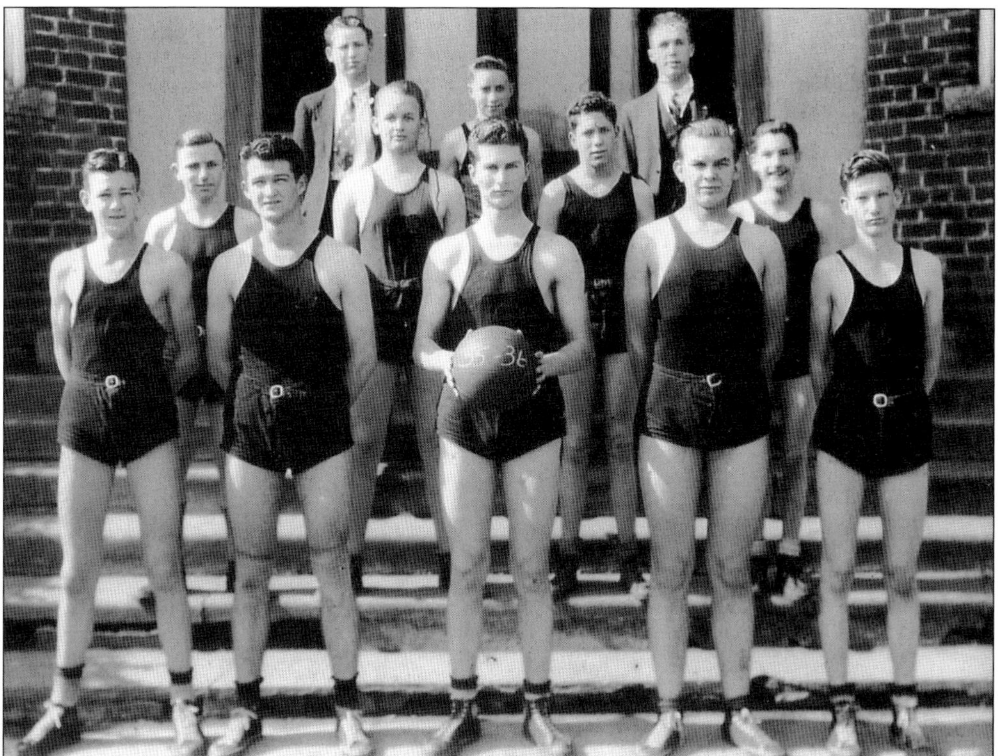

The 1936 Graham High School men's basketball team had 12 wins and four losses. Jimmy Whitfield (first row, far left) was later signed by the St. Louis Cardinals. He was killed in the South Pacific during World War II. (Courtesy of Lee Lovette.)

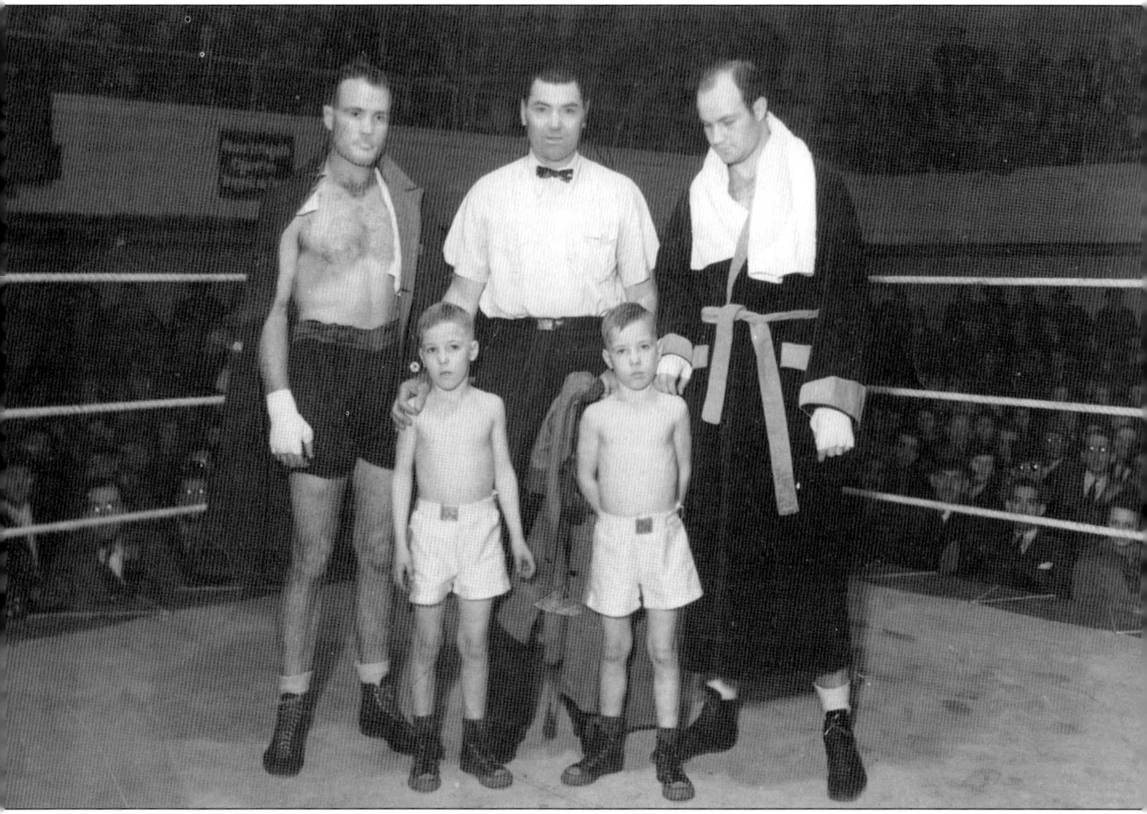

Edward "Hard Rock" Harden (left) won 63 matches and had 27 knockouts in his career. In November 1938, he faced "Navy Bill" Boyd (right). The fight was held at the armory in Durham before a packed house. Former heavyweight champion Jack Dempsey, Boyd's trainer, stands in the center. The two boys are identified as the Hanford twins. After 10 grueling rounds, Harden, the hometown favorite, lost the match on decision. The *Daily Times-News* stated that although there was no question about the ultimate outcome of the fight, the near-hysterical crowd came to its feet to cheer for Harden, "The Country Gentleman," after the match. (Courtesy of Charles Whittemore.)

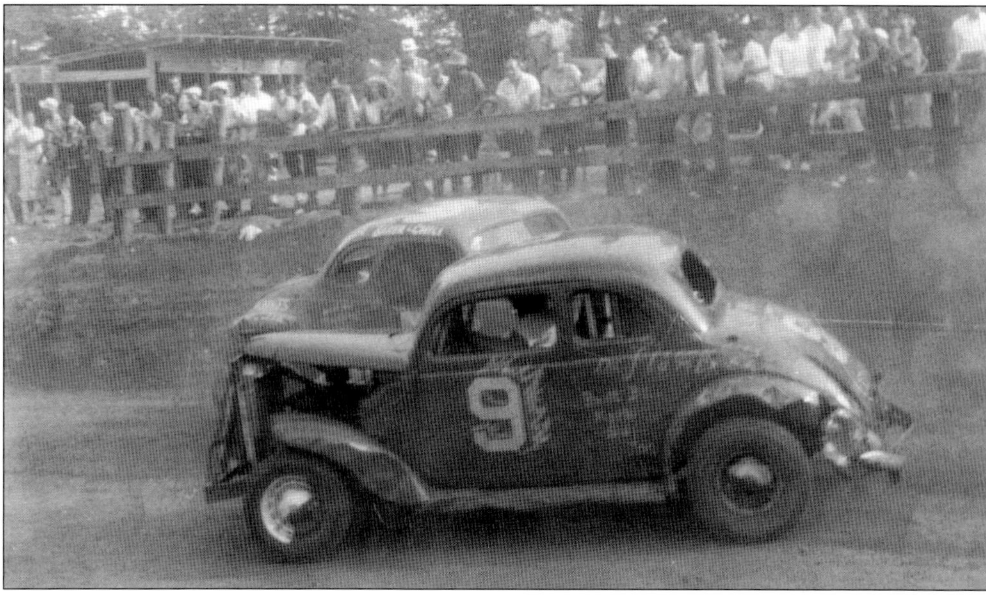

Crowds gather along Turn 1 at the Jalopy Speedway in Hillsboro to watch the Sunday afternoon action. Baker Kimrey's no. 3 car is alongside no. 9, a 1937 Ford driven by Odell Manuel of Mebane. Not everyone enjoyed Sunday racing, however; several Hillsboro churches held special revival services where ministers spoke out against the gambling and drinking that accompanied the races. The track operated from 1956 to 1961. (Courtesy of Baker Kimrey.)

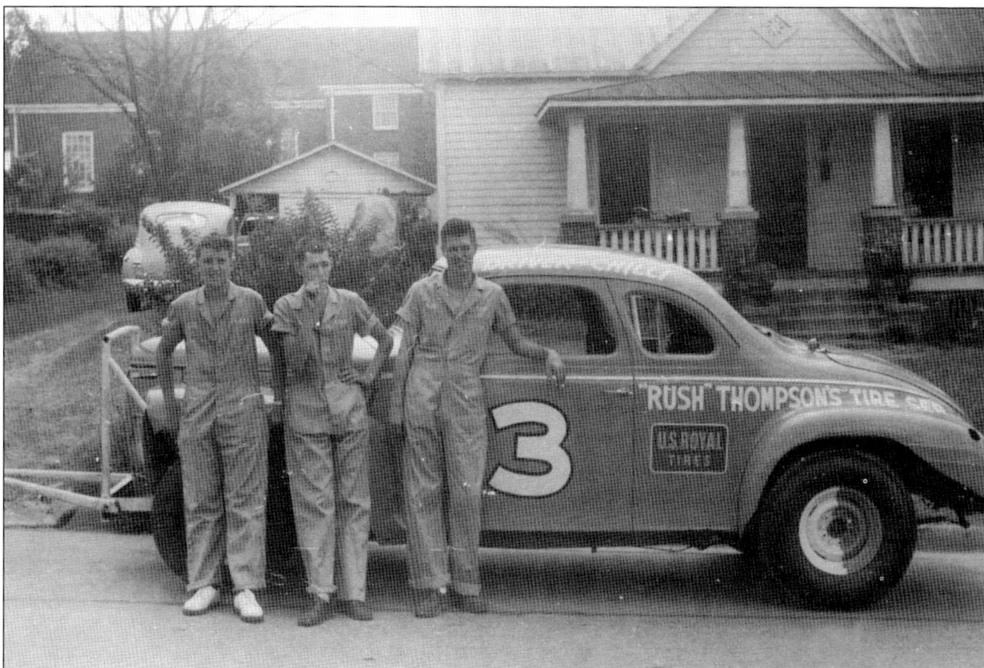

Carroll P. "Chilli" Childress owned the no. 3 car that Baker Kimrey drove at the Jalopy Speedway. The team also drove a 1940 Plymouth for Rush Thompson Tire Service. Seen here on West Harden Street, from left to right, are Baker Kimrey, an unidentified man, and Carroll Childress. (Courtesy of Baker Kimrey.)

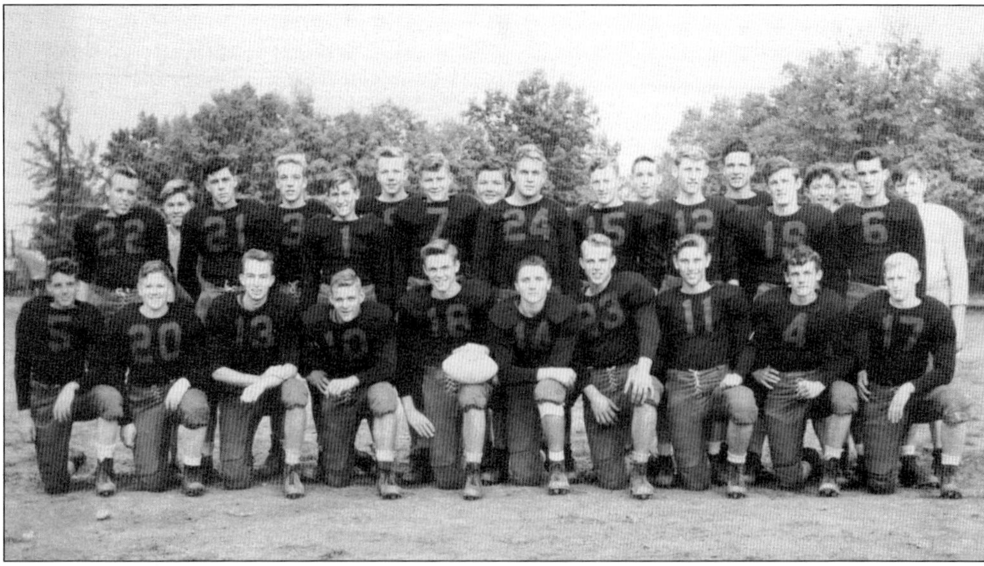

Graham High School lost their football program in 1934 as a result of the Great Depression and lack of funds. When the program was revived in 1945, the boys had never played high school football. An Army Air Corps captain, George Heckman was hired as coach in 1946. The following year, Dr. Robert C. Vincent was hired as his assistant. The coaching team led the team to a perfect season in 1948. (Courtesy of Graham Historical Museum.)

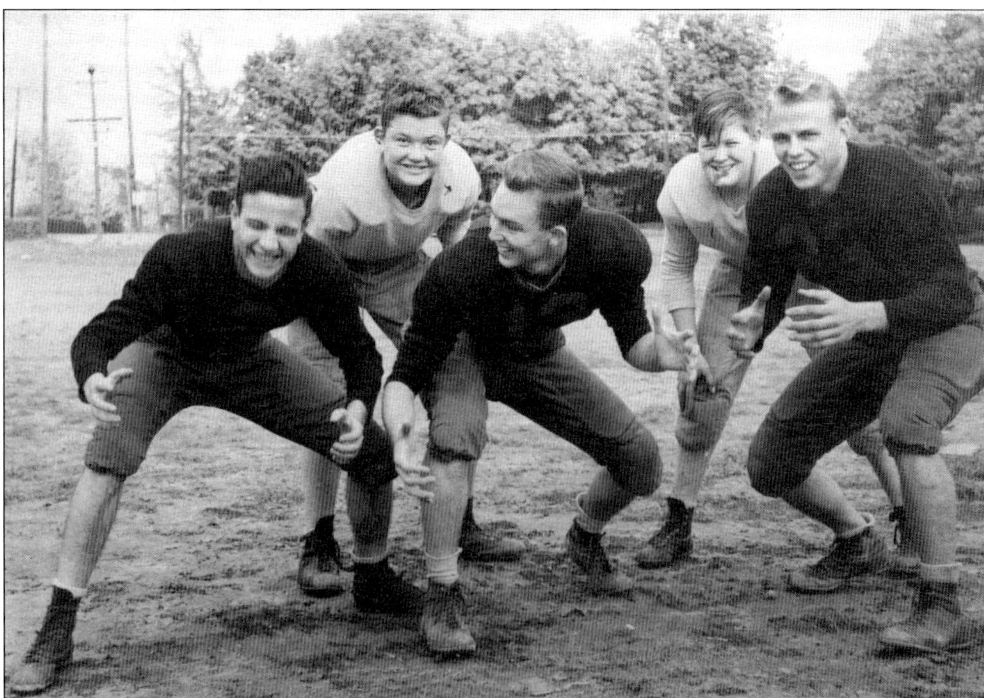

Graham High School boys are seen here enjoying football practice. Coach George Heckman is remembered for his motivational approach to football and to life. Students described him as a patient, soft-spoken man who gave players a chance to prove themselves. (Courtesy of Graham Historical Museum.)

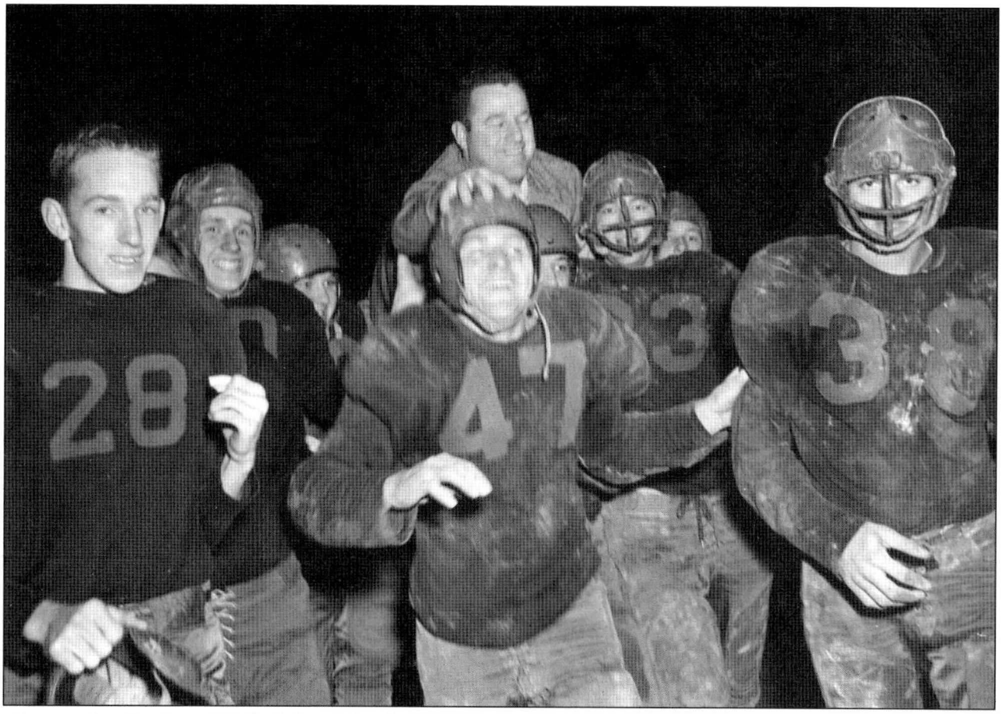

Above, the Graham High School football team carries coach George Heckman on their shoulders after winning a game in 1948. Below, in 1954, Heckman is again carried off the field after his team won the Eastern AA championship, which made them state runners-up. (Both, courtesy of Graham Sports Hall of Fame.)

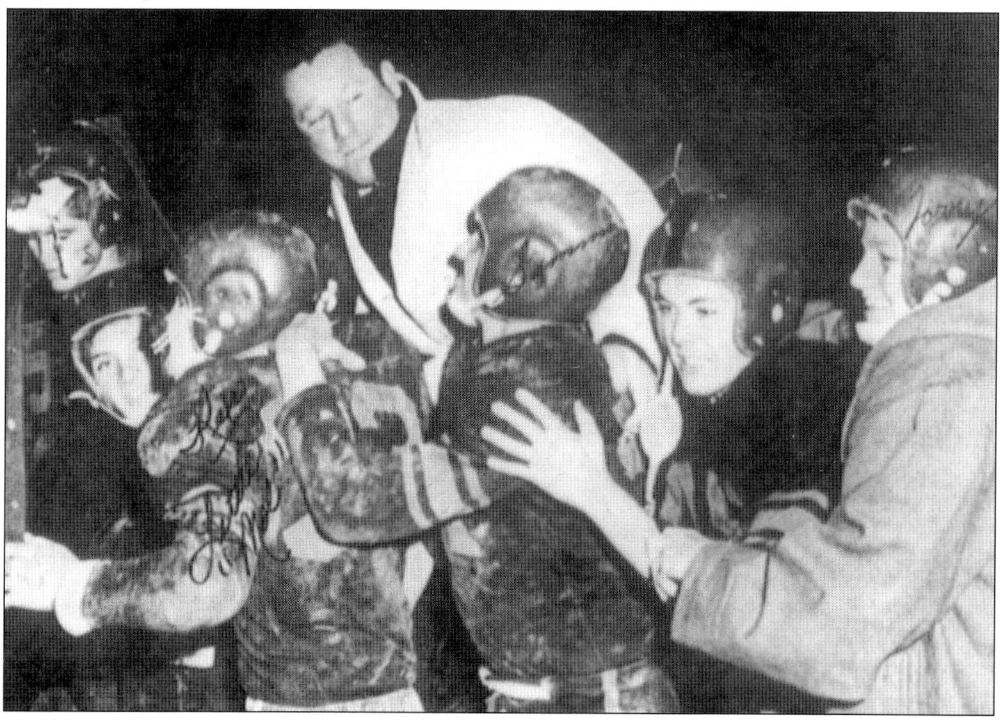

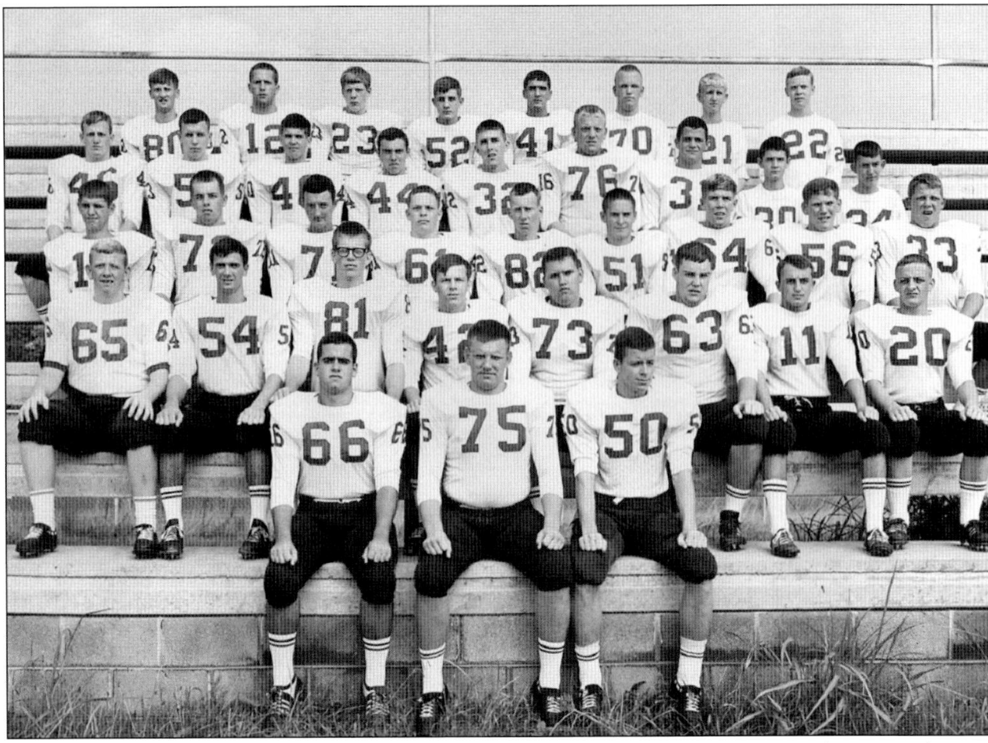

Graham High School coach George Heckman led his team to the state 3-A championships in 1965. Credited with being "the winningest coach in the state," he received the 1965 Graham Civitan Club Citizenship Award. He finished his career with 129 wins, 62 losses, and 10 ties. (Courtesy of Graham Sports Hall of Fame.)

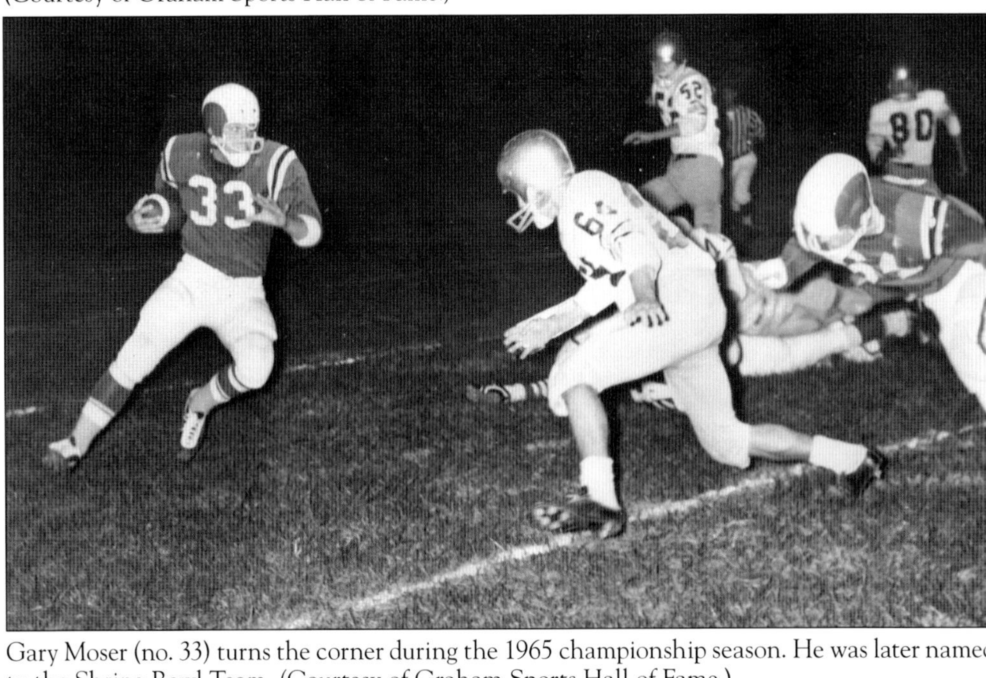

Gary Moser (no. 33) turns the corner during the 1965 championship season. He was later named to the Shrine Bowl Team. (Courtesy of Graham Sports Hall of Fame.)

Coach Heckman receives a trophy for his team after the 1948 Hosiery Bowl. He retired from coaching in 1965. As a teacher and athletic director, he served 32 years in the Alamance County school system, retiring for good in 1978. The City of Graham honored him in 1984 with George Heckman Day. The Graham High School football stadium's press box was also dedicated in his name. (Courtesy of Graham Sports Hall of Fame.)

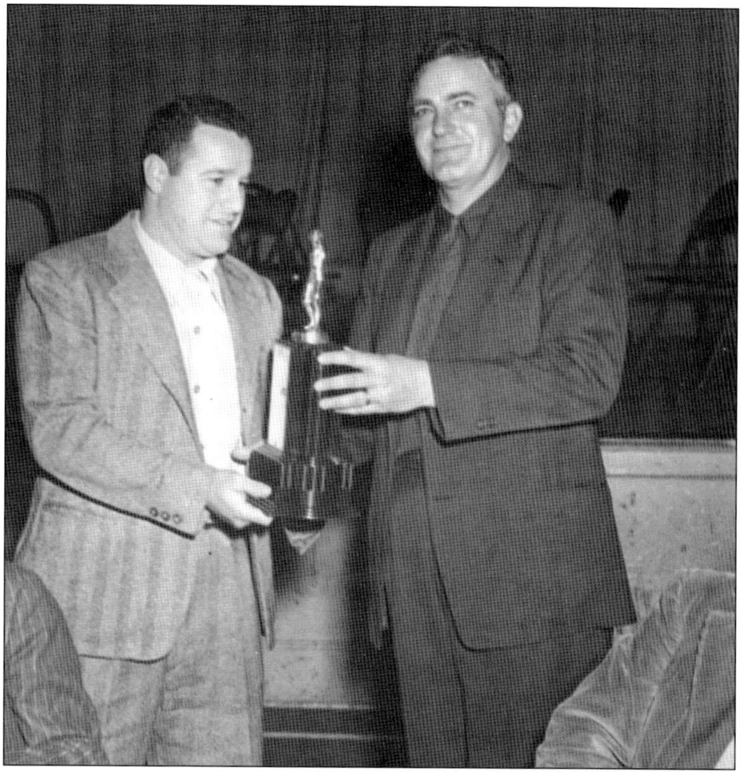

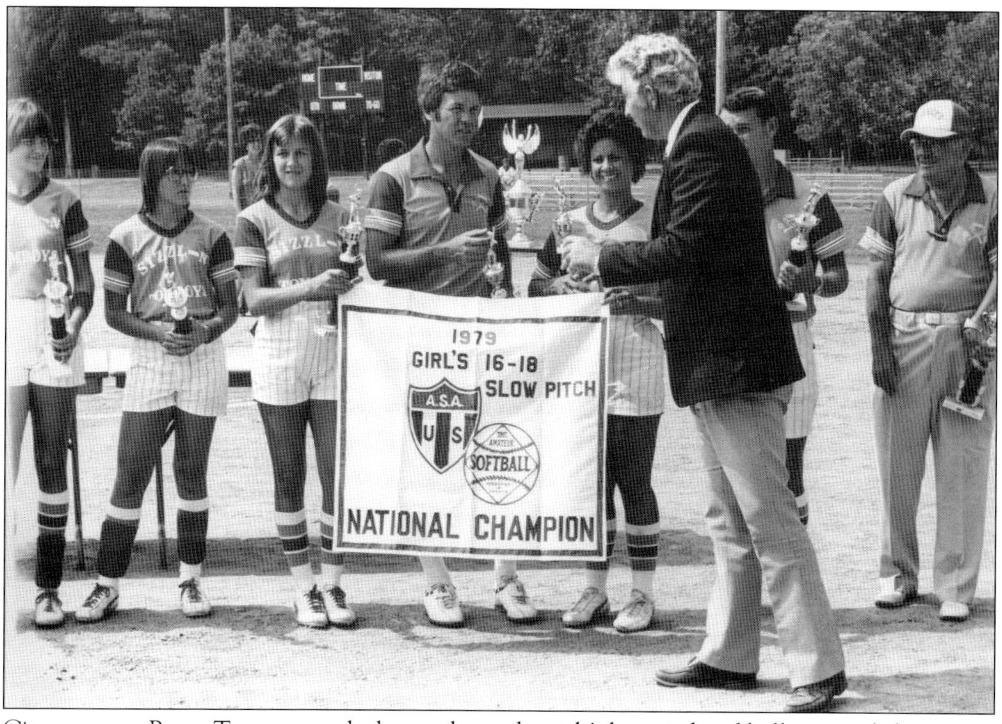

City manager Bruce Turney awards the trophy to the girls' slow-pitch softball national champions in 1979. (Courtesy of Graham Sports Hall of Fame.)

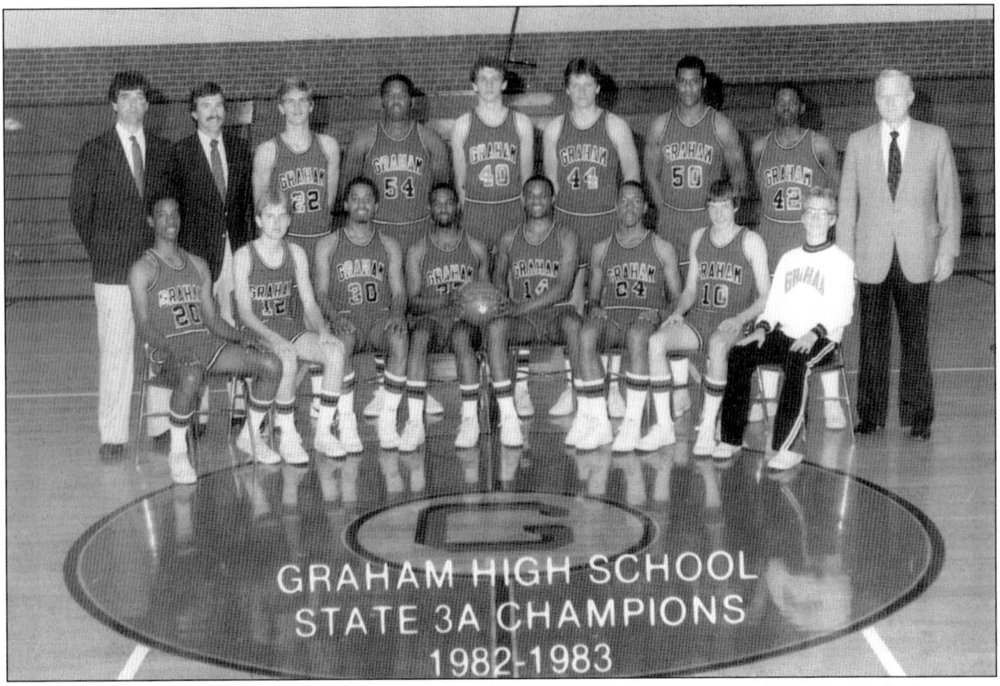

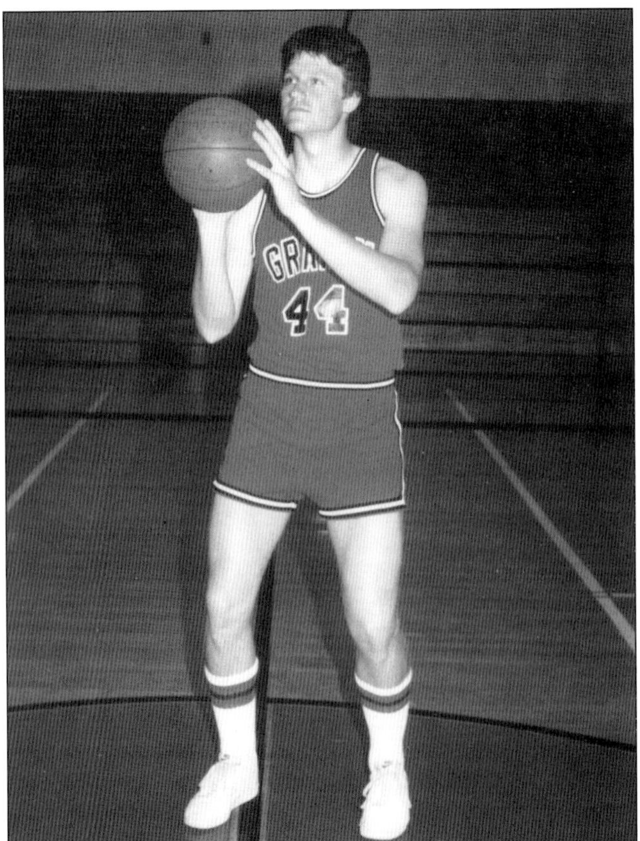

On March 26, 1983, before a record crowd of 10,000 fans, the Graham High School men's basketball team, pictured here, completed what is referred to as "the miracle of 1983," when the group of 13 underdogs captured the North Carolina 3-A championship under the leadership of coach Tommy Cole. The evening ended with a celebration at the Graham courthouse. (Courtesy of Graham Sports Hall of Fame.)

Graham won the championship game 67-61. Tim Jones finished with 27 points and was named the tournament's most valuable player. Because of his remarkable state playoff efforts, with 135 total points, he was selected for the all-state team three weeks later. Graham High School retired his number, 44. (Courtesy of Vera Jones.)

Donna Trollinger, a Graham High School women's basketball standout, went on to play for Elon College from 1981 to 1985. She is the fourth-leading scorer in Elon's history, received the Luther Byrd Scholarship, and later coached basketball at Graham High School. In 2010, she received the Distinguished Service in Sports Award, presented by the Alamance County Sports Development Council. (Courtesy of Graham Sports Hall of Fame.)

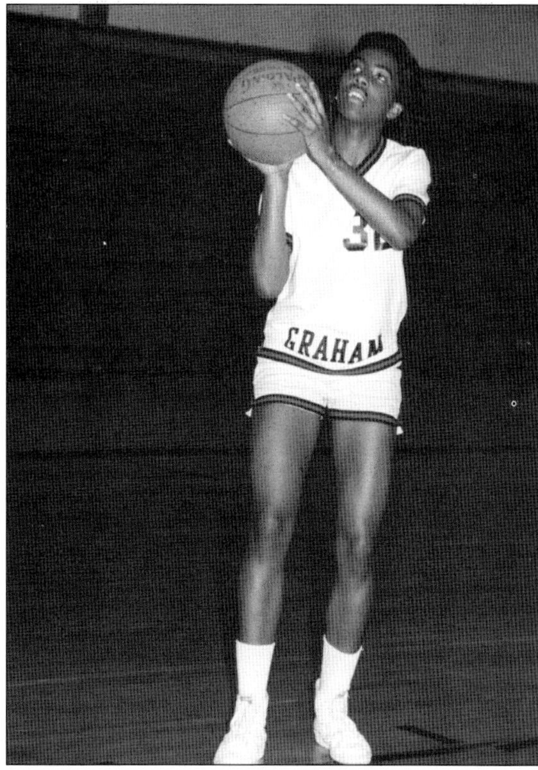

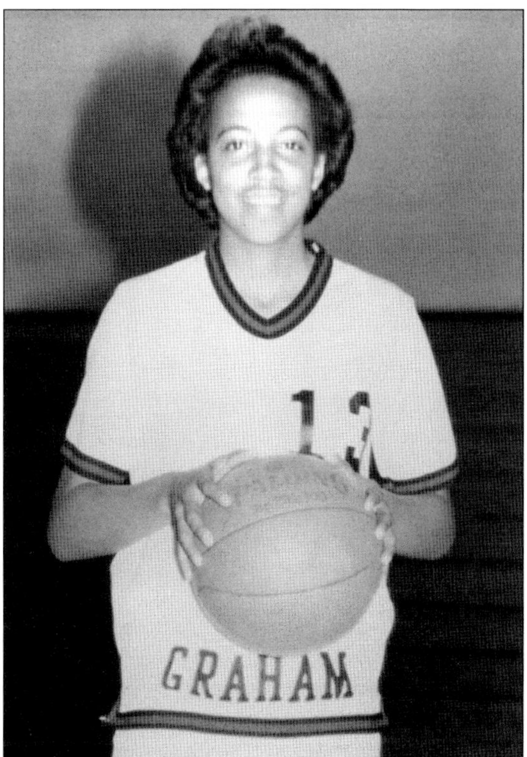

Robyn S. Hadley played women's basketball at Graham High School from 1977 to 1981. She had a four-year record of 1,138 points. She was named mid-state 3-A all-conference in her senior year. She went on to graduate from the University of North Carolina and become a Rhodes Scholar at Oxford University. (Courtesy of Graham Sports Hall of Fame.)

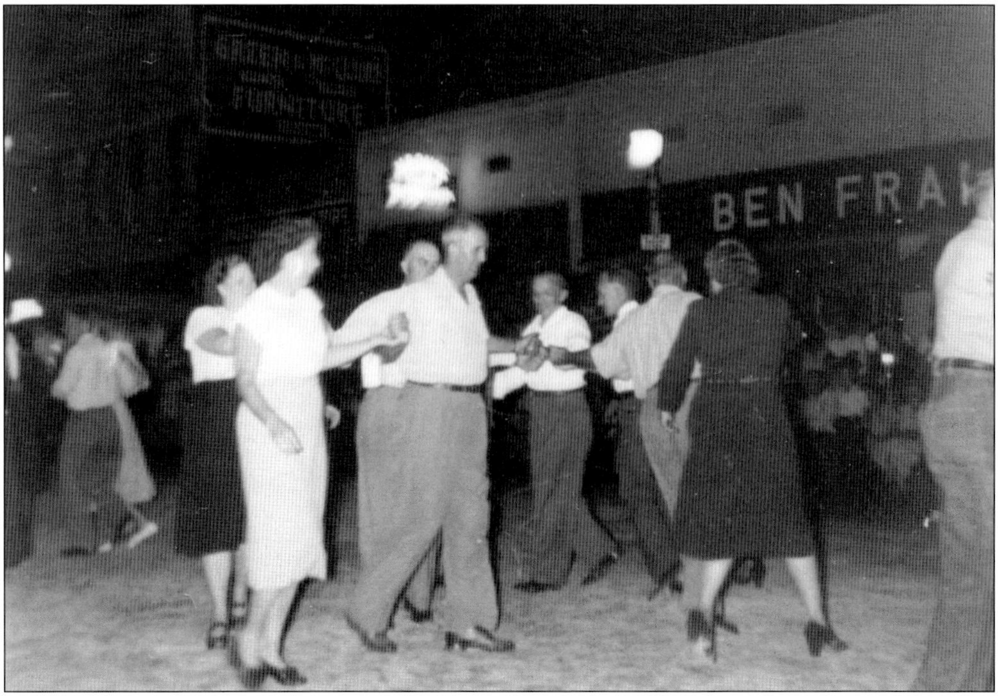

Through the decades, Graham has hosted dozens of street festivals. Square dancers are seen here having a grand old time in the 1950s on North Main Street. (Courtesy of Bartialette Thompson.)

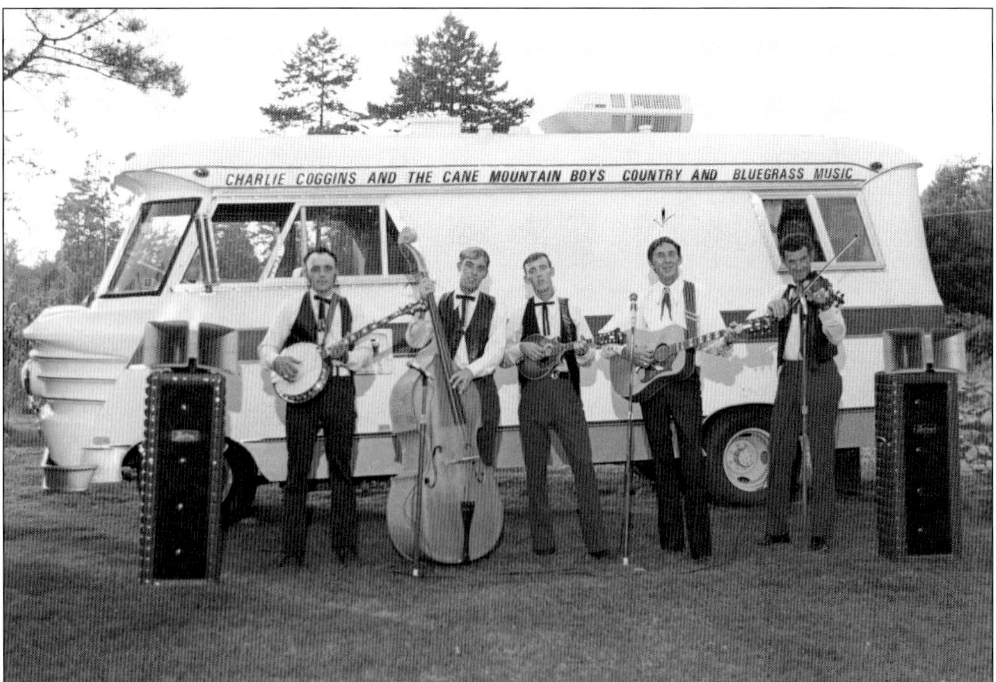

Charlie Coggins and the Cane Mountain Boys performed in the bluegrass festivals in the early 1970s. Coggins was employed by the City of Graham for more than 20 years. (Courtesy of Graham Historical Museum.)

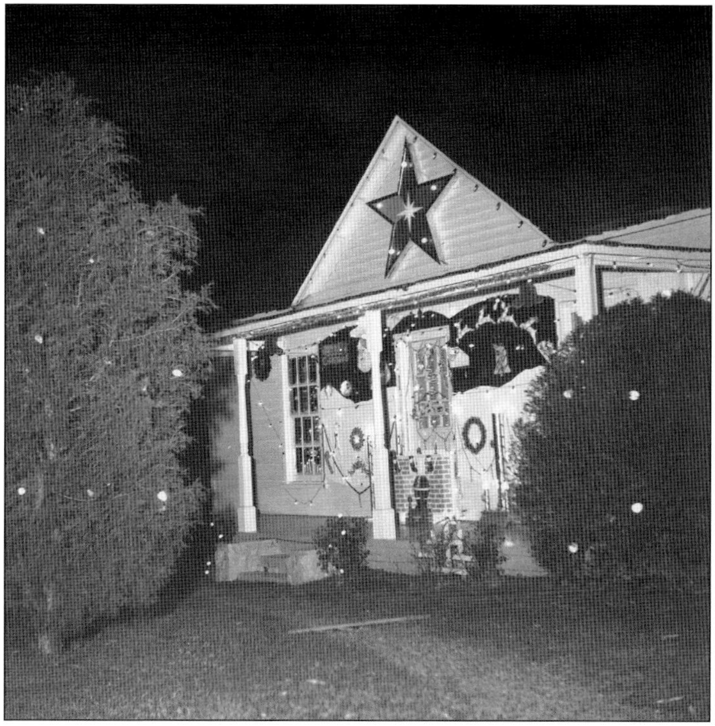

Carroll Stinson's home on Hill Street was transformed each Christmas in the 1970s and 1980s. Driving by to see the Christmas lights was an annual tradition for many Graham residents, with the only exception being 1973, the year of the big energy crunch. The brightly lit display earned him the nickname "Lightning." (Courtesy of Pat Bailey.)

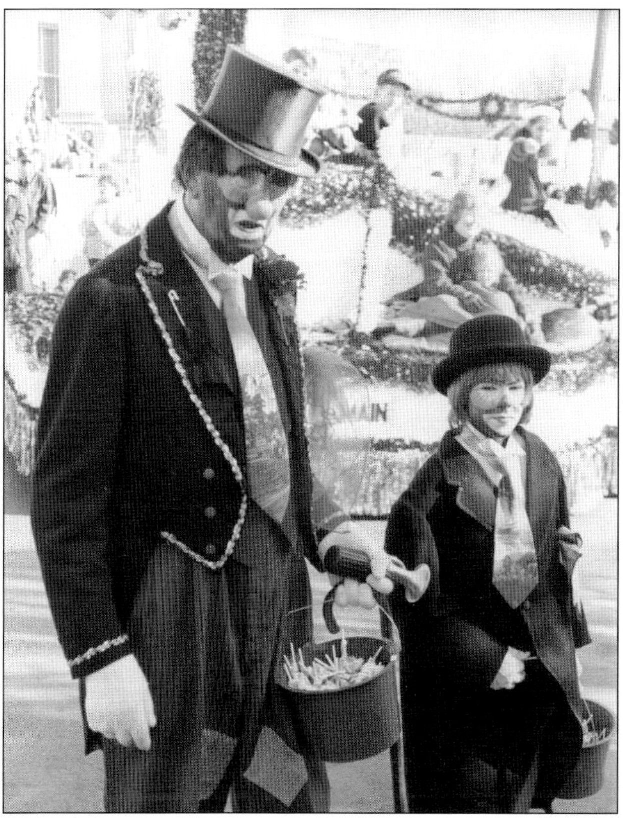

Bradley Rich, with his Riverside Café clown car, was a fixture at Graham's Christmas parade for many years. Jason Guthrie, son of Jim and Amy Guthrie walks along with him in this holiday procession. (Courtesy of Jim Guthrie.)

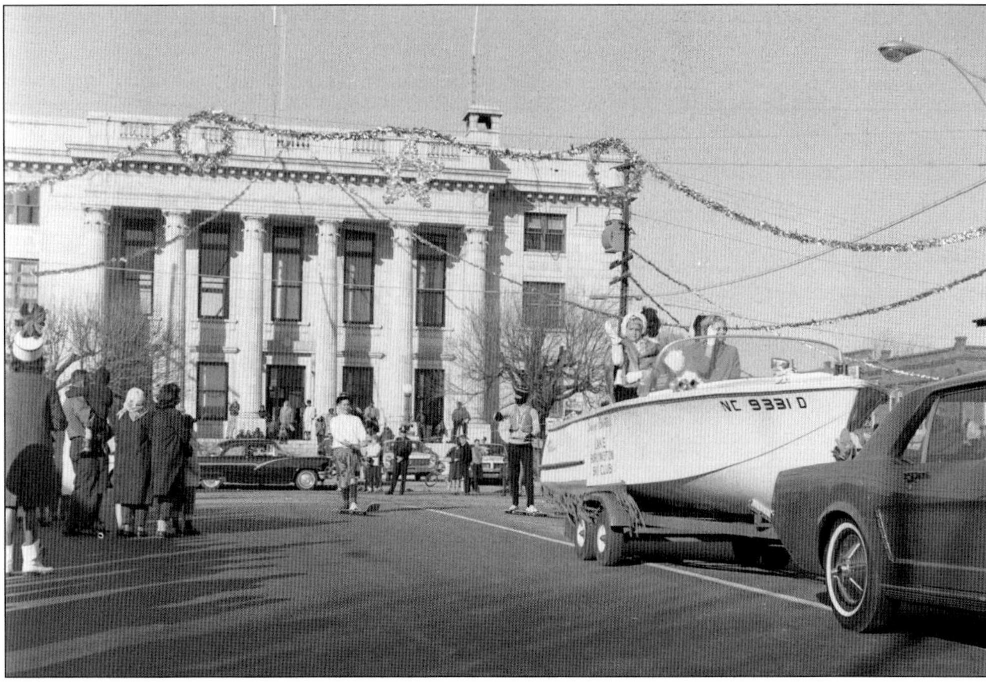

The courthouse square remains a focal point for Graham activities, and the annual Christmas parade is a favorite community tradition. This photograph was taken in the late 1960s. (Courtesy of Pat Bailey.)

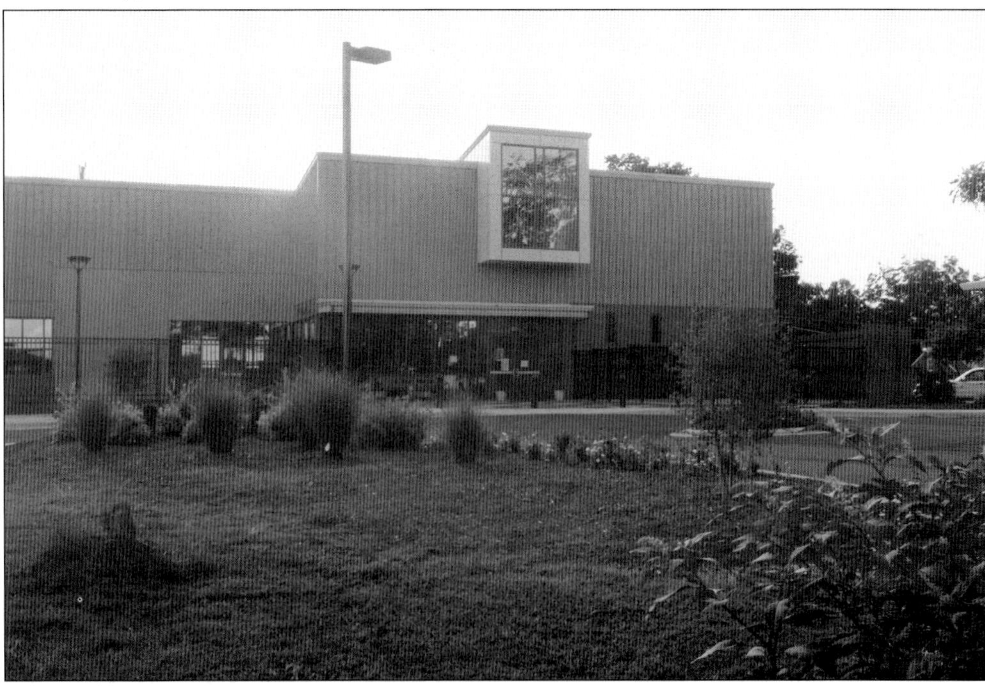

The Children's Museum of Alamance County opened in 2012 on South Main Street. The museum is a place for adults and children to expand their imaginations together and explore Alamance County's roots. (Courtesy of Samantha Barr.)

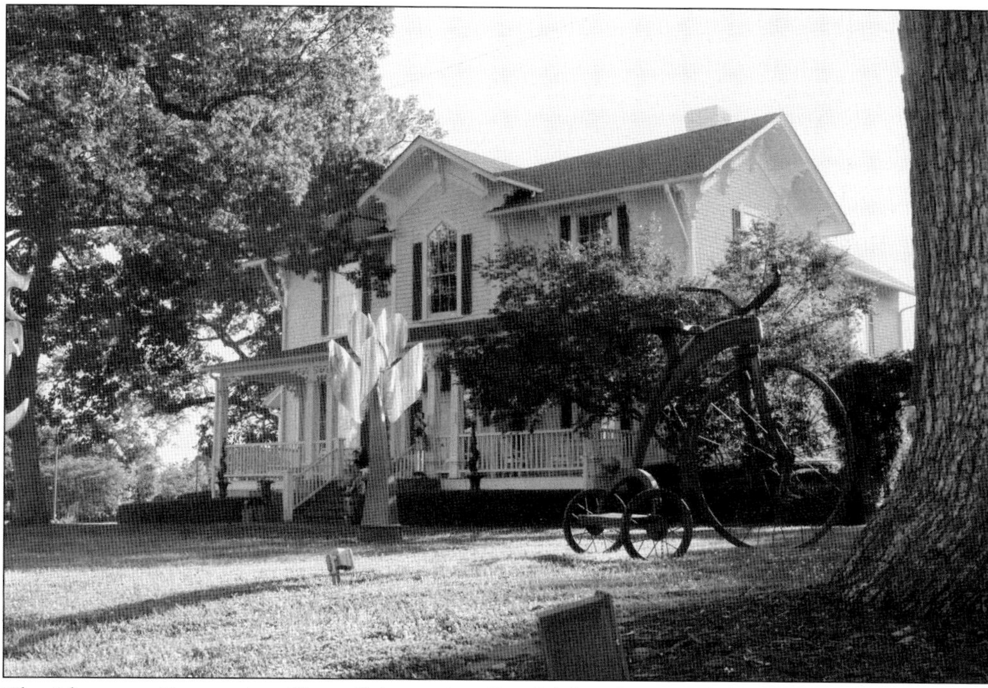

The Alamance County Arts Council, located on South Main Street, exhibits the work of local artists and maintains the beauty of the historic Captain White House. (Courtesy of Patrick Jordan.)

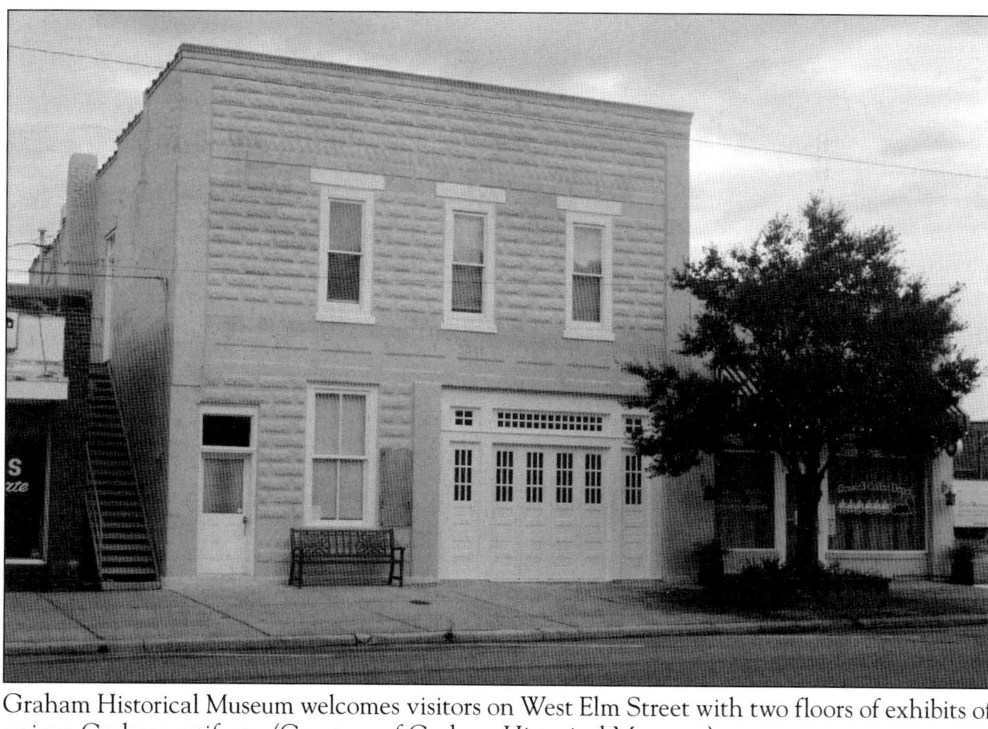

Graham Historical Museum welcomes visitors on West Elm Street with two floors of exhibits of unique Graham artifacts. (Courtesy of Graham Historical Museum.)

Bibliography

Alamance Gleaner, 1875–1947. Various issues. Graham, NC.

Alamance News Sesquicentennial Edition, 1849–1999: Celebrating Alamance County's 150th Anniversary. Graham, NC: *Alamance News*, 1999.

Bolden, Don. *Alamance in the Past, Vol. 1*. Burlington, NC: P.N. Thompson Printing Company, 1979.

———. *Alamance in the Past, Vol. 2*. Burlington, NC: P.N. Thompson Printing Company, 1981.

Euliss, Elinor Samons. *Alamance County: A Legacy of Its People and Places*. Greensboro, NC: Legacy Publications, 1984.

Hughes, Julian. *Development of the Textile Industry in Alamance County*. Burlington, NC: Burlington Letter Shop, 1965.

Lasley, William Kerr. Images of America: *Alamance County*. Charleston, SC: Arcadia Publishing, 1999.

Stockard, Sallie Walker. *History of Alamance*. Burlington, NC: Alamance County Historical Museum, 1986.

Stokes, Durward. *Auction and Action: Historical Highlights of Graham, North Carolina*. Graham, NC: City of Graham, 1985.

Times-News, 1927–2012. Various issues. Burlington, NC.

Troxler, Carole Watterson and William Murray Vincent. *Shuttle & Plow: A History of Alamance County, North Carolina*. Alamance County Historical Association, 1999.

Vincent, William Murray. *Historic Alamance County*. San Antonio, TX: Historical Publishing Network, 2009.

Whitaker, Walter. *Centennial History of Alamance County*. Burlington, NC: Burlington Chamber of Commerce, 1949.

About the Graham Historical Museum

In 2001, the City of Graham proudly opened the Graham Historical Museum in the historic 1914 Graham firehouse. Over the years, the building has also been home to city hall, the police department, a courtroom, and a jail. It is only fitting that a building that has seen so much history is now home to the city's history. The museum seeks to share the history of Graham through the collection, preservation, and display of items pertaining to Graham and its citizens.

When visiting the museum, one must see the centerpiece of its collection, a fully restored 1930 Seagrove fire truck. Other prominent exhibits include memorabilia from two local celebrities: Jeanne Swanner Robertson, Miss North Carolina 1963; and Tom Zachary, a Major League Baseball player in the 1920s and 1930s.

The exhibit *Behind Her All The Way: Graham's Miss North Carolina* honors Jeanne Swanner Robertson. She was crowned Miss North Carolina in 1963 and voted Miss Congeniality in the 1963 Miss America pageant. Jeanne generously donated her personal collection of photographs, magazines, and other artifacts to the museum. The permanent exhibit enables the Graham Historical Museum to interpret small-town Southern life in the early 1960s.

Other items of historical significance include a family heirloom belonging to the Sing Lee family. The Lees opened the Chinese laundry behind the W.J. Nicks store in 1902. Items of interest include an intricately sewn baby blanket featuring needlework by Sing Lee's wife, and a pair of Mr. Lee's traditional Chinese shoes.

The museum houses a collection of local sports memorabilia featuring the 1965 Graham High School state championship football team. Plaques for athletes inducted into the Graham Sports Hall of Fame are also on display. Visitors can also view a yearbook from Graham's Central High School signed by football great Jim Brown, who visited the school on May 30, 1964.

The Graham Historical Museum is located just off Court Square at 135 West Elm Street.